With the regards of —

J. Eldon Dorman, M.D.

2/19/97

"Confessions of a Coal Camp Doctor"

And Other Stories

by

J. Eldon Dorman, M.D.

Published by
Peczuh Printing Co.
P.O. Box 1024 • Price, Ut. 84501

First Printing 1995

Printed in the United States of America

ISBN # 0-9651094-1-0

CONTENTS

CONFESSIONS OF A COAL CAMP DOCTOR

CONFESSIONS OF A COAL CAMP DOCTOR

ANOTHER MAN'S WEST

SHORT STACKS - BONUS

FOREWORD

by Helen Papanikolas

In 1909, when Eldon Dorman was born, the frontier was said to have closed with the coming of the transcontinental railroad in 1869. Sod houses on prairie homesteads were crumbling. Weathered men, women and children maneuvered their loaded-down wagons over rutted roads looking for land and a new start in life. These were the years in our nation's history when agriculture waned as the backbone of the country and the industrialization of the East reached into the West with its coal and mineral riches.

Eldon's parents were farmers like the sojourners passing by on lonely roads, their stark homestead life matched by the precepts of their Seventh-Day Adventist religion. On their eastern Colorado homestead, eked out of sagebrush, far from neighbors, Eldon and his brothers learned to cope with the exuberance and inventiveness in the terrain of boyhood.

The reader wonders how this boy, who today would be called deprived, became a doctor. These memoirs tell us of his long, colorful odyssey. They are a unique treasure. In simple language, often colloquial, we follow the boy from his boyhood in eastern Colorado into the hard times of getting an education and through medical school and hospital training, always short of money. He leaves his hospital residency in the 1930s Depression years. Without money, without connections, he becomes a coal camp doctor in Carbon County, Utah. He follows in the footsteps of thousands of other young doctors who, unable to set up private practice, were drawn to the exploding industrialism of the nation. They used the mines, railroads, and factories as a means to make enough money to escape to cities and lucrative practices. The young man we have become drawn to as we read comes to coal country, but never leaves. Once there, he is astonished to find that Balkan, Mediterranean and Asian immigrants outnumber the American-born. Until then, the only immigrants he had known were a German farm family in Kansas where he worked one summer to make money for his schooling. In his office and in their homes, he hears the languages of Italians, Greeks, Yugoslavs and Japanese. He begins to learn their customs and their old-country hospitality; as an educated man who holds their lives in his hands in crises, he receives a touching deference.

The coal camps suit the young doctor. The combination of Mormons, other Americans and immigrants spice his life. The sagebrush and junipers, the hunting and fishing are worth the impassable snowy roads. The heat and wind help temper somewhat the tragedies in the mine and in the company houses. The names of landmarks speak of easy affection: Billy's Mountain, Joes Valley and Molly's Nipple. The young doctor fits in well with such familiarity; he feels no need for special recognition because he is a highly educated man. Through his long years as a coal camp doctor and ophthalmologist, he gathers a long list of friends: hunting, fishing and flying companions; lawyers, newspaper editors, ranchers, farmers, sheriffs and immigrants who hail him as "Little Mr. Doc." The anecdotes he tells us are humorous, sometimes sad, but they are more than that, for they again invoke a past that is forever gone.

His saga can never again be repeated; it is history at a crucial time in our nation's existence. It graphically reveals a period that has vanished. America is now a land of television, sophisticated technology and airplane travel, not the unpeopled land of the young Seventh-Day-Adventist boy and the older youth who walked miles to find work, who arrived in the coal camps with one suit of clothes and a microscope to examine blood and festerings. The immigrants who came in response to Utah's desperate need for laborers to dig coal and lay rails are gone. Their children and grandchildren are educated, many are in various professions, but their people live on in the memory of the young doctor who years later sets them down on the printed page for us.

We are not, however, reading the memoirs of an insulated doctor, important though he has been in his profession. He tells us almost nothing about his numerous activities beyond his medical practice. They are rare, people like Eldon Dorman who encompass life fully. He was one of the founders of the College of Eastern Utah Prehistoric Museum, acting as curator of archaeology for twenty years. He is a writer on medical issues, archaeology and rock art. He served as commander of Price Flight, Utah Wing Civil Air Patrol, during World War II. He also served as president of the Price National League Western Boys Baseball. He has conducted, each year for nearly two decades, multiple Rock Art Jeep Safaris to pictograph and petroglyph sites of eastern Utah. He has been honored for years of service by the medical profession and civic organizations. He sat on the board and various committees for the Utah Historical

Society and the College of Eastern Utah. Along the way, Eldon Dorman became the friend and colleague of a number of young historians who think of him with boundless respect and affection.

Many people inhabit Eldon Dorman's memory. He, in turn, continues to thrive in the memories of longtime friends and readers of his splendid memoirs. For all of us, he has illuminated almost nine decades of the West's tumultuous history, while unknowingly revealing himself as the remarkable man he is.

INTRODUCTION

This is the story of my life; I have not told everything. If I did, I would probably be in jail. And besides, it would be far too voluminous and since I am now well past my allotted three score and ten years, I might not make it.

This project would not have been possible had not my son, Jaime, given me a computer with the edict to write my life's history. It took me well over four years to get acquainted with the thing, and I still fathom only a small portion of its potential. Every day, I learn something new.

I have tried to put things pretty much in chronological order: Wray, Homestead, Greeley, Harvest Fields of Kansas and Colorado, Education, Coal Camp Doctor, WWII, Warren Peacock, Joes Valley and Joe Walker. After considerable thought, I finally decided to start out with The Coal Camp Doctor.

I have not mentioned my days in the U.S. Forest Service or the time I spent in New Mexico. Neither have I said anything about my involvement with the College of Eastern Utah Prehistoric Museum for over thirty years, twenty of which I acted as curator of archaeology and put together a book called The Archaeology of Eastern Utah, concurrently serving as a board member of the Utah State Historical Society for ten years. Nor have I cited any of my experiences as an ophthalmologist in Price, Utah, for fifty years. Another book? Probably not, so have no fear!

One article, "Recollections of a Coal Camp Doctor," has been published twice, once in Carbon County, Eastern Utah's Industrialized Island, Utah State Historical Society, Salt Lake City. Phillip F. Notarianni, Editor, 1981. Second: Medicine in the Beehive State, University of Utah Press, Salt Lake City. Henry P. Plenk, Editor, 1992.

Another document, which I called "How a Stay at Home Doctor Fought WW II in Carbon County," was published in the book, Utah Remembers World War II, Utah State University Press, Logan. Allan Kent Powell, Editor, 1991.

The rest of the material is virtually unpublished, except for Xerox copies handed out to interested friends. Some of the information was written several years ago, but has recently been rehashed. The remainder has been written within the last year.

One of my favorite authors is David Lavender. His book, One Man's West, is one of my most cherished volumes. In this book, he gives the history of his early life in Colorado and Utah.

This is my story: "Another Man's West."

ACKNOWLEDGMENTS

Jaime Dorman, my son, who about ten years ago brought me a computer, set it up and said: "Dad, I want you to write the story of your life. Get to work." My other children, Marcia, Dory and Kathy, concurred.

Maurine Dorman, my wife, who has encouraged me, corrected and often changed parts of what I have written. She has bandaged my wounds and helped me up when I fell. She proved to be my most critical critic - a master at picking up all kinds of mistakes. Many times, when a fatal crash seemed certain, she kept me airborne because she is truly "the air beneath my wings."

Helen Zeese Papanikolas, my mentor. For over twenty years, she prompted me to write, especially about Carbon County and my life as a coal camp doctor. She has helped me in innumerable ways, gently goading me when necessary. Her writings and advice have led me to try harder. I have sent her, often in rough draft, articles as I wrote them for criticism. She is a treasured friend indeed.

The Three Musketeer's of the Utah State Historical Society, Drs. Kent Powell, Phil Notarianni and Craig Fuller. They have helped in countless ways that have been beneficial. I have watched them grow in their professions and have found inspiration in their friendship, help and expertise.

Joyce Marsing, my office secretary and boss for over thirty years. She was critical of many things I wrote and would say: "This is what you said, but what you want to say is..." She was also adept at picking up punctuation and grammatical errors.

May Seaton Bertelsen, retired teacher of English, was my final scrutiny after Maurine Dorman and Joyce Marsing. She helped in countless ways to make the manuscript more presentable, even laughing at some of the episodes, especially if some of the incidents or people were familiar to her.

Dr. Nancy Taniguchi urged me to write more and used her influence to help me.

Bill Butcher, computer genius, has helped keep my equipment running and has acted as troubleshooter, at times over the phone.

Steven Montoya, assistant computer instructor at CEU came into my home many times to help and instruct. I marvel at his patience with my limited computer knowledge.

Dr. Henning Olsen, who was of great value for the use of his laser printer, which always worked when others failed. He also let me use his computer for document storage and other critical tasks and was always available for help.

Beverly Odendahl, librarian at CEU tried to teach me to scan the microfilm collection of old newspapers at the library. She was very helpful and patient.

Lynnda Johnson, editor of the Price Sun Advocate. Hers was the final word for grammar, punctuation and arrangement.

Friends and others who have helped: Dr. Milton Abrams, the Atwood Barber Shop, Karen Bliss, the late Fern Boyack, Sherril Burge, Milan and Antonia Corak, Helen Costello, Claude C. Dorman, Virginia Hanks, Donald V. Hague, Dr. Jesse D. Jennings, Douglas Johnstun, John B. "Jack" Kelley, Elva McGowan, Max G. Morgan, M.D., Art Olsen, Dr. Floyd O'Neil, Evelyn Patterick, the Peczuh family - especially Tim, the quiet, patient one, Dr. Michael Petersen, Dr. Ross Peterson, Art Rasmussen, Richard Seely, Henry and Nadine Skrinner, Helen Oliveto-Smith, Marge Sower, Monsignor Jerome Stoffel, Madge Tomsic, Al Veltri, Zelpha Vuksinick, Don and Jeannette Wilcox, Tillie Yelenich, and many others.

Once the title of the book was decided - Confessions of a Coal Camp Doctor, it seemed best to start the manuscript with the coal camp doctor stories, which make up over a third of the book, followed in chronological order by the more or less autobiographical story of important parts of my life.

In a few instances, names have been changed to protect the guilty.

Some of the coal camp doctor stories have been previously published in Carbon County, Eastern Utah's Industrialized Island and The History of Medicine in the Beehive State, and are reprinted with permission.

DEDICATION

This book is dedicated to my wife, Maurine;
my children, Marcia, Jaime, Dory and Kathy;
and to underground miners everywhere.

"Confessions of a Coal Camp Doctor"

by

J. Eldon Dorman, M.D.

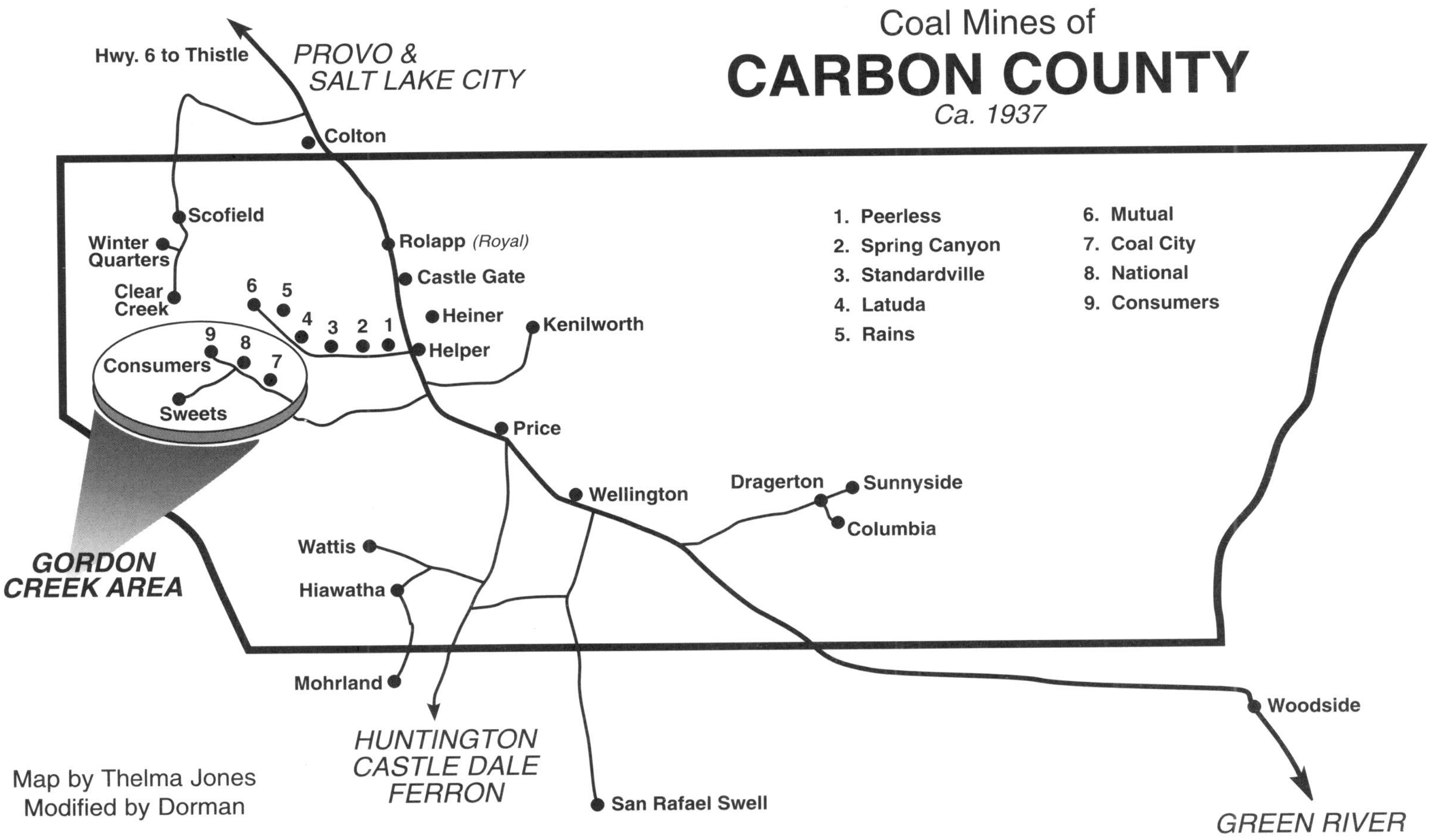
Coal Mines of
CARBON COUNTY
Ca. 1937
Hwy. 6 to Thistle
PROVO &
SALT LAKE CITY
Colton
Scofield
Winter Quarters
Clear Creek
Rolapp (Royal)
Castle Gate
Heiner
Kenilworth
Helper
6
5
4
3
2
1
9
8
7
Consumers
Sweets
GORDON CREEK AREA
Price
Wellington
Dragerton
Sunnyside
Columbia
Wattis
Hiawatha
Mohrland
HUNTINGTON
CASTLE DALE
FERRON
San Rafael Swell
Woodside
GREEN RIVER
1. Peerless
2. Spring Canyon
3. Standardville
4. Latuda
5. Rains
6. Mutual
7. Coal City
8. National
9. Consumers
Map by Thelma Jones
Modified by Dorman

The Coal Camp Doctor

During the first half of the 20th century, many of Utah's Carbon County coal mines were located in semi-isolated areas away from the major towns of Price and Helper.

If the mine was large, an active community soon grew up. There would be a mine office, a company store and usually a school. Homes for the miners early on were tents, followed by a conglomeration of shacks, which led to the term "coal camp."

Each coal camp was more or less self-sufficient, and early on, virtually all the miners who worked for that mine lived there as transportation was poor, with inadequate railroad service and roads often impassible. Eventually, schools and housing were improved, a company doctor hired, and a small hospital built for the benefit of the miner and his family.

Coal mining was (and is) a dangerous undertaking and the presence of a doctor gave the miners a feeling of security which they would not otherwise have had.

The typical coal camp doctor was young, just out of medical school. He generally intended on staying a year or two to get enough money to pay off part of his school debts and a nest egg to help start up a practice in a more desirable location. Helen Papanikolas says that Dr. Claude McDermid went to Sunnyside intending to work long enough to buy a new blue serge suit; he practiced at the mines for twenty-eight years.

Dr. Dorman was the doctor for the coal camps of Consumers, Sweets and National for three years beginning in 1937. He relates stories of his experiences in that capacity.

J. Eldon Dorman
Deseret News photo

Confessions Of A Coal Camp Doctor

I arrived in Consumers, Utah, on January 3, 1937. I was a native of Colorado, but had gone to medical school and served my internship in California. In July 1936, I went to Spanish Fork, Utah, to work for a doctor who was ill. He had recovered, and since we did not get along very well, I was pleased when, about midnight on January 2, I got a phone call from Terry McGowan, then superintendent of the Blue Blaze Coal Company at Consumers. He offered me a job as the doctor for the coal camps of Consumers, Sweets and National and asked that I report to work "for sure" at noon on the following day.

I did not quite make it by noon. As a flat-land driver, I failed to negotiate the snow-packed curve just west of old Tucker and clobbered my car when it ended up in the creek. So I entered Carbon County riding in the back of a flatbed coal truck, clutching my medical bag and rubbing my contusions.

I found patients waiting for me. I saw several sick people and handled some injuries. Before midnight, I delivered a baby boy. I received the surprise of my life when the father pressed a twenty-dollar bill in my hand shortly after I severed the umbilical cord. Never in my previous practice had I been paid so promptly. I had learned to settle many of my bills by barter – a sack of spuds, a box of apples or perhaps some eggs, butter or chickens. That crisp new bill in my otherwise empty pocket made me think I had come to the right place, and indeed, I had. I spent three of the most pleasant and enjoyable years of my life in the coal camps of Carbon County. I was called "Doctor," "Doc" or "Mr. Doc" (a title of special respect). Most frequently, however, I was "Little Mr. Doc," since I tipped the scales in those days at less than 125 pounds.

The Medical Association And The Company Doctor

Day shift gets off work. Consumers, Utah - 1936
D. Lange

Consumers, Sweets and National were the three coal mines in the Gordon Creek area, located about twenty miles west and a little north of Price, Utah. In the early 1930s, these three camps formed a medical association that was not dominated by the coal company, as were most of the others in Carbon County.

A committee made up equally of company and union personnel administered the association. The company representatives were the superintendents of each mine. The presidents of each union represented the miners. In 1937, this committee consisted of Terry McGowan and Charles Semken from Consumers, Lloyd Quinn and Ted Gentry from Sweets, plus Harry Elkins and Joe Matich from National. I attended the meetings, but had no vote, and I never had any problems with this group.

The association charged $1.50 per month for a man and his family and $1.00 per month for a single man. Money was collected by the check-off system. It was automatically taken out of the miner's wages by the company and deposited to the association, which then paid the doctor, nurse, medical bills, office expenses and hospital rent. All medicines were covered, as were office calls and house calls for any type of illness. Coverage did not extend to some surgical items:

Joe Bonto, Joe Naylor, Sr., Terry McGowan, Farny Farnsworth, Helen Memmott, Ray Naylor

deliveries were $35 extra; tonsillectomies, $15; appendectomies, $125; and simple fractures, $15. Treatment for venereal diseases was also excluded. All the Gordon Creek companies either carried industrial insurance or were self-insured.

My salary was $300 per month. Consumers provided living quarters and an office. A small five-bed hospital equipped with X-ray, microscope and other clinical laboratory facilities plus a well-stocked drug room were all operated by the doctor. Daily office hours were held. House calls were made to all three camps and visits to the Price hospital, where the most seriously injured patients were taken. During the winter, the roads were often closed by snow.

The coal camp doctor helped to contribute to the morale of the miner and his family, often making the difference in the success or failure of a mining operation. The men insisted on having someone at the portal when they were hurt. This was why I got my job, although I did not know it until after I arrived in Consumers. The previous doctor had left during the Christmas vacation without telling anyone his destination and was gone for a week. A serious accident occurred at the mine, and the doctor was fired upon his return.

Carbon County Medical Society Aches And Pains 1937 - 1950 +

After I had been here about a month or two, I was pleased to receive an invitation to attend a meeting of the Carbon County Medical Society at the old Carbon County Country Club, to be held at eight o'clock in the evening. I parked to one side of the already mostly filled parking lot at about twenty minutes before eight o'clock. In a few moments, another car pulled up beside me and Dr. Anthony R. Demman got out and spoke to me as I was getting out of my car. He said: "What time did your notice say the meeting would be?" I said: "Eight o'clock." He said: "Mine, too, but you wait and see, when we get in there we will find that the meeting is about over as the selected ones were called to meet at seven o'clock and we will be chided for being an hour late."

We went into the meeting a few moments before eight and were immediately scolded for being an hour late and told that the meeting was pretty much over. I found myself in a very hostile atmosphere. I was blamed for causing the last doctor to lose his job. I was classed as a very despicable person and a threat to the practice of medicine in the community. It was quickly decided that my application for membership in the society would be "tabled indefinitely," everyone voting against me except Dr. Demman.

What a welcome from the Carbon County Medical Society! I, of course, started asking a lot of questions in an effort to try and find out what went on. I quizzed Dr. Demman. He was a local boy who had gone to medical school and returned to Carbon County to practice. He had located in Helper about two years previously and the medical establishment had given him a rough time, just as they were now with me. Tony told me that there was a King Pin of medicine in southeastern Utah. He had taken over on the death of the wealthy Dr. Fisk, who apparently had previously ruled the roost. He volunteered the information that the scuttlebutt was that this King Pin had charged the affluent Fisk's estate megabucks to care for him on his death bed. Dr. Demman told me that the same doctor controlled virtually all the local doctors in Price and Helper, plus the coal camps of Castle Gate, Kenilworth, Sunnyside, Columbia, Clear Creek and Hiawatha. He also controlled the doctors of Emery County; Huntington, Castle Dale, Ferron and Green River. The only doctors not under his control were Drs. Richard McLaughlin and Bliss Finalyson (partners) of Price, Dr. L.H. Merrill of Spring Canyon and Dr. Ira Cummings of Standardville, besides of course, Dr. Demman and myself.

Thus, the area was divided medically into two camps, always at each other's throats, with the King Pin group being in command because of superior numbers. The relatively new (1935) Price City Hospital had been built, supposedly aided by considerable funds from the Fisk estate. King Pin had been chief of staff since its beginning. (And remained as such into the late 1940s, as each January his group would vote him in again and then adjourn the staff meeting into a poker game.)

King Pin and his group could not keep me out of the hospital since it was a community hospital and open to any qualified MD, but they sure as hell could make it miserable for me. I had a patient with a back injury in Ward 10 (it contained 10 beds). King Pin always made a big deal of making rounds - the majority of the surgical patients were his and he would command the superintendent of nurses plus a retinue of other nurses as he strutted at the head of the parade, talking with great authority, in his daily "grand rounds." He would pause at my patient's bed, shake his head and mutter loud enough so everyone could hear: "My poor man, too bad - too bad, you will never walk again."

I did not know that this was going on until Nedra Leavitt, superintendent of nurses, apparently to ease her conscience, told me about it, at the same time indicating that since King Pin was the chief of staff, there was nothing that she could do about what she thought was unethical behavior, but wanted me to know what was going on. A few days later, I walked into the doctors locker room to find Dr. Bliss Finlayson, who had just inadvertently heard King Pin make his

Price City Hospital 1935 - 1960

usual statement to my patient. He had King Pin backed up to the wall and was threatening to smack him in the kisser if he did not stop "being mean to Dorman." It was evident to me who my friends were.

I discussed the situation with Finlayson, McLaughlin, Demman and probably Merrill. They suggested that I refer my patient to Dr. Paul Richards, who at that time was considered Utah's greatest authority on back injuries. So I sent my patient to Dr. Richards, who sent him back to me as he concurred with my treatment.

Early on, another problem presented itself. I always carried a supply of narcotics in my medical bag. In the 1930s, narcotics were available only in tablet form. The various drugs came in a tiny little tube about 1/4 inch in diameter and 3 inches long, with a small cork in one end, holding about 20 pills. To give a patient a shot, a pill would be placed in a special type of teaspoon held in a mechanism over an alcohol lamp, filled with water, heated until it boiled, then drawn up in a sterile syringe and given to the patient. I carried tubes of morphine 1/8, 1/4 and 1/2 grains, plus pantopon grains 1/3 besides codeine grains 1/2 and 1. Something came up at the mine where I needed morphine 1/4 grain, but I could not find the tube. I used pantopon instead and replaced the tube of morphine when I got back to the office. Later on, another tube of morphine 1/4 came up missing and finally one day, all of my narcotics were gone. I was greatly upset and assumed that one of my coal camps was infested with a narcotic addict. One day, I chanced to mention my predicament to Dr. Richard McLaughlin. He laughed, slapped me on the shoulder and said: "I should have warned you to always lock your car when you park here at the hospital. The King Pin's office nurse tags him around a lot here at the hospital. I, and others, believe she is an addict and raids the doctors medical bags in the hospital parking lot. We have all lost narcotics. The thing to do is to carry your narcotics in your vest pocket."

Then I remembered one day at the hospital I had gone to my car to get something and had discovered this nurse in my car, but had thought nothing of it when she apologized and said she had accidentally got into my vehicle instead of her own parked next to mine. From that time on, I generally carried my narcotics in my vest pocket, which was really a very handy and safe place, thanks to the advice of Dr. McLaughlin. I treasured my association with Dr. McLaughlin as he was never too busy to be helpful and would go out of his way to give me counsel and help me in any way that he could.

As time went on, I never felt comfortable with King Pin as he continued to put little barbs into me every chance he got, just as he did to the other doctors who did not belong to his group. In about two years, I had an obese Austrian female, in her mid-forties, who developed a severe acute gallbladder attack. In those pre-antibiotic days, it was generally advised to wait out the acute episode before doing surgery. But the family wanted Dr. King Pin instead of me, so I turned the case over to him. He insisted on immediate surgery and scheduled it for the next day. In an effort, I guess, to impress me about his great surgical ability, he invited me to scrub in. His chief assistants were, as usual King Pin's favorites, so once again as in intern days, I was a mere piece of protoplasm on the end of a retractor. King Pin struck a fine pose, slashed an eight inch gash with the scalpel though skin and three inches of fat right down to the peritoneum. After the greatly swollen and edematous gallbladder area was exposed, he started to rip and tear instead of slowly and carefully dissecting. His actions made me think of a bull in a china closet as he pulled and tugged. Eventually, the patient died from a peritonitis. I was greatly upset, more so when the family seemed to blame me for her death. I never scrubbed with him again.

I was not able to figure out how King Pin had developed the reputation that he had as a surgeon. I finally decided it was just plain guts on his part and a gullible public. One of his favorite excuses, if something went wrong, was: "She/he was just full of cancer!"

After I had been in the coal camps for nearly three years, I decided to go back to school and specialize. I went to a residency in Washington, D.C., and the Graduate School of Medicine at the University of Pennsylvania, spending a year at each place in eye, ear, nose and throat. Then, in September of 1941, I returned to Price, Utah, to practice in my new specialty, being the only specialist as such in all of eastern Utah. I found King Pin more entrenched than ever in his command post.

World War II, with all its problems, came and went. Dr. King Pin and I more or less ignored each other, so things went smoothly, even though always a little tense. J. Bracken Lee had been mayor of Price for twelve years and was thus the ultimate boss of the Price City Hospital. But in 1948, Lee was elected governor of the state of Utah. A.D. Keller was the new mayor. He soon called a meeting of all the doctors. He stated very bluntly that a certain doctor had been chief of staff at the Price City Hospital for twelve years and he wondered if such a thing was the right thing to permit. Therefore, he had called a special meeting of the staff for a new election to determine the new staff under his regime. He further stated that many people in the community, himself included, were concerned about one specific medical group being in charge at the hospital for so long, so he was calling for an election to see what would happen and opened the floor for nomination of a new chief of staff. The room was very quiet – not a soul opened his mouth. It seemed that everyone was afraid to speak. I piped up and nominated Tony Demman. That broke the ice, Tony was put in by acclamation, other officers were selected and the meeting closed, I thought in an amiable manner, albeit with a gleam of satisfaction in the eyes of the minority medical group after over twelve years of domination, mostly by one man.

The following morning, I went to the hospital to see my patients. I checked my charts at the east side nursing desk and turned to walk to the west side. I had taken perhaps three steps when someone forcibly tapped me on the shoulder. As I turned, I was hit on the point of my jaw by the doctor's right fist with great force. I was cold-cocked. The next thing I knew, I was on the floor of the adjacent drug room, with King Pin on top beating me with his fists and Dr. King trying desperately to separate us. The nurses were screaming at the top of their voices. In reply to the calls for help, John Moyle rushed from the X-ray department and (he told me later) seized King Pin's collar with his left hand and with his right hand, reached between his legs, securely grasped his testicles and tossed him some twenty feet down the hall. Moyle then half carried me downstairs to his laboratory.

I came to after Moyle had bathed my face with cold water. I said to Moyle: "That SOB hit me, didn't he?" and took off up the stairs hunting for King Pin. I found him, surrounded by some of his cohorts, in the X-ray room. I tore into him, hitting him any place I could, but especially in the region of his right eye, making a cut to the bone above his eyebrow with the ring on my left hand. I was pulled off him by his friends and my friend, John Moyle. The ironic thing was that King Pin was president of the Utah State Medical Association that year and had to appear at the annual meeting the next day in Cedar City. I was told that he concocted a beautiful story about a car accident and hitting his head on the steering wheel on the way, to explain the black eye and the inch long cut with stitches.

I began to get warnings from many people - nurses and other hospital personnel, even some of King Pin's buddies - that he was threatening to kill me and was carrying a gun for that purpose. One person reported to me that he had seen him (alone) out by the airport, practicing with a pistol, which was a 9mm Luger, my informant had later picked up some of the spent shell casings. I doubted that he was a very good shot, but also concluded that he might just be crazy enough over his dethronement to try such a thing. So I started carrying a gun. Dr. Quinn A. Whiting, as a token of his friendship, had brought me from Germany, where he had been stationed during the war, a beautiful Walther PPK automatic pistol. I kept this pistol tucked under my belt when I was at the hospital, on the street, etc.; pretty much all the time. When I was in surgery, the gun was in my locker. King Pin and I avoided each other and never met face to face. I kept hearing some hanky-panky about the $50,000 charged by Dr. King Pin at the death of Dr. Fisk. So I hired an attorney, Duane Frandsen. He got into old court records and found out that, indeed, Dr. King Pin had billed Fisk's estate for $50,000 for one shot of adrenaline as the man was dying. But the doctor had settled for $17,500 and Frandsen brought me a copy of the check. I carried a weapon for over two years, but that ended when I eventually became chief of staff at the hospital and he started kissing my ass for any favors that he could get.

Incidentally, I carried the pistol mostly in a legal manner. I had started to carry the gun when Sheriff Joe Dudler called me into his office one day. I thought I was going to get hell, but he said: "I know you are carrying a concealed weapon and I know your problem, so let's make it legal." He called the county clerk, Brig Young, downstairs, swore me in as a deputy sheriff complete with a two-inch sized nickel-plated badge, which I never did turn in even after the crisis was over!

One other little item that I think is precious, especially since Dr. King Pin's universal remarks to his appendectomy patients was: "We got it just in time - it ruptured right in my hands." In 1953, Dr. Kenneth Castleton was president of the Utah State Medical Association. The United Mine Workers Welfare and Retirement Fund was supervised by Dr. William Dorsey and Ada Kruger. They had set up a meeting at the Price City Hall, more or less calling a lot of the doctors in this area on the carpet, especially about unnecessary surgery. Officials of the state medical association were called in, so Dr. Castleton and others were here. I was involved because I was one of the board of directors of the association that year. Each doctor involved was called in, shown his hospital charts and asked to explain if there was a problem. Shortly after lunch, Ada Kruger came to me tearing her hair. She said that they had seventeen appendectomy charts on the good doctor, fourteen of which were normal, but that during the lunch hour all of his charts had disappeared!

Dr. King Pin had a very large practice with extremely loyal patients. I asked one old gal about him one day and she let me know with considerable force: "You bet he is my doctor - why he has already cured me of cancer five times!"

You can't beat that!

Physical Examinations For Miners

As winter progressed, the demand for coal increased. My office was flooded with men waiting to be examined so they could go to work. The age limit was forty-five years. Strange as it may seem, I never had a patient who was over forty-five years of age. They would actually hide their canes and crutches outside my office. The physical examination was just a rough screening test. There were no pre-employment X-rays of chest or back, and anything that fooled the doctor was "legal." But welfare was not yet a way of life. All a coal miner asked for was a chance to work – to dig the coal to pay off his debts, feed and clothe his family and perhaps send his son to school. He never missed a shift. Often, he fought in line to get an extra shift or doubled back to work overtime without extra pay.

I hold a personal respect for the old-time Austrian, Italian, Greek and Welsh coal miners. I still recall their nicknames - Flat Nose Mike, Fat Mary, Tony Bolony and Mexican Joe. Each camp had several men known as Big John. The nicknames were always appropriate. A man called Buffalo came into my office one day. His incredible size prompted me to ask him the size of his pants. "Well, Mr. Doc," he replied, "these are fifty-six, but they're getting a bit snug."

One Mistake I Made

I had a mine telephone in my office and one at home. If an accident happened, I was frequently requested to meet the more seriously injured at the portal. It was quite an uphill walk, so I started driving my car. No road exist-

Consumers, Utah - 1937
photo by Art Van Wagonen - Dorman Collection

ed, but I could drive almost to the mine entrance. The entrance stood in view of the entire town, however, and every woman in camp recognized my car. Soon, each was standing on her front or back porch, wringing her hands on her apron and wondering if her husband or son was hurt or killed. I only drove up there twice. The ever-present fear of death in mine accidents, explosions or afterdamp already haunted the families enough.

Medicines

The practice of medicine was quite different in those times. No sulfa drugs or antibiotics were available. At Consumers, we had a new portable oxygen tent which was extremely useful for treating pneumonia.

Of the various types of cough medicines, syrup of wild cherry was the most popular. It cost $2 per gallon and I used to buy it in ten-gallon lots. One day, I was over helping Dr. Ira Cummings in Standardville and I mentioned the popularity of this syrup. He set me straight in a hurry. "You're stupid," he said. "Do you realize that a good portion of that syrup goes on these people's pancakes?" His statement was literally true. I watched for it and saw it happen. So, I thought I would stop this practice. I bought syrup of white pine tar, which had essentially the same ingredients, but tasted terrible. The patients put up a fuss when I tried to switch. Elixir cheracol was another cough medicine used for pancakes. Elixir terpin hydrate with codeine (TH&C) cost $8 a gallon then. It contained 40% alcohol, which is equal to 80-proof vodka, and almost two grains of codeine per ounce. TH&C was a popular medicine. It cured a lot of things besides a cough.

The five kinds of aspirin came in different colors. The white and the green worked best for me. The pink and orange did not seem very popular. Dr. Orson Spencer found it best to use the variegated color.

Mail-Order Nurse

When I first went to Consumers, I was unable to find a nurse to assist me. I finally phoned California and, by offering $125 per month, was able to hire a registered nurse away from her $85-a-month job.

Over the years, I continued to have nursing problems. One Catholic RN quit when I asked her to set up a tray for a male sterilization operation. It was simple: She said, "If you are going to do that kind of surgery, I quit." She walked out the door, literally leaving me with my patient's pants down.

In those days, there were various correspondence schools offering nurse's training. At least one woman in camp took such a course. She was a young married woman, and I used her a lot both in the hospital under the supervision of the RN and to help me out with home deliveries. She was pleasant, willing and hard-working.

I was glad to have her with me when I experienced a problem home delivery. The patient was in her early thirties. She had one child, a boy, about eleven years old. Eight previous, more or less full-term pregnancies had ended in stillbirths. She had come to me in about her fourth month of pregnancy. I had found her Wassermann to be a 4+, had treated her with mapharsen and had hopes of getting a live baby. But when I next saw her, there was a new problem.

My nurse and I found that the baby was well on its way with the head partially exposed, but the labor pains had stopped. I was afraid that the baby might start to breathe and choke to death in the birth canal. So I handed my nurse a 10-cc vial of pituitrin and a 2cc syringe and said: "Give her 2 minims right away." I thought I would have a few minutes for this drug to act, so I rushed into opening the sterile O.B. bundle and getting out sterile sheets, my sterile gown, gloves and other necessary items. Somehow, I chanced to look up just as the nurse injected the medication into the patient's arm. I stood spellbound with my mouth open, but unable to say a word as I saw 2cc instead of 2 minims, or sixteen times the amount I had asked for, being injected. I did not get my gloves or gown on, but caught the baby in my open arms against my chest as it shot out of the birth canal like a shot from a cannon. It was alive and apparently healthy.

The baby's cord Wassermann was negative, but the people moved away, so I had no real follow-up. I do not think I even scolded my nurse. It was my fault for not checking whether or not she knew the hypodermic dosages. I continued to use her when she was needed and appreciated her help.

Measles And Mumps

The acute infectious diseases were a great menace in the coal camps. If one child showed up with the measles after a weekend visit to friends or relatives in Castle Valley, the disease spread like a plague to all the children of the three camps. Otitis media, a middle ear infection, was an almost certain complication of the measles in those days. I carried a myringotomy knife in my medical bag and opened many bulging eardrums as I made house calls. The adults did not escape the childhood diseases. I vividly remember an epidemic of mumps that swept like wildfire and resulted in the tragic illness to two young men that certainly changed their lifestyle.

Looking up (west) Main Street Consumers, Utah - 1936
D. Lange

Active immunization clinics were held each year for diphtheria, whooping cough, tetanus, typhoid, paratyphoid and smallpox. In general, the response to these clinics was good.

'One Night With Venus...'

The venereal diseases also posed a problem in the coal camps. The per capita rate of VD, however, was probably no greater in the coal camps than in Salt Lake City.

The biggest problem, of course, was that we did not have proper medicines to handle these diseases. Gonorrhea often had to be treated for a year or more to effect a cure. Lues, or syphilis, was more serious. It was treated by various arsenicals such as "606" or mapharsen. Injections of mercury were often used in the chronic stages, which led to the well-worn medical cliche of the 1930s: "One night with Venus and the rest of your life with Mercury."

Each new case of venereal disease afforded considerable interest to the camp doctor. By simple observation and deduction, he was able to trace its progress and to discover, often with surprise and amazement, who was doing what to whom and approximately when. Any coal mine doctor could have been a blackmail expert. For me, however, keeping the medical and social secrets of the camp was part of the fun.

Pool Table Surgery

I never dared to leave camp on Saturday nights. These towns really cooked on weekends. Parties, fights, brawls - you name it - they did it with enthusiasm.

I was new in the Gordon Creek area when I received a midnight call on Saturday night to rush to the beer parlor at Sweets. This beer joint was something special. Its floor was covered with several inches of sawdust hiding the blood and gore of previous Saturday nights. I found an older man sitting in a chair against the wall, with his head hanging down against his blood-covered chest. When I spoke to him, he raised his head and revealed a cut on his throat from ear to ear that gaped open an inch or more. To my amazement, I discovered that it was a superficial cut through the skin that exposed, but did not damage the major blood vessels of the neck. I also noted that my patient was inebriated.

I was disgusted, since I had already patched up several bloody noses and left quite a mess back at my office. There would be a problem transporting a drunk and bleeding patient to the office, probably in my car, to sew him up. Since there was a pool table in the saloon, I decided to work there. I took out a couple of small sterile towels and the necessary instruments and proceeded to sew the man up. This, despite the helpful and sometimes critical audience, did not take too long. The thump of the jukebox never died and the drinking, smoking and revelry only paused momentarily while my stitches were inspected.

As I did my barroom surgery, I heard most of the story. I was surprised and chagrined to learn that my patient was the mine foreman.

He loved to drink and he loved to play poker. He had been doing plenty of both while the jukebox was pounding out polka after polka. Due to the chronic shortage of females in the Sweets beer joint, many of the Austrian men were dancing with each other. One Austrian fellow kept asking the mine foreman to dance with him, making quite a nuisance of himself. Finally, the foreman, more interested in poker and booze, cursed and told the fellow in no uncertain terms to leave him alone. The Austrian left, but soon returned with an open clasp knife, stood behind the foreman's chair and proceeded to cut his throat from left to right.

I had finished my throat repair job and was patching up the hand of Osby Martin, who had grasped the open blade of the assailant's knife as he wrestled it away from him, when somebody suggested, "Maybe you had better go see Sam" - the knife wielder. Then I found out the rest of the story.

When business was good, the right-hand end of the bar held an open case of warm beer. When he removed a cold beer from the cooler, the bartender could replace it with a warm one from the top of the bar. In the excitement of the knife episode, the bar patrons had proceeded to break thirteen full bottles of beer over Sam's head without knocking him out. I saw broken glass on the floor and dried foam on the low ceiling.

I found Sam at the bunkhouse, squatting in a galvanized tub of water and holding a bloody washcloth to his bleeding, lacerated scalp. I asked him how he felt. He looked up and said, "I feel pretty good, but I do got a leetle bit headache!" I spent the next few hours picking glass out of his bald head. I got back to my house in Consumers just in time to hear the celebrants at the boarding house next door greet the dawn with loud, discordant verses of "It's Only A Shanty in Old Shanty Town."

Osby Martin

Osby Martin was a bachelor who lived in the Sweets mine bunkhouse. It was said that he had killed a man and served time in the Colorado penitentiary and that he had been an exhibition shooter for the Winchester Repeating Arms Company.

Everyone in Sweets was scared of Osby. On occasion, he would take his .30-.30 Winchester 94 rifle, stand in the main street in front of his bunkhouse, toss ordinary glass marbles in the air and break them one by one. Many heated arguments in Sweets came to an end when Osby threatened to get his "turty-turty."

Osby had quite a racket going. The main line in the mine at Sweets used electric locomotives for haulage, but horses were still used for dispensing and gathering the coal cars to and from the various working entries. Osby Martin was one of the drivers who dispensed the cars. The miners at Sweets were paid fifty-five cents per ton for hand loading, but without coal cars, they could not load the coal. If Osby failed to get his proper "cut" on payday, the miners failed to get the cars they needed. Eventually, the situation became tense and a union meeting was called. The problem, however, was resolved outside the meeting. The Sweets union hall was reached by a narrow footbridge five or six feet above the small drainage creek that ran through the bottom of the canyon and was fed by the kitchen sinks, dishpans and slop jars of the cabins lining its banks. Under several inches of slimy gray dish water was about a foot of malodorous primeval ooze that not even a trilobite could live in.

Sweets Mine - 1937. Looking east, down canyon
Photo by Clyde Stevenson - Dorman Collection

The problems of the union hall boiled over onto the footbridge. A little five-foot-six-inch, 135-pound miner named Elmer Brinley confronted the brawny Osby. He landed a haymaker on Osby's chin that staggered him back against the flimsy railing. Osby sailed through the air, landing flat on his back in the ooze and slime.

Then the miners sent for me. I never understood why they didn't call the sheriff, the mine superintendent or the mine foreman in these situations. Perhaps they thought my services were about to be needed and that I should be handy.

When I drove into Sweets at early dusk, I found an armed camp. A man standing behind the corner of his house holding a six-shooter waved me up the road. The closer I came, the more belligerent the situation looked, with a shotgun here, a deer rifle there and an automatic pistol or two in the hands of determined coal miners. I was flagged to a stop by a couple of armed men shielded by a building. They told me that Osby was in his room. I was the logical one to go in to talk to him, they explained, since he might have been hurt in his fall from the bridge. I pounded on his door. There was no answer, so I pounded again and said, "It's Doc." The door was unlocked and opened. Osby set the .30-.30 by the doorjamb. He had just finished taking a bath in a galvanized washtub. I hastened to sympathize with, and even magnify, his leg and chest injuries. I convinced him to go with me to the hospital at Consumers for X-rays and other first-aid treatment. We did not see a soul as we drove through and out of Sweets with the .30-.30 upright between Osby's legs.

I X-rayed him and bound up his wounds. When he complained of pain, I gave him some "pain" pills well laced with sleeping pills. It was now dark outside. I let him get a little drowsy and he forgot about his .30-.30, which I had put out of sight. I delivered him back to his room and tucked him in. After a couple of days, I took his gun back to him. I was told that the episode finished Osby's days of extortion at Sweets and Elmer B. was the camp hero.

Father Ruel's Request

In 1937, the Catholic priest at Price was Father William A. Ruel and his assistant was Father Jerome Stoffel, just out of the seminary. They came to

Consumers to see a patient for whom I had given up all hope. When the young six-months-pregnant woman had become seriously ill with pneumonia, the community was snowbound. I had her carried to the small mine hospital, where I put her in the new oxygen tent. Without penicillin or other antibiotics, my only hope for her was oxygen, but she had gone steadily downhill. The roads were cleared, but it seemed unwise to move her to the Price hospital, which had nothing more to offer than oxygen.

Quite early one cold snowy morning, Fathers Ruel and Stoffel appeared and administered the last rites. But about this time, another complication came up: she had gone into rather active premature labor. I explained the situation to Father Ruel and his quiet, somewhat shy, young assistant. It looked as if the mother was sure to die; she might, while breathing her last, give birth to an infant who might live but a short time.

I became busy with my other tasks of the day, pausing frequently to check my patient. At dusk, I answered a somewhat demanding knock. It was Father Ruel, who needed to talk with me about a matter of great importance. He indicated that he, too, was a busy man and many duties required his presence back in Price. He and his assistant had spent the entire day in the camp waiting for the baby to be born in order to baptize him, but they must leave at once." Therefore, he wanted me to baptize the new baby if he was born alive. Since I had been raised under a rigid Protestant family and educational regime, my face must have indicated some question. Father Ruel hastened to assure me that this procedure was ethical and honorable. He had me memorize the words that would save a tiny soul from purgatory. I was further concerned when I thought I discerned a hint of skepticism in the eye of Father Stoffel, as if he, as surely I did, doubted my ability to say the proper words at the proper time and in the proper sequence. Perhaps someone up above was skeptical as well. In any event, within a few hours, the premature labor pains stopped and the patient went on to a rapid recovery from her pneumonia and eventually a normal full-term delivery.

Dental Practice

I was routed out of my bed early one Sunday morning by an older Austrian fellow still somewhat inebriated from a Saturday night party. He held his lower right jaw in both hands and swung his head back and forth and up and down as he moaned and groaned with a toothache. He could not stand still, but paced my office floor in agony, swinging his head in rhythm with his steps. I offered him pills or even a shot of morphine for his pain, but he had brought his own painkiller and proceeded to gulp at frequent intervals from a bottle of Old Crow.

Consumers, Utah - 1936, Typical "tar-paper shack"
D. Lange

He demanded that I pull the offending tooth. I explained that I was not a dentist and he should visit one in Price or Helper. He objected strongly and pointed out several dental forceps in the glass-enclosed instrument case in the corner. He also informed me that a previous doctor had pulled a tooth for him with no problem. I argued against playing dentist while he took turns pleading and berating my ability. Finally, I reluctantly selected a formidable forceps as he pointed out the offending second molar with his forefinger. I thought his selection was questionable, since several other teeth looked worse. He insisted, however, so I applied the forceps and started to pull, twist and yank. I gradually backed the patient and the chair against the wall, put my knee on his chest and eventually ended up with the tusk. The patient spat out a mouthful of blood in my wastebasket, took another slug of booze and thanked me profusely as he backed out the door.

When I saw the patient on the street the next day, he ignored me completely. The following day, the same thing happened. I wondered if he had been too intoxicated to remember what had happened. I could no longer endure his ungratefulness, so I asked him if he did not appreciate what I had done. He let forth a tirade of blasphemy, shook his fist under my nose and said he had gone to see Dr. Joe Dalpiaz in Helper because I had pulled the wrong tooth!

Dr. Claude McDermid

Recent medical school graduates often came to Carbon County to work for mine companies, staying just long enough to accumulate enough money to return to the East and open up a practice. Utah historian Helen Papanikolas says that one of these young doctors, Claude McDermid, arrived in Sunnyside in 1911 to assist Dr. Andrew Dowd. After the financial deprivations of his schooling, he intended to stay only long enough to afford to buy another blue serge suit. He stayed.

After a year in Sunnyside, he became the Castle Gate company doctor and won the miners' respect. Florence Reynolds recalls waiting in his office when a new manager stormed in, bent on economizing. It was a cold day in winter, and the manager warned Dr. McDermid that he was going to turn off the electricity in the miners' company houses.

"You are not," said the young doctor.

"I am," the manager answered. "They don't need it and don't deserve it."

Whereupon, Dr. McDermid rose to his full six-foot-six, hit the manager with his fist and sent him sprawling.

Dr. McDermid practiced in Carbon County for twenty-eight years and was the Castle Gate company doctor at the time of the tragic 1924 explosion that took 172 lives. He and his three sons were left with rheumatic hearts from a bacterial epidemic, and he died soon after leaving Carbon County.

I did not have the physique or the ability to be as aggressive as Dr. McDermid, but this story illustrates how many of the early doctors were willing to jeopardize their jobs with the companies that hired them, in defense of the coal miners and their families.

Baxter

Baxter was a he-cat spelled with a capital C. He was given to me, three-fourths grown, by the wife of Samuel W. Georges, MD of Spanish Fork, Utah, for whom I had worked for about six months while he was ill. Dr. Georges was from Persia (now Iran) and the cat's parents had been imported from that country. When I first went to Consumers, Baxter raised so much hell, yowling and fighting the other cats in camp at night, that I decided to cure the infernal nocturnal noise. One evening after office hours, I stuck his head in a coffee can filled with ether-soaked cotton, put him to sleep and emasculated him. I will never forget the terrible look that he gave me when he came to and he would have nothing to do with me for several days, but gazed at me with malevolent eyes.

Baxter soon reached maturity. He stood well over a foot tall at the shoulders. He had a large head, with erect tufted ears. His hair was over an inch long, a tannish yellow color with white stripes. His tail was long and bushy. He had a ruff of longer hair about his neck which, together with his tail and the hair all over his body, would swell up to tremendous size when he was upset. He soon whipped all of the abundant tomcats in camp. One good-sized long-haired mongrel got his baptism of fire one day when he tried to chase Baxter. He immediately found the cat astride his head and neck, trying to scratch his eyes out with his forepaws while his hind feet dug out hunks of fur from his neck and shoulders, all the time screaming feline invectives. Soon, all the other dogs in camp were quickly intimidated, too. Even the biggest, fiercest dog would tuck his tail between his legs and head for home if Baxter snarled and spit at him with ruffled up fur and expanded twitching tail as he strutted up the narrow coal town street. My surgery did not seem to slow down the cat at all. He would lounge around the house all day, but toward evening, he would disappear, not to show up until the wee hours of the morning, when he would yowl at the front door to be let in. So that I would not have to get up in the middle of the night, I put a 2x6 plank extending from the open bedroom window to the ground, thus he could come and go at will. In the morning, I would frequently find dead ground squirrels, mice or birds on the floor beside my bed. Several times, there were half-grown cotton-tail rabbits. In warm weather, he might not show up for several days at a time. He roamed the entire town and adjacent hills at will.

Eventually, he invaded the mine, generally after midnight when the hustle and bustle of mining was at a low ebb. There were two shifts, morning and evening, of about a hundred men each. But in the middle of the night, there might be perhaps only a dozen or so men underground in the maze of tunnels, cross cuts and rooms that extended several miles into the mountain, even below and beyond Beaver Creek. Men would report to me that Baxter was often seen two or three miles beyond the portal, probably hunting mice that were there because of the discarded lunch bucket morsels. Pump men or shot-fires, on their lonely duties at night in the mine, would get the daylights scared out of them when they chanced to come across him staring at them from the top of a timber or a ledge in the mine. Several men thought he was a bobcat or a lynx. One fellow told me he thought that he was seeing a mountain lion ready to pounce on him and took off running and yelling for help at the top of his voice. After the element of surprise was over, there was a mutual coal miner-cat adjustment with no further problems.

When I left Consumers in late 1939 to go back to school at the University of Pennsylvania, I gave Baxter to the Ray Johnson family. He lived for 18 years on their farm, a part of their household, but still his own CAT and boss. QUITE A CAT! Many years later, Tommy Johnson told me: "Baxter was my buddy when I was growing up; he was better than a dog."

Bozo

Bozo

Bozo was a pedigreed English bulldog that I purchased in Salt Lake City as a companion for Baxter. He was built like a brick outhouse – very sturdy. In spite of his formidable and ferocious appearance with bowed legs and underslung protruding lower jaw with long exposed teeth, he was the opposite of the cat in temperament - most of the time. Bozo and Baxter got along well, often sleeping cuddled up together on the living room floor. He was friendly toward most people and liked to be petted and made over. But he would diligently guard my small daugh-

Marcia "Snookie" Dorman, 1938

ter, Marcia, as she played on the boarding house lawn, one of the few spots of green in the coal mining town of Consumers. Under his care, she was safe from anyone.

My dentist, Dr. Lyman Kofford, and I concocted what we thought was a brilliant idea. I used to bring Bozo to town with me and would sometimes walk him up and down the main streets of Price or Helper. Dr. Kofford and I thought it would be great if Bozo had a gold cap on one of his massive, inch-long lower canine teeth. This would make his otherwise fierce look more sophisticated and note-worthy. So we coaxed the dog into the dental chair to take an impression for the crown. But Bozo abruptly changed our minds; he suddenly had us backed against the wall and we felt lucky to get out of the room alive…

Sister Billy

Looking down (east) Main Street Consumers, Utah - 1936, D. Lange

One of my favorite patients was Mary. She came to me early on in her pregnancy. She was a tiny, slender beautiful blonde gal who tipped the scales at about a hundred pounds. Mary and I hit it off well from the beginning. She was married to Goldie. They had one child, a boy, about four years old, named Kenneth. She had one commanding obsession; she wanted the new baby to be a girl – a baby sister for her son. Each time she came to my office for her monthly checkup, she wanted me to predict the sex of the new baby and always informed me that she would not settle for anything but a girl. I would tease her and say that she ought to be happy for another boy who could grow up to be a coal miner. But she always insisted, in no uncertain terms, that the new one would have to be a girl. In order to tantalize her, I began calling the expected one "Sister Billy." Soon, the whole coal camp became aware of my name for the new baby and joined in the good-natured bickering. As her pregnancy wore on, Mary and I would squabble more and more about Sister Billy in a good natured way. Mary's mother operated the boarding house next to my office so we saw a lot of each other even between her maternity visits. Every time I saw her, I would inquire about Sister Billy.

Her due time was in March. At mid-afternoon on a Sunday, I received an emergency call to go to her home. It was a bright sunny day, exceptionally warm for that time of year. The snow was melting and the one dirty street was filled with more than a foot of mud and water. I soon got stuck in my car so I had to walk the remaining quarter mile, carrying my big OB bag that contained my sterile instruments, sheets, gloves, gown, etc.

I was met at the door by a concerned Goldie and Mary's mother, Anna. They were upset because Mary was not due for another two weeks. I had to work fast as the baby was on its way. Mary was having violent labor pains so I quickly opened a can of ether, saturated the gauze on the large metal mask and placed it over her face, with directions to one of my helpers to keep pouring the ether. I got into my sterile garb and soon delivered a beautiful new baby girl.

The residence was a two-room wooden shack. There was a small kitchen and a larger combination bed-living room. The only source of heat was a coal-fired kitchen stove which had an exposed brick chimney. I immediately carried the baby into the warm kitchen and started cleaning it up, checking the newly severed umbilical cord and getting it into its swaddling clothes. Standing next to me, against the chimney, was Luke, Mary's stepfather. He was trying desperately, but vainly, to get the cork out of a new quart bottle of Old Crow so he could properly celebrate the arrival of his new granddaughter. Suddenly, there was a terrible noise; the whole house shook and shuddered. There was a shower of half-bricks which hit Luke on the head. The baby and I were covered with chunks of mortar and the room was filled with dust. I dashed into the other room. A giant round boulder, three feet in diameter, had become dislodged from its high cliff perch due to the unseasonably warm day. It rolled down the mountainside and hit the Day home. The headboard of Mary's bed was against the north wall of the room. The missile had passed within a foot of the side of her bed, right where I had been working when I delivered her. She was still half asleep and groggy from the ether and wanted to know what all the noise was about. The path of the boulder was like that of a bullet; the entrance hole by Mary's bed was three feet in diameter, but it took out most of the south wall along with numerous pieces of furniture.

After I had checked the utter devastation, Luke finally got my attention to look at his head wounds, which were bloody but not serious. He threw his hands in the air, said "Dooo Gummit – I am getting the hell out of here before the whole house falls down!" and took off down the mucky canyon road. The bad part of it was that he took the bottle of booze with him!

The new baby was named Golda, but for several years, was known most frequently and affectionately as Sister Billy…

Nineteen years later, I was invited to her wedding reception.

Bill Hall

The Gordon Creek grade school at National served the three coal mining towns of Consumers, Sweets and National. Bill Hall was one of the teachers there. His parents were from Hiawatha, but he batched in one of the Blue Blaze Coal Company apartments across the street from my home and office in Consumers. He was in his early twenties; he was a slender 5 ft. 8 in. tall, tipping the scales at less than 130 lbs. He was a good teacher, well liked and respected in the community.

Bill Hall, awarded Congressional Medal of Honor

In the late 1930s, there was a band mania in Carbon County. This condition extended to all of the coal camps in the region; even grade schools had their own marching bands, complete with often elaborate uniforms. The Gordon Creek school participated enthusiastically in this program. Bill Hall was in charge of their band.

One Friday, a special practice was called at Price in preparation for the upcoming band contest. Shortly after noon, Eddie Martin, the school bus driver, loaded up the kids, with Mrs. Joe (Gussie) Bonto as chaperon, accompanied by her daughter, LaRue, and took off for town. Bill Hall drove his own car alone as he wanted to do some shopping before he came home. Toward evening, there was a terrible spring snowstorm which caused considerable consternation among the parents waiting at home. The storm increased in fury; it got dark and still no bus. Finally, it showed up several hours late; LaRue Bonto was on the bus, but her mother was not.

I was in my office about ten o'clock that night, having just taken care of a mine injury. I was about to lock the outside door when down the steps, half falling, came Bill Hall. He was bleeding profusely from both mouth and nose, with blood all over his face, hands and clothes. One eye was greatly puffed up and starting to go black. There were swollen bloody abrasions on both cheeks and forehead; his lips, tongue and mouth were cut and bleeding. He carried in his hands a .22 caliber pump action Winchester rifle.

As I patched him up, I got the story. Because she had wanted to buy something in a store in town, Mrs. Bonto had come home with Bill instead of on the bus. He had driven his car into his garage located beneath his apartment. As he got out of the car, he was clobbered by Joe Bonto who said: "So you are the guy who is messing around with my wife!" When he got up, he was knocked down again.

Joe Bonto was a big man. He was the mine foreman. He could whip any man in town. Everyone knew this so he was seldom challenged. The ethnic miners called him, in grudging admiration, "The Bonto." Being a bit of a womanizer, he was extremely jealous of his wife. Under the circumstances of the sudden snowstorm and the uneasy waiting, I could understand his anxiety, but Bill Hall did not see it that way.

Bill was pretty upset and rather wild. He told me as soon as I treated his injuries he was going to shoot Joe Bonto. He was swearing, throwing his arms about, raving and ranting about the injustice of the whole situation; he had only helped Mrs. Bonto out by giving her a ride and had, of course, never even touched her. He asked me to hurry up with the first aid so that he could go and shoot Joe Bonto right away. I had taken his gun and placed it in a corner of the room. As I was finishing my job, he picked it up and was about to be on his way. I explained to him that his condition might be more serious than first anticipated because of the multiple, traumatic injuries to his head. I had already given him a small dose of morphine for his obvious pain, but it only seemed to stir him up and make him more wild and determined to go immediately and shoot Joe. I continued to try to appease and calm him down, but to no avail. I again took the gun, but he jerked it back away from me. I would take the gun from him – he would again wrestle it away. I kept talking and telling him that the worst thing he could do would be to commit murder. I kept reasoning, finally got the gun, gave him some pain pills and told him to go home to bed with ice packs to his head. He eventually left, leaving the gun behind. I had just placed it out of sight in a cupboard when he showed up again, demanded the gun and said that nothing was going to stop him from shooting his assailant. He had started to bleed again so I had him sit down while I once more worked on his wounds. I gave him three grains of Seconal and fibbed to him, saying that it would help stop his continued bleeding. Soon, he became drowsy. I helped him to his feet, guided him across the street and upstairs to his apartment and tucked him in. He was sound asleep when I left.

There is no doubt in my mind that he would have tried to kill Bonto if things had not worked out as they did. Late the next day, he showed up in my office for treatment. He was still very much upset, but thanked me for preventing him from doing something that he would have regretted the rest of his life. But I did not give his gun back for a couple of weeks.

Years passed by. The United States suffered a terrible blow at Pearl Harbor on December 7, 1941. In a few months, she was fighting for her very life in the Pacific and getting the hell beat out of her most of the time. But the battle of the Coral Sea turned the tide. Bill Hall helped win that battle. He was a Naval Reserve pilot from the aircraft carrier Lexington on patrol May 7, 1942. He dived his plane at a Japanese aircraft carrier, contributing to the destruction of the vessel. The next day, he took on twelve Japanese planes and downed three of them.

For these heroic deeds of personal bravery above and beyond the call of duty, he was awarded the Congressional Medal of Honor. In part, his citation reads: "Though seriously wounded in this engagement, Lt. (j.g.) Hall, maintaining the fearless and indomitable tactics pursued throughout these actions, succeeded in landing his plane, safely."

The Congressional Medal of Honor was created during the Civil War, to be awarded by the president "in the name of the Congress of the United States" and is the highest United States military decoration that can be awarded. Since its onset, over 2,500 people have received this citation.

I have quoted from a paper presented at the annual meeting of the Utah State Historical Society in 1993 by Linda Thatcher. She further states that Bill Hall was one of only five people to ever receive the Congressional Medal of Honor from Utah. A sixth person, not from Utah, but adopted by the state because of his death at Pearl Harbor on the U.S.S. Utah, also received the medal.

It was not too long before Bill was back in Carbon County on R&R and to recuperate from his wounds. I saw quite a bit of him and we did considerable reminiscing about coal camp days. He also told me that his plane was shot up so badly that it was pushed overboard after he landed on the Lexington. We cooked up a party or two at the old Country Club in Carbonville, in which he quietly participated. He was a great guy and fun to be around. I was proud to know and associate with him.

I always felt, in my own selfish way, that I had contributed a great deal to the war effort. Instead of shooting down Japanese planes and bombing their aircraft carriers, Bill might well have been languishing behind bars at the Utah State Prison had I not stopped him from trying to commit homicide on Joe Bonto!
(Reference: 3)

Marko And Tillie Yelenich

Tillie Yelenich at Dr. Dorman's retirement party.

During the winter months, I had to make house calls at Sweets, located about a mile away from my office at Consumers. Frequently, the roads were bad: lots of snow or mud or a combination of both. I would drive down out of Consumers toward National, then make a right turn to Sweets. I would stop at the Sweets Mine office where Lloyd Quinn would give me a list of the calls for me to make. Generally, I could drive a bit beyond the "beer hall" to a sort of intersection close to the "Jap boarding house," where I would park and take off on foot, carrying my heavy medical bag. Most of my visits were to see sick kids, usually babies or preschoolers or an occasional housewife who thought she was too sick to come to my office.

I would often make these trips about 9 a.m. I would really be tired and exhausted after trudging by foot all over the camp in the deep snow. Then Tillie Yelenich would save my life by waving me to her home, where she would have something for me to eat. I enjoyed my visits with her; it gave me a moment to rest my tired legs and aching back besides giving solace to my hungry stomach. She would give me a couple of slices of home-

Sweets Mine - 1937. Looking west, up canyon
Photo by Clyde Stevenson - Dorman Collection

made bread with jam, a cinnamon roll or perhaps a bowl of hot soup. During the holidays, I would get some fresh baked "potica" with generally a loaf to take home. Tillie was married to Marko Yelenich, a quiet spoken man, older than Tillie by several years. Marko was from the "Old Country" - Yugoslavia - where he had been born and grown to adulthood before coming to America. When I first knew them, they had two children: Martha and Tony. I was soon to deliver Marko Jr.; daughter Helen was to come later.

When Marko Jr. was about 6 months of age, he developed a very severe pneumonia. I put him in my portable oxygen tent, as that was the only treatment we had in those pre-antibiotic days. I despaired for the baby's life, as he seemed to get worse and worse. I would drive over to Sweets a couple of times a day to see him. After several days, he was no better. I saw him one evening and his temperature had gone up to 106 degrees F. and his breathing was very labored. Earlier that day, I had been so concerned that I suggested to the parents, whom I knew were Catholic, that perhaps they should call a priest. Fathers Edward F. Dowling and Jerome Stoffel from Price, over 20 miles away, responded. They had just baptized the baby at the time of my visit. From the sad look in their eyes, I could tell that they, too, shared my apprehension. That night, I could not sleep for worrying about him so I got up, dressed and went to the Yelenich home about 3 a.m. As there was a dim light glowing, I tiptoed into the home.

Marko and Tillie were asleep, completely exhausted from their vigil of tending little Marko, day and night for several days without rest or sleep. At first, I thought that the baby had died. But when I raised the flap of the oxygen tent, he was breathing quietly and his forehead was cool. I knew that the crisis was past so I quietly left the house. When I returned the next day about 10 a.m., no one knew that I had been there during the night as they, like the baby, had passed the crisis in the slumber of exhaustion. Everyone was overjoyed at the fortunate turn of events.

Some unorthodox methods of coal mining were engaged in at the Sweets Mine. A few of the men, anxious to make an extra dollar or two for their families, would go into the mine and work on weekends. Loading another ton or two of coal at $0.55 per ton meant more to them than resting on Saturday or Sunday. Probably this semi-illegal procedure was tolerated by the management in its desire to get all the coal it could during the heavy demand of winter months. Also, there was always a handful of legitimate workers in the mine, around the clock, doing maintenance work, watching the pumps, hauling in props or perhaps working on the rails, even on holidays.

One Saturday night, about 10 o'clock, I got an urgent call that there had been an accident and that I was wanted at the portal of the Sweets Mine at once for an emergency situation. I was all dressed up in suit clothes, white shirt and tie, but took only time to grab my hard hat and medical bag, as I had been told that maybe I would need to go underground as some miners had been buried by coal. I was met by Grant Charlesworth, who was standing by a small electric mine locomotive. He explained that a small crew of men were already in the mine in an attempt to rescue the injured. He urged me on top of the locomotive, told me to lie flat with one arm over my medical bag to a hand hold and the other hand to a grip on the other side of the locomotive. He warned me that there were some low spots in the tunnel so under no circumstance was I to raise my head or "You will get your damn brains splattered all over hell!" The ride was a rough one; the machine lurched and swayed and nearly lost me a time or two, Grant was in a hurry.

We reached a spot where he stopped the locomotive. He helped me off the top and ran ahead of me toward the accident site. I had trouble keeping my balance on the uneven floor, my head-lamp giving a very poor light in the inky blackness of the mine. Soon, we reached the room where the men had been working. There were three or four men already digging furiously at an immense pile of coal that had caved from the working face and roof. Three men had pretty much been buried by the coal and rock. By the time I got there, their heads were uncovered so that they could breathe, but most of the rest of their bodies were out of sight. They were all badly crushed by the debris. I pitched in to help uncover them a little more so that I could give each one a shot of morphine; all the while, more coal kept falling from the roof and rib. For a time, it seemed that rescue team and all might be buried in a massive cave-in.

Sweets Mine tipple on right, 1937.

The men were Marko Yelenich, John "Bulldog" Mikulas and another one whose name I have forgotten. When I got to Marko, he looked up at me, smiled and said: "Mr. Doc, I am going to have to have a little talk with you – don't you know better than to come into the mine with a suit and white shirt on!"

All of the men were seriously hurt. Besides his other injuries, Marko had one Achilles tendon severed by a sharp edge of rock as if by a razor blade. I sewed it back in place at the Price Hospital and he, undaunted, was soon back to work. Thereafter, Marko would proclaim far and wide that he might not be alive if it were not for me. In later years, he would introduce me to his friends as: "Mr. Doctor Dorman - he save my leg and maybe my life in the coal mine at Sweets." And then, of course, he would tell about Marko Jr., too. He sure helped pump up my ego.

Marko told me one story that I will always remember. It seems that one time, during the terrible depression years, his total Sweets paycheck for the month, after deductions, was about $2.50. Since he and Tillie were recently married, he bought her a new pair of bedroom slippers for $0.80, a file to sharpen his pick for $0.25 and gave $1.00 to the union! I also remember Marko's white rubber boots that he wore when he stomped the grapes for his homemade wine.

After the mine closed at Sweets, Marko and Tillie operated a hotel-boarding house in Helper. I used to visit them. In one of the bedrooms, they had the world's greatest brass bed. The style was four poster in type. It was made of real polished brass, the posters being about 4 inches in diameter, each capped by a removable ornament. Legend had it that this bed, at one time, had belonged to a madam at one of Helper's brothels. She had used the hollow brass tubing to stash her cash and other valuables.

Years later, Maurine and I were invited to celebrate Marko's 90th birthday at the Slovenian Home in Spring Glen. Once again, he touted my praise to anyone who would listen. The highlight of the evening was when Marko (who said he could not dance) danced with Tillie. All of Marko's children and grandchildren were there, except one son, Tony, who had died at a young age of Lou Gehrig's disease (amyotrophic lateral sclerosis) a few years previously.

Marko passed away February 16, 1988. Tillie's 80th birthday was celebrated by her family and friends March 6, 1993 at the Slovenian Home in Spring Glen. The polkas were danced perhaps just a wee bit less vigorously than in previous years…

Crazy Jim

One thing about "Crazy Jim" was that he, in my opinion, was sure as hell crazy – like a fox. He was a Greek man who had a miserable flock of moth-eaten old ewes that he ran in the Gordon Creek area of Carbon County during the years that I was camp doctor for the coal mining towns of Consumers, Sweets and National. I always marveled that his scroungy band of about a hundred ancient ewes could make it through the tough winters. On my way to Price, I would see him on horseback as he drove his emaciated flock, in the foot deep snow, seeking forage in the sagebrush flats east of Coal City. I do not remember that he had a dog. His eight- or ten-year-old daughter acted in place of one. He sat on his horse and directed her, as she, her feet and legs wrapped in gunny-sacks, rounded up the strays. One day, after a storm, I watched as this little girl, struggling in snow up to her knees, broke trail for Jim and his horse.

It is doubtful, in my mind, if he had any legal right, under the Taylor Grazing Act, to herd his miserable band of sheep where he did. But in any event, in search of better food for his flock, he moved his sheep into upper Consumers Canyon, early one spring. The ewes, which had produced a crop of unusually beautiful plump lambs, were put to graze around the springs that supplied the drinking water for Consumers. Terry McGowan, superintendent of the Blue Blaze Coal Company, ordered the sheep away from the culinary water source. Then Jim put his flock in Mine Canyon which was adjacent to the mine portal. Terry again ordered him away because of the danger to men and equipment. But the feed in Mine Canyon was lush, apparently not having been grazed for several years. Jim would drive his sheep over the hill toward National, but they kept ending up once more in Mine Canyon. Finally, Terry cussed the sheepman out and threatened dire circumstances to him and his sheep if they were ever found in Mine Canyon again.

Jim wanted that luxuriant grass for his flock of hungry ewes and robust growing lambs. One day at dawn, he eased the herd over the ridge into Mine Canyon and took off for places unknown, apparently thinking that if he could not be found, his untended sheep could eat to their hearts content. In the late afternoon, the mantrip came roaring out of the mine with Dave Stonebreaker at the helm of the mainline locomotive. The men jumped out of the coal cars into a bunch of woolies. Terry nodded his head and mine foreman Joe Bonto shouted: "Okay, boys, get out your pocket knives and go to work."

I was told later that fourteen lambs bit the dust. It is certain that most of the camp enjoyed fresh meat for several days. I was not forgotten; I found a fine serving of neatly wrapped lamb chops left in front of my door. Needless to say, Crazy Jim no longer tried to put his sheep on forbidden ground in that area.

Many years later, I asked Joe Bonto if he remembered the episode. "Yes," he laughed. "There was a sheep pelt under every rock in camp - the dogs kept digging them up for the next six months." He added: "We were a bunch of reprobates in those days. We tormented the local bishop for his participation when on the mantrip the next day, we chanted: 'Go to church on Sunday, kill a sheep on Monday!' "

(Reference: 6)

Coal Miner Detoxification

Bill Weston's drinking habits were of great concern to his family. His wife and daughters contacted me to see if I had any suggestions about helping him dry out. Mrs. Weston told me that when he came out of the mine, he would go directly to the pool hall and drink for several hours. Frequently, he would consume enough booze that someone would have to help him home. Then he would go to bed in a drunken stupor and it was difficult to arouse him in time for work the next morning. Mrs. Weston was greatly concerned as the situation was getting worse and she feared that eventually he might lose his job. She begged me for some magic potion that perhaps she could slip into his coffee that would cure his worrisome habit. I told her that I knew of no such medication. She insisted that I try to do something. I again told her that I knew of no wizardry of that kind.

She motioned me to her home the next day when I made house calls at Sweets. She asked me if there was something that I could give Bill that would make him sick to his stomach. She said she knew, from past experience, that if he became nauseated and had to vomit, he would not touch any hard liquor for a long time. But she said: "No matter how much he drinks, he never seems to throw up. But I wish he would as that would cure him." I told her that there was a medication that I could give him by hypodermic injection that certainly would make him vomit. I emphasized that it was a very powerful drug and not without its dangers because of its severe emetic action. She was overjoyed and insisted that I come back that evening when her intoxicated husband came home. I returned as planned. Sure enough, Bill was home in bed, partially dressed and inebriated to the point that he hardly knew me. The family had followed my directions and was prepared for a mass upheaval by covering the bedroom floor with a conglomeration of #2 and #3 galvanized wash tubs, dish pans and wash basins, some borrowed from the neighbors. Newspapers were between these vessels and on the chairs and other furniture and extended into the living room.

Bill did not protest when I gave him 1 c.c. of apomorphine. We sat down and waited while he snored away in his stupor. We waited and waited and nothing happened. I was about to give up in disgust at the failure of the medicine to work. All of a sudden, there was an explosion of booze-filled vomitus that sprayed the low ceiling and eventually, everything in the room. We, too, were hard put to dodge it. Pretty soon, his stomach was empty, but he continued to heave and retch. I left in about half an hour, leaving the family to clean up the mess. Mrs. Weston did not seem to mind; in fact, she was very happy and said: "Thank you, thank you, doctor, I am sure this will do the trick. I am certain he will not drink again after being that sick to his stomach."

I returned the next morning to confront a very disgruntled housewife. When I quizzed her, she started to laugh and said: "You know Bill awakened bright and early this morning and said that he felt better than he had in years. He did not remember getting a shot nor did he recollect you being here. Worst of all, he did not recall being sick to his stomach and went off to work more chipper than I have seem him in a long time!"

Let that be a lesson to conniving housewives and doctors.

Milan and Antonia Corak

Milan and Antonia Corak were a young, recently married couple who lived in Sweets. Shortly after I came to the mines, I was called to their home. I think they just wanted to size me up and invented an imaginary illness for

Antonia to justify the house call. Anyway, I could find nothing wrong with her and my visit became a sort of social call, as we visited and talked about many things.

Eventually, we became good friends. Milan and I used to sneak over to the remotely located Oman Ranch to try and find a pheasant or two to poach. We would drive there in my old beat-up 1929 Model A Ford. We at times saw some pheasants in the alfalfa fields there, but generally at a distance, or sometimes people were at the ranch so we didn't have any luck in our nefarious activities. One day, we were driving home across the sagebrush flats when we flushed a couple of sage hens. Milan was a better shot than I and downed a very large sage hen which, being a generous person, he gave me to cook with instructions how to do so.

I smuggled the bird into my apartment, cleaned it out, hiding the feathers in a paper sack for disposal in the garbage. I washed the dark-meated fowl multiple times under running water. Then I soaked it overnight in a mixture of saltwater and vinegar. I was awakened during the night by the odor of sagebrush, which permeated the entire apartment. The next morning, the smell was still strong so I thought it best to soak the thing another twenty-four hours, with frequent changes of the salt-vinegar mixture. I then decided to cook the bird, stuffing the carcass with a mixture of bread crumbs and onion. The cooking process really brought out an odor that bordered on a stench and filled the entire apartment house and wafted out into the narrow coal camp street, causing passers-by to sniff the air in puzzlement. The bird was finally done as tested with the tines of a fork. I cut off a slice of the black breast meat for a sample. It tasted exactly like a mouthful of sagebrush!

My friendship with Milan and Antonia progressed over the years. I became better acquainted with Milan as I had to put his nose back in place a time or two after some sort of a weekend argument. He was a scrapper and would not take the lip of any of the Serbian men in the camps. Milan's parents had come from a different part of the "Old Country," adjacent to Serbia, and he apparently had inherited a hatred of the Serbs.

Eventually, Antonia became pregnant and I insisted that she go to the Price Hospital for her first baby as she was a small, slender woman and her pelvic measurements were, I thought, questionable. Mila Lee was delivered with no problems in January of 1938. Antonia's total bill for a week in the hospital was

$31.75, which included a $10.00 charge for the delivery room, $21.00 for seven days in the hospital, $0.75 for medicines and an additional charge of $1.00 to cover incidentals. My fee for delivery was $35.00 and Milan paid me $15.00 on account January 25, 1938. I have copies of these bills and receipts, which are of considerable interest in these days of exorbitant medical and hospital charges! *(Reference: 7)*

Helper - 1937

I went to Price more often than Helper. This was because I frequently had patients in the Price City Hospital. But I loved to go to Helper to shop; I purchased many things there besides groceries. John Skerl Sr. of Helper Mutual Merc. often frequented the Gordon Creek camps, selling many things. He would visit with me at times and I purchased from him new linoleum for my office floor. He peddled, generally close to payday, many items from his car and would take orders for anything for future delivery. Joe Corak told me he purchased a .22 rifle from him at five dollars down and five dollars a month.

To me, Helper was a wonderful place to go on a payday Saturday. The streets and stores were crowded with a polyglot population, pushing and crowding, with two dozen or more languages from Arabic to Zulu filling the air. People of all sizes, color and description mingled in the noisy crowded streets, laughing and joking as they spent their hard earned cash. Helper's more than twenty "beer parlors" were filled to capacity, with bar patrons lined up two deep, the gaming tables full and the slot machines playing sweet music to the owners' ears. Raucous sounds and strange music issued from the overcrowded Greek coffee houses. Italians engaged in animated conversations, using their arms and hands as much as their voices. Musical Spanish blended with the more harsh Slavic voices, while other unrecognizable languages added to the cacophony of the city's streets.

I purchased groceries at the Success Market, dining room furniture at Helper Hardware, a washing machine at Skerl's and a fine woolen mackinaw, to keep me warm while making house calls, at Lowensteins department store. I would go into the McGonigal Drug store for a coke, where I made an annual purchase of cough medicine called Syrup of Wild Cherry (later changed to Syrup of White Pine Tar) in ten gallon lots. I found the Helper people friendly and easy to get along with. Numerous miners from my camps lived there and I made many house calls to their families, when I could find the homes, which was difficult in Helper's mixed up streets. At least twice, I ended up in houses of ill repute, much to my chagrin. Helper was also a railroad town so that especially on payday, the city really cooked, was fun to watch and be a part of. When a strident whistle echoed off the cliffs to the north, many people would hasten to the depot to watch the gigantic steam locomotives come and go. I was glad and proud to be accepted as one of the crowd as I heard many friendly greetings of "Hallo Meester Doc." A little different than Price, where the more sanctimonious sometimes scrutinized one's appearance for signs of tell-tale garments. But Carbon County was only 30% to 40% Mormon in those days, so it was not too bad being a Gentile.

Henry Skriner says that during World War II, he came home on furlough before being shipped overseas. His goal was to have a drink in each of the twenty-seven bars which lined the west side of Main Street. He started at the north end of town, but only made it as far south as number twenty six!

Industrial Injury

One night near midnight, I was awakened by a pounding on my apartment door. There was a man saying he had been hurt in the mine and wanted my help. I took him downstairs to my office. Generally, I was warned of any injuries by a phone call from within the mine. I had never seen the man before; he told me his name was Tony Kutkas. He lived in Price and would be on his way home as soon as I cared for him. He was a big man with rugged good looks, quick to smile and joke in spite of his injury.

He said he was on the night crew, that a piece of rock had fallen from the roof and cut his head. He removed his hard hat to reveal a two inch cut on the top of his head through the scalp to his skull, with little bleeding. I asked him why his hard hat had not protected him. He said "Oh, it got knocked off in my trying to get out of the way." As I shaved his head around the wound, I noted that it was a clean cut and did not contain any coal dust or dirt, as it should have from a roof fall of a sharp piece of slate. Two questions crossed my mind: Why had I not been called from the mine? Why did the wound look too clean? My problem was soon solved. Terry McGowan, mine superintendent, returning from town, saw the lights on in my office and stopped in to see what was going on.

Terry greeted Tony by name. It seemed that there had been an altercation in the mine. Tony's headgear had been knocked off in the scuffle and he had been clobbered over the head with a two-by-four. Terry asked who his assailant was and then said he did not like the man because he was a troublemaker and asked Tony if he had taken care of him. Tony assured him that he had and told a few details.

With a question on my face, I pointed to the pink "Report of Industrial Accident" form that I had started to fill out. Terry said, in his quiet Irish brogue: "With a name like Tony Kutkas, he can't be Irish. But he fights like an Irishman, so go ahead and fill it out! I guess it was part of his job to do what he did." I never did see Tony's partner in combat. He apparently nursed his injuries at home or sought medical help elsewhere.

Black Jack

A fellow named Harry called me to my office one Sunday midmorning. He removed his hat and bowed his close-cropped head for my inspection. I saw five or six three-quarter inch long wounds that were identical. They were sharply outlined and looked as if they had been made with a sharp knife, through the entire scalp. I was puzzled that they would all look the same. Immediately, I thought of the knife wielder Sam Kovich, but doubted he could do such a neat job.

Harry set me straight. He had participated in a party at the Silver Dollar Club the night before that had gotten out of hand. A Price cop had broken up the commotion with a blackjack. The incident was my introduction to this type of injury, which I learned to immediately recognize in the future.

Stretcher Case

One afternoon about two-o'clock, my mine telephone rang and I was asked to report to the mine portal at once. I was told that there had been a back injury, probably serious. To complicate matters, the power had gone off and the entire mine was being evacuated. This meant that all one-hundred or more miners underground would have to walk approximately three miles or more out of the mine. I was told that they were on their way and would soon reach the surface, carrying the injured man on a stretcher.

I did not have long to wait. Terry McGowan, mine superintendent, led the exodus, followed by Joe Bonto, mine foreman, who with five other men was carrying the injured man on a stretcher. Before the stretcher was put down, Joe gasped that it was a long three miles to carry a man, even if a couple dozen or more miners had taken turns. The stretcher bearers were out of breath, panting with streams of sweat running down their coal-blackened faces. The stretcher was carefully lowered to the uneven ground to be immediately surrounded by a horde of sympathetic miners. The body on the cot was covered with a blanket, head and all. I raised the covering from the man's face. He looked at me and the crowd, grinned, jumped up, dusted himself off and laughingly said as he walked away: "Thanks, fellows, that would have been a long walk." Joe Bonto started to swing his fist, but was restrained. By this time, fifty or more men had gathered about and watched in amazement as the young man strutted jauntily down the hill with never a limp.

Empty coal cars going back into the mine, Consumers, Utah 1937 - Dorman collection.
Dave Stonebreaker, motorman - Ike Morgan, nipper

All the men, but especially the carriers, stomped, cussed and swore as only upset coal miners can when they have been duped. A few days later, I asked Terry if the man had nerve enough to show up for work the next day. "Yes," he said. "He showed up as cocky as ever, but a funny thing happened. It was a day set aside to search the men for matches. (There was an ironclad rule that anyone found carrying even one match into the mine was fired.) You know that guy had five or six matches in his clothes! Now, Doc, do you suppose there was an outside chance that someone could have planted the matches on him?" …

1929 Model A Ford

I had wrecked my Pontiac on the way to Carbon County. I had it repaired, but it never worked right so I soon purchased a new Ford V-8 coupe from the Standard Motor Company in Price, operated by the Stamoulis brothers, Milt and Harry, for $800.00 on payments. It was a good car, but a little low slung. I was stuck too often in the deep snow, especially on house calls to the three camps.

Facing my second winter, I dropped in to the Redd Motor Company to inquire about a car to help me get around on the bad roads I had to face in making house calls. Their salesman, Ben Black, showed me a 1929 Ford Model A that had been taken in on trade. It was a sorry-looking two-door sedan. He said he would sell it to me for $35.00.

But there was a problem: the rear end was shot and would have to be replaced. So I went to Harry Gordon's junk yard in south Price and purchased for $15.00 the differential of a Model A Ford pickup truck. Bud Gilbert, of Sweets, was taking a course in auto mechanics at Carbon High School. He installed the parts for me, getting credit at school and giving me a very serviceable vehicle to get around in for winter snow and muddy roads, where my regular car would not go. I named it "Jalopy" because of its dilapidated appearance. I used it a lot in making house calls in the upper end of Consumers, over to Sweets and to National, where I previously had to walk as Jeeps and other 4-wheel drives had not yet been invented. It was high off the ground and had mud tires so I would go places with it that an ordinary car could not. I often put on heavy duty chains in the winter months.

The truck's rear end gave it a lot of power, but it would not go over 40 miles per hour downhill with a tail wind. I found it very useful in the summer months too, getting up the steep ridge to Beaver Creek for fishing, where my regular car would spin out. I only turned it over once on the way there, but Lee

Semken and some youthful friends, out for a hike, put it back in place and I made it to the top after sorting out my bulldog Bozo, my rifle and fishing equipment that had been mixed up in the turnover. My rescuers, with a mixture of scorn and mirth, declined a ride in my mountain climbing conveyance. I was a poor fisherman, spending most of my time disengaging hooks from my clothing or untangling my line from the willows of Beaver Creek.

I lost a rear wheel once going at top speed toward Coal City for a now forgotten reason, maybe just a demonstration of my all terrain jalopy, with Joe Bonto, Goldie Day and Dave Stonebraker. Even with the loss of a wheel, I was able to keep it under control, although the ride was a bit rough until I got it stopped in the barrow pit beside the road. The rear wheel had sailed down the road ahead of us, so it was retrieved and reinstalled by spare lug-nuts with my husky passengers holding up the left rear wheel area because my car jack was missing.

I was ashamed to be seen in it in town, so I restricted its use to the Gordon Creek area. When I left in 1939, I sold it to Ted Gentry for $50.00, half down and the rest on next payday. He drove it for many years.

Big John

Every coal camp had its Big John. Consumer's Big John was a timberman in the mine. It was his job to put up the wooden props that supported the roof. Terry McGowan, mine superintendent, chanced on him one Monday morning during his inspection tour. He noticed that the man was mumbling loudly to himself, in at least two languages. Terry concluded that the timberman apparently had a monumental hangover from a very wet weekend and asked what his problem was. He swore again and said: "Mister Terry, I have sawed this damn thing off three times already and it is still too short." The story was the source of amusement for the entire camp and was Big John's one claim to fame as he was teased unmercifully for several days.

Sweets' Big John was really big. He stood about six-foot-six inches tall, with shoulders nearly as broad. It was hard to tell where his shoulders left off and his head began as his short neck was as large as his head, which looked as if it had been screwed in place atop a massive cement foundation. His entire body rippled with bulging muscles. He was not fat; everything was muscle.

I was called to my office about three o'clock on a Christmas day. Big John was in my waiting room, accompanied by a couple of Austrian buddies who looked like midgets in comparison. One of the men spoke for Big John as he did not speak English too well. It seems that about four or five Austrian miners had got together for a Christmas celebration. They were all bachelors and had pooled their resources for an "Old Country dinner" consisting of a small roasted pig, complete with apple in mouth. All of their talents were lavished in the production of this feast, accompanied, of course, by the consumption of considerable wine and hard liquor of several varieties. They gorged themselves on the repast and soon became nostalgic about their homes in the old country. They had all come from the same general area in Yugoslavia, but each started to brag about his own specific town of origin. The arguments waxed strong and loud and even led to fisticuffs. Big John and a fellow by the name of Sam Kovich became especially incensed with each other about the respective merits of their hometowns, to the point that Sam drew his clasp knife and stabbed Big John.

Loaded coal trains below Consumers, Utah 1937

I sized him up as he stood before me. He had come to my office under his own power. I thought he looked pretty good, maybe a little pale. I admired his gigantic stature and well muscled body as I asked him where he had been stabbed. He pointed to his right upper abdomen, but I saw no blood. In those days, zippers were just coming into use. He was wearing a beautiful tan colored woolen shirt, closed by a zipper. I reached up and grabbed the zipper and pulled it downward. Much to my amazement, out rolled about a quart of purple colored clotted blood, which I thought, for a moment was liver. But it was not. He was no longer bleeding from his wound. There was a stab wound about an inch in size which extended through the skin and deep into his thick abdominal muscles, but did not penetrate the peritoneum. Big John was lucky! He had been saved by his own heavy muscles. I sent him home with a caution to avoid Sam Kovich, who had a reputation as a knife wielder.

Sam Kovich

Sam Kovich was a problem. He made a lot of extra work for me as I had to sew up the victims of his knife. He was an Austrian man, a bachelor who lived alone in one of the rooms in the Sweets bunkhouse. He seemed to be mad at the world: he was a surly individual, pretty much of a loner. I never saw him smile.

For me, the first victim of his knife was at the Sweets beer hall, when I had to sew up the throat of a man who Sam had cut. The next episode was when he stabbed Big John in the belly during an argument about their respective homes in the old country. There was considerable speculation about other incidents, including one that Sam had killed a man and disposed of his body in a culvert. However, no body was ever found. I was greatly upset when a third victim was brought to my office. Sam had stabbed this man (Pete) in the back three times. The wounds penetrated the kidney area. I had considerable difficulty controlling the bleeding so I put the man in my small hospital where I could watch him constantly. The patient's life was in jeopardy as there was considerable blood in his urine and I feared he might get an infection from an obviously dirty wound which had penetrated the kidney area. The only medication that I had to give him, in those pre-antibiotic days, was Sulfanilamide.

I had Pete in the hospital for about a week and I thought he was doing pretty well, but he started to bleed again. I was called to his bedside at dawn one morning. The mine dayshift had gone to work, so the street outside was relatively quiet. Suddenly, I heard a loud voice: "Where the hell is that G-D doctor. I am going to find him right now." There was a loud noise on the hospital stairs and the outside door burst open to admit a wild looking man. I thought it was Sam Kovich after me. I had threatened to report him to the authorities because of the multiple stabbings, and a friend of mine from Sweets had told me that Sam said he was going to kill me. So, I thought that Sam was after me to fulfill his promise. Pete's bed was adjacent to my X-ray darkroom, where I had placed a pistol just in case. I seized my pistol, pointed it between the intruder's eyes and started to squeeze the trigger. But the man shouted "No, no, I am not Sam!" And sure enough, he was right. He was a person who was frequently mistaken for Sam, nicknamed "Watermelon" because of the oblong shape of his head. He had smashed his hand in the mine and was looking for treatment. And I had almost pulled the trigger. Watermelon sure as hell did look like Sam.

I was greatly upset by this episode. It was obvious that the community knew about Sam's threat to kill me. Everyone considered Sam kind of crazy and a dangerous man and was afraid of him. I finally reported him to the authorities. He was arrested, jailed and was soon called into Judge J.W. Hammond's court, which at that time was upstairs in the Silvagni building. All three of the stabees testified and the judge sentenced him to two years in the Utah State Penitentiary. Before he left the courtroom, Sam shook his finger under my nose and said: "I kill you when I get out."

The court proceeding was held a short time before I left my coal camp doctor job of three years to return to school. When I returned to Carbon County some two years later, I was concerned about Sam's whereabouts because of his threat to me. I found out that he had been let out of prison early, had gone to Rock Springs, Wyoming, where he had got into a lot of trouble and had been killed in a brawl.

Many years later, I heard another story about Sam from my friend, Delon Olsen. Although Delon was primarily a rancher and stockman, he supplemented his income in the winter, as did many others in the area, by working in the coal mines. In fact, in 1924, he had been a member of the rescue team from Sunnyside who had helped bring out the bodies of the 172 miners killed in the tragic explosion at Castle Gate. He said that in about 1936, he had gone to work at Sweets. He had been put to work with Sam Kovich as a partner. He was very unhappy working with Sam, as he felt that Sam did not abide with the safety rules and was surly and hard to talk to. He repeatedly asked his boss to be given another partner, but was refused. So he took his problem to the higher ups at the time and raised quite a fuss in general. He was called into a union meeting and was "blackballed" out of the union for "discrimination against a fellow workman." He was never able to get a job in a union coal mine again.

Coal Miner Deer Hunt

I dearly loved to hunt deer. Joe Riche and Jack Smith were friends of mine, about my age, and I hunted with them a lot, but had not had much luck, legally or otherwise. I was pleased one fall when I got wind of a hunt that was planned by some of the mine personnel, so I sort of invited myself to go along. Joe Bonto, mine foreman; Ray Johnson, assistant mine clerk; Luke Millich, husband of Anna Millich, boarding house operator; and one or two others were the instigators. The big reason that this hunt was so desirable, to me at least, was because it was to be held at Luke Millich's homestead at the head of Johnson Creek, which was a tributary of Beaver Creek and was supposed to be lousy (overrun) with abundant deer. In fact, Luke bragged that the area was infested by big bucks, just waiting to be shot. Besides, Luke was supposed to have a desirable set up with a cabin or two, a small barn, complete with a spring with potable water for man and beast., in short, all the requirements and an ideal location for a successful deer hunt, plus the luxury of a cabin for cooking and sleeping.

Joe Bonto seemed to be the chief honcho for this hunt. I sensed that he was not too enthusiastic about me being part of the supposedly seasoned and experienced hunters going on this safari. But it was hard for him to turn me down since, after all, I was the camp doctor. He, in a way, tried to make me feel welcome. But I could tell that he, and others, were not too happy with my semi-self-invited presence. But the group, in good grace, located a saddle horse with all the fixings for my use.

Joe had splurged for a new gun for this special hunt. He had purchased in town a brand-new lever action Winchester rifle in caliber .348. This was a new gun on the market, touted by the experts to be adequate for any animal up to and including grizzly bear, as it utilized a cartridge about the size of a man's forefinger.

The only way, at this time of year with snow on the ground, to get to Luke's place was by horseback. The day before the season opened, we were busy making the final preparations. About ten o'clock in the morning, Luke took off on horseback, leading a couple of pack horses with all our groceries and liquor supply, the purchase of which Bonto had supervised and saw to it that there was a bottle of Old Crow for each person plus a spare or two, just in case. Luke was accompanied by Sam Pavich. I never did figure Sam out completely. He was an older Austrian fellow, maybe a retired miner, perhaps in poor health, who lived with the Millichs. He seemed to be a general flunky around the boarding house, washing dishes, carrying in coal, shoveling the walks and doing other menial work about the place. Luke took Sam along, expecting to get a lot of work out of him helping out with the chores in camp. Sam was a known boozer and drank anything he could get his hands on, even if he had to swipe it. He was an expert at finding someone else's booze supply and consuming it with great relish.

The rest of us took off a little after noon. We were bidden bon voyage by a considerable portion of the coal camp of Consumers, with lots of advice and suggestions about where and how to hunt, etc. It took us several hours to get to our destination. We rode up Consumers Canyon to the top of the ridge into Beaver Creek, then down Beaver Creek to Johnson Canyon, then up Johnson Canyon to Luke's homestead. I had been to most of the area previously, but had never been to Luke's place as I could not drive that far in my Model A Ford. I was impressed with Luke's set up and stayed outside to help unsaddle the horses, feed them and do other necessities in an effort to earn my keep. Bonto and a couple of others had gone into the cabin. Pretty soon, I heard a lot of very loud cussing and swearing so I went into the house to investigate. Sam was sprawled out, dead drunk. Bonto was shaking him and asking in no uncertain terms where he had put the whiskey. It seemed that, when Luke had turned his back or was otherwise occupied, Sam had hidden all the whiskey and was now too drunk to tell where it was. Here they were, on the edge of a memorable hunt, but not a drop to drink in salute. I did not imbibe in those days, but Joe and Luke were very much upset as were most of the others. Everyone, but especially Joe, had very unkind things to say about Sam as he snored blissfully on in his drunken stupor. But Sam could not be roused; neither could the booze be found, although the search was prolonged and exhausting.

Joe mumbled and grumbled a great deal while we pitched in and cooked a semirespectable supper. After we had eaten and cleaned up the dishes, Joe again shook Sam and questioned him about the location of the liquor, but to no avail. Sam snored on in his happy intoxicated coma and in no way responded to Joe's questions and threats. A poker game started up to the hissing of a Coleman lantern, and Joe and the others continued grumbling about the missing liquid refreshments. I was tired so I rolled into my sleeping bag in the adjacent, unheated small cabin. I nearly froze to death in my newly purchased "genuine down" Alaskan sleeping bag, which was an obvious fraud of feathers instead of down. Also, the ruckus of the volatile poker game next door was not conducive to sleep. Everyone, but Sam, was up and ready to go before dawn of the opening day of the hunt. Sam was still out like a light. Bonto was even suspicious that he had somehow consumed more booze during the night and kept mumbling what he was going to do to Sam.

After a hasty breakfast, we were soon out hunting, except Luke who we left in camp to keep an eye on Sam. We were hunting close to camp. Ray Johnson was sent to cover an area where the rest of us would be conducting a drive. We trudged along in the snow, making considerable noise. Suddenly, we heard four shots in rapid succession. Bonto said: "That's just Ray. You don't need to worry about him; he can't hit any thing." We completed our drive and at the end, found Ray with four dead deer, their throats already cut. Now there was a problem. All of the deer were does and it was a buck only hunt. Ray, of course, was scolded and cussed out. He explained that all he did was pull the trigger with his .35 caliber Remington automatic aimed in the general direction of the deer. He confessed that he had never previously killed a deer, although he had put a lot of lead through his automatic trying to do so. And he did take a certain amount of pride in his recent marksmanship. We were not about to let the meat go to waste, as there were a lot of people back at the mine who could use the food. Bonto left us to do the butchering and went to once again check up on Sam.

We hung up the animals, taking considerable care to put the remains out of sight as much as possible. We then returned to camp for a midmorning snack and coffee. We found Bonto greatly elated; he had found out from Sam where about half of the supply had been hidden as Sam had been too clever to put it all in one place. But for the moment, Joe and the other drinkers were happy. I asked Joe how he got Sam to fess up. He said that when he got back to camp, Sam was sort of half awake so he slapped him a couple of times to awaken him the rest of the way and put the muzzle of his rifle to Sam's head and threatened loud and clear, with a few expletives thrown in, to pull the trigger if Sam did not tell where the liquor was cached. His method worked and Sam produced about half of his hidden horde, which was enough to pacify the thirsty hunters at the moment.

We fixed a lunch and then went hunting again, this time on horseback. We rode west of camp and were soon on some of the higher ridges toward Scofield. We tied up the horses and hunted on foot. I soon ambled off by myself as I felt that the group was a little critical of my hunting ability and methods. Walking slowly and quietly through a grove of quakies, I spotted a nice three-point buck standing sideways to me not twenty-five yards away. I was so excited that I nearly wet my pants. I steadied my gun against a tree, put the cross hairs of my scope on the deer's neck and squeezed the trigger of my .257 Roberts Model 70 Winchester. Down the deer went, so I hurried to it, placed my rifle against a tree and started to cut the buck's throat. But instantly, the deer was on his feet and pushing at me with his horns. I was pushed backward between two small quakies with great force. Lucky for me, the trees were separated by about twenty inches at waist level, but came together at the roots. I backed through this opening, grasped the deer's antlers with both hands and pulled his head down in the V-shaped opening by the the two trees, grabbed my .22 Colt Woodsman pistol from my belt and shot him between the eyes. Then I cut his throat, cleaned him out with some difficulty and braced him against a tree, with a dead quakie stick propped to keep the chest cavity open so that the meat would cool off properly.

I found the men back with the horses. They were tired and disappointed, as no one had even seen a deer. We packed my animal back to camp, getting there a little after dark. The men were more anxious to drink than to eat. Luke had guarded the booze from Sam so it was safe, even if Sam was very disgruntled and sullen. Luke had a stew going and fried up some fresh liver. But to me, the evening was spoiled because the men drank too much and tended to be noisy and quarrelsome as they worried about getting the illegal meat home without being detected.

The next morning, we quartered out the does. Two were left with Luke for future use and the rest were packed back to Consumers, arriving well after dark with no complications, perhaps because the horns of my buck were prominently displayed.

Harlot's Haven

I was no little surprised to learn that the Sweets Mine community was, at times, a haven for some prostitutes from the Rock Springs area of Wyoming.

I never did find out all the particulars. But once or twice a year, one or two or three of these soiled doves would show up for a variable stay at the Carbon County coal mining town. I got the impression that they had relatives or friends there. Possibly, they were in trouble with the law in Rock Springs so they had to be out of sight for a while. Maybe they had contracted a social disease or were otherwise ill, or perhaps they were just enjoying an R&R. The ones I saw looked well worn, with a lot of mileage.

Sweets contained, during the busy winter mining season, more than its share of bachelors. Many would rent a tar paper shack and form a communal relationship for shelter and cooking. Others would board with a family or at a regular boarding house, like Eva Corak's, who would feed as many as twenty-five or thirty. There was the "Jap boarding house" for two dozen or more Orientals who kept to themselves. The more confirmed bachelors stayed in the Sweets bunkhouses - three wooden shacks perched on the north slope of the narrow canyon, each containing four rooms entered off a long slender porch. The rooms were small with a cot; small, square coal stove, makeshift table, and often powder boxes for chairs.

The denizens from the red light district of Rock Springs livened things up a bit. They were not above free-lancing their wares. This was a good deal for them because they would not have to split their take with a madam or pimp, which often resulted in tempting bargain prices. The occupants of the bunkhouses perhaps benefited the most from this opportunity of cut-rate, on-site pleasure.

Osby Martin called me to my office one Sunday about 10:00 a.m. He had in tow one of the visiting ladies of the night. He said he was concerned about her and wanted to help her out. Osby told me his story, sparing no details. The two of them had met at the Sweets beer joint and participated in the usual Saturday night brawl. They spent the night drinking and dancing innumerable times to the deafening juke box throb of the "Beer Barrel" and other polkas. There had been a fistfight or two to vary the usual whooping and hollering and carousing of a Saturday night in the Sweets beer parlor. The boisterous gathering lasted until near dawn, when they left the party together. Osby jingled a couple of silver dollars in his pocket and they ended up in his room. She was, he thought, a little reluctant so he placed two silver dollars in her hand. Everything went as anticipated until he tried to withdraw. He was unable to do so. He said that for a few moments, he thought it was "great fun." But as time went on, he became apprehensive as he repeatedly tried to separate. He recalled, in considerable concern, of seeing a bitch dog being "hung up" with her mate for perhaps a day or more. He felt trapped in their togetherness and fearfully wondered what to do. He said that this precarious situation persisted for perhaps a half hour, while his anxiety increased, gradually approaching a state of panic, as he tried to stand up, but could not. Eventually, they broke apart, much to his relief.

The woman gave her age as thirty, but to me she looked a dissipated fifty or sixty. She would not look me in the eye, but her face portrayed toughness, a touch of defiance, a bit of arrogance and perhaps contempt, combined with more than a hint of desperation. She said that "her problem" had developed in Rock Springs after an especially vigorous winter season and her madam had suggested she take a vacation. She had not seen a doctor; the situation interfered with business and she wondered if there was anything I could do to help her. She was a hard looker, skinny, her hair unkept, wearing worn soiled clothing and tattered shoes. Her winter coat was thin, frayed and threadbare, with a torn sleeve. She appeared utterly devoid of sexual attraction, at least anything that was visible.

I gave her a thorough examination, with expected results. Part of my medical training had been at the 2,300-bed Los Angeles County Hospital, located in the L.A. slum area, that devoted nearly an entire floor to prostitutes in all types and stages of distress. Osby's friend had a condition known as vaginismus, a severe spasmodic contraction of certain muscles of the female pelvis, sometimes curable by complete rest.

I could only advise her to indefinitely prolong her "vacation."

Emergency Surgery

The Gordon Creek mines were often snowed in during the winter months. Generally, this was only for a day or two and caused no great

Road at Coal City, winter 1936-37
Photo by Tom Burgess - Dorman collection

inconvenience except for the lack of mail and fresh food such as milk, vegetables, etc. Even a minor snowstorm accompanied by wind could be a problem and I frequently had to use a scoop shovel to clear the drifted road on my way to the Price Hospital, especially at Coal City, where I would meet the mail truck on its way up to the camps.

But one time, we had a real blizzard and were isolated for several days. I had a young male patient, who lived in the bunkhouse, develop appendicitis. He had all the classical symptoms, including an elevated white blood count that kept getting higher each time I took it.

Houses at Coal City, Winter 1936-37
photo by Tom Burgess - Dorman collection

I was faced with a dilemma. Try to get to town with my patient, maybe get stuck and freeze to death, or attempt to do surgery, all by myself at my little hospital? I found that I had adequate instruments with the exception of abdominal retractors. But I did not have sterile bundles of sheets, towels and other cloth items. The instruments could be boiled, but I did not have a steam sterilizer to properly prepare the cloth articles for surgery. One final phone call confirmed that the roads were absolutely impassable and should not be attempted under any circumstance. So the necessary cloth items were put in a bundle and baked in my electric kitchen oven several times at high temperature. I obtained from the mine shop tailor-made strips of copper cut to the right size and thickness to use as retractors. One final white blood count showed another 2,000 elevation, so I went ahead with surgery, supervising my RN nurse as she poured the ether while my "mail order nurse" helped me hunt for the appendix which was soon found and proved to be "hot." (But it did not rupture in my hand!)

The patient made an uneventful recovery with no signs of infection from my unorthodox sterilization method, which was indeed a blessing in those pre-antibiotic days.

Peed On

Helen Papanikolas tells the story about the mine official, who at the height of the 1933 strike and the rumble between the National Mine Workers and the United Mine Workers, was taken down, robbed of his gun and "peed on by six big Austrian women." My friend, Milan Corak, tells me his mother, Eva Corak, was the woman who seized the man's pistol. He said that he had the pistol, a Colt automatic, for many years, but has given it to his daughter, Mila Lee, for safekeeping. It is still in her possession.

The above incident ruined the mining career of the well-known official involved. Prior to this time, he had been looked upon with respect as a superintendent of a large coal mine whose every order and whim were instantly obeyed as if he were God. Once the word got around that a bunch of Austrian females had thrown him to the ground and peed on him, he was the laughing stock of the community and had to be replaced as no one obeyed or respected him anymore. Terry McGowan took his place as superintendent of the Blue Blaze Coal Company at Consumers.
(Reference: 3)

Getting Away

When the mines were busy, it was hard for me to get away for even a momentary change of scenery. It often seemed that my life was a routine of going to the hospital in Price, making office and house calls, often at all hours of the night. I even got in trouble because of my hospital calls. One time, I barely finished a problem delivery at the hospital and had to rush back to National for another delivery in the home, where the expectant mother chewed me out for "almost" being late. Another time, I was at the Price Hospital when there was a man killed in the mine at Sweets. My tardy appearance at the portal was met with glum looks on the faces of the miners who had carried the victim out of the mine. I got the feeling the men thought that if I had been there to give the injured man a magic shot, maybe he would have lived. Unfortunately, there is no way to cure a completely broken neck sustained in a roof fall.

I had purchased at Zinick's Sporting Goods in Salt Lake City a .22 Hornet rifle. The purpose of this gun was to surprise the prairie dogs along the side of the road on the way to town as it had more than double the range of a .22 long rifle cartridge. These animals knew exactly how far a regular .22 rifle would shoot so they taunted all hunters from just beyond that range. The .22 Hornet was the answer and I sent many a prairie dog to prairie dog heaven who thought he was out of range. Having pretty well cleaned out the local dog town on the road to Price, I ventured one Sunday away from camp to Miller Creek, where I really surprised a bunch of uninitiated dogs.

When I drove back into camp, there was a man and his son waiting at my door. He was very angry. His six-year-old son had found one of my .22 Hornet brass shell casings and had swallowed it. He was upset for two reasons: First, I was responsible for the shell and second, I should not have been absent when needed. He complained to the Medical Association about my dereliction of duty.

I never dared leave the area on Friday or Saturday night as there was often considerable activity that required my services. So I stayed close to camp most of the time, but would sometimes go for a drive on Sunday afternoon if everything was quiet. It was fun to watch the camp activities, especially on weekends: people coming and going, arguments both general and family. Others perhaps showing off their new car or cleaning up the old one. There would be a gathering at the boarding house next door to eat, drink, sing songs, gossip and outtalk each other. If the weather was good, people would gather on the apartment house porches or in the street to laugh and joke and communicate with each other.

My living quarters were in the "big" apartment house that housed all the topnotch mining officials in contrast to the "lesser" apartments across the narrow street that sheltered, according to strict coal mine pecking order, the less important officials. My apartment was on the ground floor so that all who left or entered Consumers passed my living room window. This meant that I had a front row seat to observe, in my leisure time, all the drama of a coal camp town. Great stuff! Always fascinating.

Underground

I was greatly interested in the coal mining process and was curious about what went on underground. Soon, Terry McGowan took me into the mine. I wore the hard hat of a man who had recently been killed. This was supposed to be bad luck, but I was not impressed by superstition, as later I inveigled Terry into taking women guests into the mine which was a No-No in those days and upset some of the ethnic miners.

We rode in a coal car pulled by the mainline locomotive. The company had recently purchased a new Joy loader and Terry wanted to show me how it worked. We went into a room where the monster operated. There was an operator assisted by a helper who managed the mechanical marvel. The noise was so loud that voices could not be heard; communication was by a referee type whistle blown by the helper, in short and long bursts, plus multiple sounds of one long, two shorts, two longs, a long and a short, etc.

The din was unbelievable. The arms of the mechanical apparatus scooped up massive and small lumps of coal and deposited its load into waiting coal cars, all the while moving forward, backward and sideways on its always moving tracks. Sprayed water kept the dust down, but the noise never abated.

Terry left me there for perhaps twenty minutes while he went to his other duties. I scrambled to keep out of the way of the men and equipment and finally found a place off to one side, where I seemed to be out of the way. Terry soon picked me up and this ended my first trip into the mine. I showered and returned to work in my office. About two hours later, I was called to the portal to care for the injured Joy loader's helper. He said that he had been standing in the exact spot where I had been when a roof fall buried him and broke his back! He ended up a semi-invalid. I went back into the mine at Consumers several more times, for some reason having no fear. I guess I was stupid.

Some coal miners homes - National, Utah 1936 North Fork Gordon Creek in foreground. Photo by Dorthea Lange

I went underground several times with Frank Morgan, mine foreman at Sweets. I found it fun to make rounds with him while the mine was working. I was especially interested in watching him tap the roof with the long cuelike stick he carried, to judge the safety of the roof. Sweets still had horses underground and I was impressed at the way they worked, backing up or going forward at the command of the driver. I watched as the "rope riders" took their lives in their hands each time they ascended and descended on their steel cables in the steep dips guided only by their whistle signals.

I only went in the mine at National once. There was a new boss there who invited me into the mine with him more or less on his maiden voyage of inspection. The mine was not working that day and we managed to get lost and ended up in some old abandoned workings, finally crawling on our bellies over fallen debris to escape the caved in area. I felt lucky to get out, as I know he did.

Sweets and National used some horses or mules in the mines. Consumers was mechanized and was also experimenting with Joy loaders. But nearly all of the coal in the three mines was hand loaded at $0.55 a ton... "Sixteen tons and what do you get?"

Lonesome

I was roused from my sleep at 2 a.m. by Eddie Martin, the night watchman. He told me there was a very sick man at National who I should see right away. He also told me that the worst storm of the year was raging outside. I tried to get my car out of the garage, but the snow had drifted two feet deep in front of the doors, so I decided to walk the more than a half-mile to National, carrying my heavy medical bag. The icy wind blew with such force that I could hardly stand against it, whipping the snow into my face with galelike force, making it difficult to see. I had trouble finding and staying on the road as it passed beneath the Consumer's tipple and I had to use a flashlight to find my way to my patient's abode.

He was a bachelor and lived alone. He offered me a drink from a bottle of booze, but did not apologize for getting me out in a blizzard. He said the storm had kept him awake so that he got to worrying about his health and decided to call me. I listened to his story and examined him. He had no fever, his lungs and heart sounded good, but his belly was a little tender in the epigastric region, where his pain seemed to be located. I made a mental diagnosis of chronic peptic ulcer and finally asked him how long he had suffered this pain. He said since 1928, about a 10-year period!

I got a little upset and asked him why he had to call me at two o'clock on such a miserable night. He then said he was lonesome and needed someone to talk to... The only things that kept me from freezing on my return home were my often repeated cuss words hissing through my teeth as I struggled through the icy snow laden blasts.

Another time, because of impassable roads, I walked to a home in upper Consumers late on a Saturday night because the woman's husband was out drinking and she got really lonesome and needed someone to talk to, so sent her twelve-year-old son to call me, supposedly for a necessary call. She greeted me with tears of joy and said she just had to have someone to talk to. So we talked.

Long Walk

There was one location I dreaded being called to because I had to walk so far. There were two families who lived in Sawmill Canyon above the tipple at Sweets. I could drive my car as far as the tipple, then walk the remaining half mile. The shacks these people lived in were terrible: leaky roofs, poor floors (some dirt), broken windows and walls that let the cold in and heat out. One family was Austrian and spoke little English; they did not call me unnecessarily as there was always some one deathly sick, so sick in fact that I had to have one patient carried out and hospitalized.

The patriarch of the other family was a giant hillbilly from Alabama or Tennessee who was widely known as the laziest man in Sweets. In spite of his title, he had about ten or twelve kids. He would often send two or three at a time to call me, usually at night or on a Saturday or Sunday. Most of the calls were for frivolous matters, but I always felt I had to go "just in case." I was not as smart as Dr. Frank Colombo who, after I left Consumers, lived in Columbia as camp doctor, but went to the Gordon Creek mines two or three times a week to give medical care to the people in that area. Many years later, I asked him how he handled the overbearing indolent hillbilly. He said that every time he was called to make the distant house call, he would insist that the father return with him to the office so that he could intrust him - and him only - with the proper medicine. He bragged that a couple of trips cured the lazy one.

Birth Control

There was a demand for birth control information so I started fitting some of my female patients with diaphragms. I got a set of fitting rings and put in a stock of the most frequent size contraceptive devices. This procedure had never been taught in the Gordon Creek area, so business was brisk for a time and I even picked up some customers from Price and Helper.

One day, a patient from Sweets questioned me at great length about the efficiency of this policy. She was a buxom woman in her mid-twenties who already had three children. Did it work? Was it safe? Was it guaranteed? How much did it cost? How long would it last?, etc, etc. She finally signed a deduction slip for the mine to take out a total of five dollars, on two paydays, from her husband's future earnings. I sent her home with a new diaphragm in a neat little box with complete detailed instructions, both verbal and written.

I did not see her again for about six months. I was making house calls in Sweets when she called me to her home. She greeted me with a scolding voice as I entered her one room dwelling. She was obviously pregnant and very unhappy about it. She berated me for the equipment I had sold her, which she said was worthless even though it had cost five dollars. I did not know what to say, so asked her if she always used the diaphragm. She took me to her bed, indicating a shelf above it on which rested the diaphragm box. She pointed a finger at it and said: "There the damn worthless thing is, on the shelf right above my bed where I keep it all the time and it has not protected me at all!"

O.B. Practice

I had an active obstetrical practice. Most deliveries were in the home; the rare patient was hospitalized because of some feared complication. It was most difficult for a doctor to deliver a baby in the ordinary bed, which was much too low and had no semblance of stirrups. The doctor had to be an acrobat to get in the position for what was going on. Kitchen tables were used at times, but tended to be so slick that there was fear of losing the patient. I purchased, from a surgical supply house, what was called a portable obstetrical table. It was a mechanical miracle – a true Rube Goldberg contraption – that converted the ordinary bed into a delivery table of sorts, complete with stirrups. I found it very helpful.

Besides the three camps, I delivered babies in Spring Glen, Price, Miller Creek and Wellington. I enjoyed my O.B. work very much. Even in unwanted and unplanned pregnancies, it was wonderful to see the true mother love that shined above everything else when a mother first saw her newborn babe.

Early on, I had several women I had never seen before call me when they went into labor. They seemed to think nothing of having no prenatal care. I tried to make up for it by giving them especially good postnatal care, which they seemed to appreciate.

The public health nurses from Price would come up every few months and help out with well baby clinics. We would try and immunize as many kids as possible and as young as possible.

My total charge for pre- and postnatal care and delivery was $35.00.

Bony

Bony was the anathema of all coal mine operators. Bony was rock that got mixed in with the coal. It generally showed up as streaks or thin horizontal layers of rock in the coal seam. Carbon County coal mines had layers of coal that varied in thickness of four feet or less at Peerless to more than twenty feet at Castle Gate. Some mines were relatively free of bony; others were plagued with more than one seam of the cursed rock that could come and go with the whim of the prehistoric seas that had originally produced the coal.

All big companies hired what were called "bony pickers." These were low men on the totem pole at a coal mine, being the lowest paid and the butt of many jokes. It was their job to pick the bony out of the coal passing endlessly by on conveyers, so that a clean product could go to market. The late Amando Salzetti worked on the tipple at Consumers for several years. He told me that the salary of a bony picker was $4.70 for an eight-hour shift. Each mine had its "bony pile" containing countless tons of discarded worthless rock and coal, sometimes on fire.

From the beginning of time, bony was an item of contention between the coal miner and the mine owner. Prior to about 1940, lump coal was the sought after product, to be burned in the stoves and furnaces of Salt Lake City. But if a big lump of coal had a one inch strip of rock going through its center, the miner had to break the lump and clear the bony away. If he did not, his car of coal would be penalized at the weigh station and he might receive no credit for that load.

There were a few "old" people in the camps, living out the rest of their lives with some of their children. One of these was a retired coal miner who was well past his three score and ten. He had worked in the mines in Wales as a child and had come to America as a youth, spending virtually all of his life in the coal mines. He was partially ill and I saw him often as his blood pressure was very high. As part of my visit I would quiz him about his life as a miner in the old days. He would tell stories about the Winter Quarters disaster that killed at least two hundred men on May Day 1900. He claimed that many more than the official count of two hundred were killed and described with gruesome detail some of his experiences in that mine. He told me about the Chinese miners in the Clear Creek mine – how they virtually lived underground, maintaining that they cooked, ate and slept in the mine. He described their beautiful arches in the mine, handmade by pick. He told about participating in rounding up the Orientals, locking them in a boxcar which was sent down grade. He said the boxcar had left the tracks a few miles down canyon and there was nary a trace of the celestials ever found, only the busted up boxcar.

Price Insurance man Walter M. Donaldson says that he lived with his parents and 4 siblings in one of these tents at Consumers for 1½ years, 1929-1930. He calls it "one of the happiest periods of our lives. Even in winter, we were as snug as a bug in a rug." D. Lange

I asked him how old he was when he first went to work in the mines. He said six years, which seemed awfully young to me. I had heard of eight- and ten-year-olds helping load coal, so I asked him if that was not a pretty young age to be doing heavy physical labor. He looked at me, grinned and said he would let me in on a well-kept secret. Each morning before going into the mine, his father would scrape the soot from the underside of all the stove lids and mix it with water in a bucket. Once the coal was loaded, his job was to use the lampblack to paint over the streaks of bony so that it would not be seen by the company weighman!

(Reference: 7)

Max And Elsie

Max and Elsie were high school sweethearts and very much in love. Max lived in Consumers. Elsie lived in Sweets, where Max seemed to spend most of his time. Elsie got the mumps, so I put up a quarantine sign and sent Max home. I told him he would have to stay away or he, too, would get the mumps.

A couple of days later, I went to see how Elsie was doing. As I entered the front door, I heard the back door slam, so dashed quickly there to find Max leaning nonchalantly against the wall with a rebellious look in his eye. I chastised him and told him in all probability he would get the mumps. He just grinned at me and shook his head.

He did get the mumps, so I teased both of them frequently about not obeying my quarantine.

The years went by and they went their separate ways. Elsie married, but divorced. Max married, but lost his wife to a brain tumor. Eventually, the high school sweethearts were reunited and married to live out their golden years together. When I see them, they always remind me that I am no longer their mumps truant officer.

The Company Store

All three of the mines in the Gordon Creek area maintained a company store. The ones at Sweets and National were relatively small and seemed to contain the bare necessities. The one at Consumers was quite large and although narrow, extended deep along the canyon floor.

By the late 1930s, the heyday of the company store was over. The companies encouraged, but did not insist that the miners use the company store exclusively. Many miners did not own cars, but would hitch a ride or send a list with friends to town on Saturday to do the bulk of their grocery shopping. Some relied on the company store as it was very convenient to pick up scrip at the company office, then spend it at the store. All of the mines issued their own "money" as scrip, which was redeemed at full value at their stores inflated prices. This same scrip would be accepted at many of the stores or bars in town, generally at about 80 cents on the dollar.

The store at Consumers was a popular place; gossiping housewives, miners off shift, noisy kids at the candy counter. Nearly anything could be purchased there, from a miner's hard hat to a deer rifle. There was a well-equipped and stocked butcher shop and grocery store. Semi-legal punch boards were plentiful and their merits were constantly touted by the clerks. There was a slot machine or two, with the handles being pulled by a slovenly housewife whose husband was slaving underground at that moment to support her gambling pleasure. The company store served as post office for the community so for that reason alone was a busy place.

Blue Blaze Store D.Lange

The company store had another convenient purpose: even though one purchased most of his groceries in town, it was a handy place to buy a pound of bacon, a loaf of bread or a quart of milk. It was also a suitable meeting place to gossip about ongoing subjects or just pass the time of day.

Skullduggery

One time, I had a patient brought in with his face pretty well smashed in. I chanced to remark that I wished I had a human skull to aid me in getting the facial bones back in place in a better way.

The following Monday morning, I found a gunny sack in front of my door. It contained, of all things, a human skull. It was a beautiful specimen; the bone was firm and well preserved, with complete upper and lower jaw and intact decayed teeth. It took me only a few days to learn of its origin, since the perpetrators could not keep quiet long.

Two young miners from National showed up. They said they had gone pheasant hunting in the Uintah Basin the previous Sunday with several friends. While going from one field to another, they had crossed a sagebrush flat. One of the men noticed as they walked across an area that it seemed hollow underfoot. With their curiosity aroused, they checked things and discovered an underground cavern. This subterranean pit was about ten feet in diameter and three or four feet deep. It was covered by wooden poles, with about a foot of dirt on top. They were amazed and surprised to find it contained three skeletons, an old saddle and some bows and arrows besides a very ancient looking rifle. The men realized that they were probably in a Ute Indian grave. They became frightened, thinking they were possibly on Indian ground, so started to cover up and conceal their intrusion. Then one man remembered my desire for a skull, so he retrieved one, put it in a gunny sack beneath a pheasant they had shot and hurriedly left the area to finish their hunt in distant fields.

Actually, I did not pay too much attention to the skull until I returned to graduate school in Philadelphia. There, I had meticulous studies of the head and neck, so found it very useful in my school work. I painted each bone of the skull a different color in order to more easily tell them apart. I sawed the top of the skull off to reveal the contents of the brain cage. I sometimes carried it to class with me in a paper bag to share with my classmates as few owned a skull. We learned everything there was to know about a skull. When I returned to Price, I operated on one side of the skull to show my patients the different kinds of sinus and mastoid operations. It was a very valuable tool and occupied a spot in my treatment room for over fifty years. I did not fully realize, until I began to study archaeology, that the men who obtained the skull for me had desecrated a historic Indian grave.

Beer

One Saturday night, well after midnight, I was called to my office. I was met by a young couple from National. She was repeatedly retching and trying very hard to vomit. He was carrying a beer bottle in one hand and a small wrapped package in the other.

It seems they had been out on the town and decided to share a bottle of beer before retiring. They both had a couple of swigs when, to their horror, they discovered a mouse floating in the unconsumed beer. They become violently ill, but managed to fish the carcass of a very dead mouse out of the beer bottle, which they now displayed to me. The husband proceeded to reinsert the animal into the bottle which he shook up and down to show me how they had discovered their calamity. All the while, the woman was retching and gagging and complaining of stomach pains. The husband, too, seemed a little white around the gills and made repeated attempts to vomit. Both looked only slightly less bedraggled than the dead mouse floating in the half full beer bottle. I gave them medication to "settle their stomachs," which they promptly lost.

The couple broadcast their plight far and wide, showing everyone the mouse in the bottle in an attempt to stir up a lot of sympathy before they went to court to sue Clara Miller, the local distributor of Fisher Beer. When they confronted her, she claimed they had purposely put the mouse in the beer in an attempt to make some easy money.

There were people who thought the occurrence had its funny side. Terry McGowan did not like Fisher beer. He said: "Of course the mouse died. Nothing could live in bottled horse pee!"

Exit Coal Camp Doctor

All of the major coal mines in Gordon Creek area were owned and operated by absentee landlords for the purpose of making a profit. A.E. Gibson did the original prospecting in the early 1920s that resulted in a mine on the north fork of Gordon Creek. This mine was first called Gibson, but later a company called Consumer's Mutual Coal Company was formed, so the name was changed to Consumers. Two other rather large mines were shortly opened in the area: The Sweet Coal Company, controlled by the prominent coal mining family of that name in Salt Lake City; and the National Coal Company, owned by Carl Nyman of Price. At the height of the midwinter coal mining season, around 1937-38, Consumers employed about 300 people, Sweets close to 150 and National 100.

A railroad was built to the area about 1924 and before long, the Consumers property was purchased by the wealthy Raddatz interests who had made their money in hard rock mining at Dividend, Utah. The name of the company was changed to the Blue Blaze Coal Company, but the town name of Consumers was retained. The Blue Blaze Coal Company spent a lot of money modernizing the mine inside and out with new equipment and bringing it thoroughly up to date, including on the surface two large cement block apartment houses, a new mine shop, tipple improvements, mine office, etc.
(References: 1,5)

One early spring day, (John Milovich says 1938) right at the very peak of all the hustle and bustle of a busy coal mining season, we received word that the mine was closing. I had examined that morning about a half-dozen new men to go to work. By noon, I was suddenly told: "No more, the mine is closed!" What a shock; no one could believe this news. Everyone was stunned. One moment, the future was filled with promise of fat paydays; the next, the reality of being out of a job and facing hunger for yourself and family. It was utter devastation for nearly 300 people and their dependents.

We heard conflicting stories about the situation, but apparently the major stockholders, obviously wealthy people, of the Blue Blaze Coal Company, wanted to get out of the coal business. They supposedly had been advised by their attorneys that they could take an income tax loss of several million dollars if they folded up the mine. In any event, it was done, like a snap of the fingers.

Terry McGowan was put in charge of liquidating all the assets of the company. Virtually all of the homes in the camp were owned by the company, so people were asked to move out and the houses were put up for sale. Several were moved to other locations, but most were knocked down for the lumber and other building materials. A frequent price for a tar paper shack was $15.00 to $25.00. The tipple was largely dismantled and most of the rails pulled from the mine, the steel being sold to Japan at $20.00 per ton. The two large cement block apartment houses were retained intact for several years. I was permitted to maintain my office and the hospital for the benefit of the rest of the community of Sweets and National.

I stayed there until the fall of 1939. After the closure of Consumers, it became evident that it would be difficult for the other two mines to support a full-time doctor in residence. I wanted to specialize anyway, so made arrangements to go east for that purpose.

Sweets, National and the few people at Consumers decided to give me a farewell party. The hat was passed, two giant barrels of beer were purchased and the entire community was invited to the Union Hall at Sweets. The free beer was gulped in prodigious quantities, while the juke box pounded out polka after polka. When the "Beer Barrel Polka" was repeatedly played, the stomp of the dancing shook the floor, walls and the very rafters of the building. As the consumption of beer progressed, the hilarity of the crowded building increased to the eardrum bursting point. Several speeches were attempted, but could not be heard. I was hoisted to the shoulders of a half dozen stalwart miners and paraded several times around the room to the shouts of "Leetle Mister Doc, goodbye, goodbye, thanks for everything - goodbye, goodbye." From my precarious perch, I surveyed my friends of many nationalities, the coal miners of Carbon County: the most wonderful people in the world!

Sweets Union Hall, 1939
Photo from papers of J. E. Brinley

Later on, WWII erupted and Terry McGowan was able to salvage enough of the mine to produce coal there during the war and until about 1948. *(References: 1,7,8)*

Immigrant Sons

Helen Papanikolas points out that "insults to the miners' dignity were commonplace." But the browbeaten first-generation immigrant could attain instant status and respect if he educated his son to be a doctor. One reason this was true, I believe, was that the camp doctor was one of the most respected people in the community.

A large number of Carbon County immigrants' sons became medical doctors and dentists. Often, two sons in one family entered the respected professions. Second-generation Italian-American Charles Ruggeri, Jr., became an ophthalmologist, while his brother James practiced dentistry. A.R. and John Demman were another pair of Italian immigrant sons who practiced medicine. Drs. Nick and Mike Orfanakis were sons of a Greek immigrant. The Austrian Gorishek brothers, William and Frank, opened their practices in Carbon County. Today, a number of second and third generation sons continue to contribute to the professions.

Resumé - Then And Now

Two hundred miners died in the explosion at the Pleasant Valley Coal Company mine at Winter Quarters (Scofield) in 1900; another 172 men died at Castle Gate in 1924, not to mention dozens of smaller life-taking disasters and countless amputated arms and legs, shattered bones and broken backs. Life was cheap. Workmen's Compensation did not exist. After the Winter Quarters catastrophe, families received $500 for the loss of each life. The amputations of an arm or leg sometimes brought $300 to $500, if the company paid. It had been said that in the early days of coal mining, the life of a miner approximated the value of a prize mine mule. These conditions no longer exist, but they are still part of the coal miners' heritage and must not be forgotten. Death still lurks in the mines: the Wilberg Mine fire of December 19, 1984 (6 days before Christmas) killed 27 people, 26 men and 1 woman. This disaster cast a dark shadow over the entire community because these people were our friends and neighbors.

In 1994, Utah mined over 24 million tons of coal. Carbon County alone produced nearly half that amount. But not too long ago, Carbon County was the Appalachia of Utah, the bastard child. But without its coal, Utah's industries and power plants would grind to an abrupt halt.

Carbon County is also Utah's melting pot. At one time, its immigrants outnumbered the "native" Americans. Thirty-two nationalities are recorded as having lived in Helper during the early part of this century. Due to its polyglot population - refined and tempered in the melting process - Carbon

County supports a broader, more tolerant and cosmopolitan lifestyle that sets it apart from the rest of Utah. The Greeks, the Austrians, the Italians, the Welsh, the Finns, the Japanese, the Chicanos and the "native" Americans have all left their imprint on its rough, often cruel, yet proud heritage.

I am glad and proud that I had a chance to participate in the formation of this heritage. I am glad and proud that I lived and worked in Carbon County.

“Another Man’s West”

Another Man's West

I often look back on my eighty-five years of living and the small boy I once was on a homestead in eastern Colorado, my life in Greeley, Colorado, and my progression through high school, college and medical school to become a coal camp doctor in Carbon County, Utah. Later, I returned to school to become a specialist and to eventually practice as an ophthalmologist in the same office in Price, Utah, for fifty years. I retired in 1991.

About ten years ago, my eldest son, Jaime, gave me a computer and said: "Thanks, Dad, for a college education. Now I want you to write your life's history." I was intimidated by the machine, especially because I had never learned to type. The following is a product of my "hunt and peck" system, thanks to the grudging forgiveness of my P.C.

Wray

I was born at Wray, Colorado, December 16, 1909. Wray is a tiny town located in northeastern Colorado on the south fork of the Republican River a few miles west of the Nebraska line. My parents had settled there in the 1890s, prior to their marriage on October 30, 1892. I had four brothers: Myron, born October 4, 1893; La Verne, March 25, 1899; Earl, July 20, 1902; and Claude, March 5, 1915.

Memories about my life at Wray are somewhat vague as my family moved to a homestead at Squirrel Creek, Colorado, when I was about five and one-half years old. Some things I remember.

The house at Wray was a rather large one, with a front porch and a large upstairs veranda facing the railroad tracks across the street. I remember a large luxuriant garden with a grape arbor where I used to hide in seclusion with my prize possession, a small dog. Jack was a black, trimmed in brown, rat terrier dog that was a recent gift to me.

We had a windmill in the back yard with an associated wooden water tank, elevated on stilts to give water pressure to the house and garden. My mother had a greenhouse filled with all kinds of plants, flowers and vegetables. This building was heated by a wood and/or coal stove in one end with the stovepipe extending the entire length of the ceiling to exit at the opposite end in order to more evenly heat the structure in winter. My mother took a great deal of pride and pleasure in her greenhouse so that it was treated with much respect and a hands off attitude by everyone. Mother knew all the Latin names for the flowers and rattled them off with considerable expertise and pride.

We kept pigs in those days in spite of my parents strict Seventh-Day Adventist abhorrence of eating pork in any form. One time, I was rescued by the seat of my pants by my father from the anger of a ferocious old sow as I tried to get a close look at her brood. I remember getting a swat on the backside and threatened with more punishment if I ever got into that pig pen again as "that old sow will eat you."

I was overjoyed one day when a new pair of bib overalls was delivered to the house for me by horse and buggy from a local store. I sometimes walked with my father across the tracks and over the bridge on the south fork of the Republican River on the way "uptown" to the small collection of stores, a bank, etc., that made up the town of Wray in those days.

There were forbidding "sand hills" bordering our property to the north. Somehow, to me, the sand hills represented the great unknown. They were supposed to be largely unproductive, with farming being difficult, if not nearly impossible. I did hear stories that some people could grow large, luscious, sweet-tasting watermelons some place within their mysterious cactus-covered sage brush hills. Today, the same sand hills are very productive for cattle and crops, with the discovery of underground aquifers and the development of pump and spray type irrigation.

We kids were very often sent to scrounge for any pieces of coal that may have fallen off the passing trains. I do not believe that we were instructed to make obscene gestures to the train crews to encourage them to throw pieces of coal at us from the tender on the engine, but I am sure that it probably happened.

I looked up to and respected my brother, La Verne, who was ten years my elder. He was ahead of his time in that he had a telegraph set in his room. He could communicate with a telegraph key "clickety clack" with some of his friends across town via makeshift telegraph lines of purloined wire and barbed wire fences. I was greatly intrigued by the sounds of the telegraph keys. One day when I thought he was not home, I heard the clickety clack of the keys which he kept locked in a desk. I pried the hasp open and started to monkey around with the key. I no sooner got interested in flipping the key up and down when I was suddenly seized by my older brother, turned over his knee and given a resounding spanking. Now a spanking by my brother, La Verne, was something to be remembered. He not only hit with great force, but at the same time, gave the cheek of your fanny a very forceful squeeze with his fingers. He called it a "Dutch spanking." No wonder I respected him! That incident ended my fooling around with his telegraph outfit.

I was taken down to the railroad yard to see the big red boxcar that had been fixed up to transport our possessions for our anticipated move to Squirrel Creek, where my father had recently taken up a homestead. One end of the boxcar had been partitioned off for the animals. There were stalls built of lumber for several horses, at least one milk cow and a flock of chickens, complete with hay and other feed. The rest of the car was filled with furniture and other essential needs. Primitive beds had been made on the floor for my father and brother, Earl, as the trip to Pueblo, Colorado, would take several days.

I recall the night my brother, Claude, was born. I was rudely awakened in the middle of the night, made to get partially dressed, semilocked in the living room where I sat in considerable confusion listening to all the racket of the coming and going of strange people, including our family doctor, whose name was Claude Cecil Crockett. Eventually, I was taken into Mother's bedroom to see my new baby brother. This was quite an experience for me as I had no prior idea of what was going on.

My parents firmly believed in "spare the rod and spoil the child." It seems that my brother, Earl (five years my senior), got into considerable trouble at school and elsewhere. We were all told repeatedly, "If you get a licking at school, you will get another one when you get home." Earl got busted at school: word of his problems had preceded his getting home and Dad was waiting for him. I can still hear his frantic yells of pain punctuated by the resounding whacks of a razor strap. His painful yells and screams reminded me to always be a "good boy." We all soon learned to yell long and loud when being punished to help prove that said punishment was indeed effective. Periods of punishment were rare, but when it did happen, it was generally deserved. Today's kids could use a little more rod, I do believe, but it would probably be called parental abuse! I personally wonder if perhaps parents don't really abuse their kids more in the long run by not spanking their butts when they need it, thus perhaps keeping them out of future trouble.

Homestead Experiences
1915 - 1918

Why did my parents move to Squirrel Creek? The story my father told was that my parents wanted to get their children away from the evils of the world. They felt that their children would be better off away from the temptations and problems of a city. Wray's population then was probably about five hundred to maybe one thousand.

During the middle of the second decade of the 20th century, there was a great movement toward a return to the land. The U.S. government opened up millions of acres of land throughout the west for homesteading. Thousands of acres in east central Colorado were put up for grabs. All that was required was to pick your spot, build a house, break up the sod, plant crops and live on your farm for three years. After you had "proved up," the land was yours.

Most of this "homestead mania" was a mistake at that time (1915). Certainly, Squirrel Creek (shown on the maps as Black Squirrel Creek) should not have had its sod broken up. The land was good for grazing, but not for farming. There was just not enough moisture to sustain and mature the crops, and there was the incessant wind so that once the ground was plowed, the top soil was soon blown away. The first year the ground was plowed and the sod broken up, there seemed to be enough retained moisture and nourishment to produce better crops than in following years, which were meager indeed.

To The Homestead

I well remember the trip from Wray to the homestead, which was located about thirty-five miles northeast of Pueblo, Colorado. This was a flat, treeless area, extending roughly from the base of the mountains eastward into Kansas. It was once the home of buffalo and the Plains Indians, but after their extinction had been utilized extensively and successfully as a cattle range. Our property was located right in the middle of a vast cattle empire controlled by the Drinkerd(?) family.

It is easy to fix the approximate date, as my baby brother, Claude, was three months old when we settled there. He was born March 5, 1915, so we probably moved in the month of June. In previous months, my father had gone to the area, filed the necessary papers and began making preparations. He built a very fine two-story barn, complete with haymow (which never contained any hay). He had broken up the prairie sod and planted the first crops of corn and pinto beans. My brothers, Earl (five years my senior) and La Verne (ten years older than me), were with him.

My mother, with Claude as a babe in arms, and I traveled by train to Pueblo. I was fascinated by my first train ride and remember the lunch Mother packed, including a banana which I considered a special treat. I enjoyed the train ride with its whistles, smoke, cinders and the hard working chuff-chuff of the steam locomotive as it pulled the uphill grade between Denver and Colorado Springs. It took us the better part of a day in the chair car to get to Pueblo. We stayed all night with friends and early the next morning, set out in a real covered wagon to complete our journey. The wagon was new, cover and all, and was heavily laden with supplies. I was crowded in the spring seat with my father, who had met us in Pueblo, and Mother, who carried Claude in her arms or on her lap. It was a beautiful spring day. The prairie grass was luxuriant and green, the cacti were in bloom and the meadow larks sang as they flew about in the warm sunshine. Jack rabbits bounced over the sagebrush and prairie dogs barked with their high pitched staccato yaps. There were a few scattered range cattle. All in all, I thought it was a pleasant and romantic scene and with a little imagination, I could see Indians in war bonnets riding in the distance as fast as their ponies would go.

It took us most of the day to travel the thirty-five miles to our new home. We stopped several times along the way to stretch our legs and have a lunch. Five miles before we reached our destination was Squirrel Creek. It is shown on the maps as Black Squirrel Creek, but we always referred to it by its shortened name. It was a dry creek bed running from north to south. I never remember seeing running water in it, only rare stagnate pools in the shade of the low bluffs that made up part of its banks. The creek bed was sandy and loaded wagons often got stuck. When we finally arrived at the homestead, the only building present was the brand new barn, where we lived the first year. My father had partitioned off two small rooms from the barn proper; one was a combination kitchen and living room, while the other served as a crowded bedroom. Earl, and sometimes others, slept in the haymow if the weather permitted.

I remember the living quarters in the barn as being very dark, with only one or two small windows.

Dad and others had already fenced part of the ground to protect our property from the range cattle that roamed the semi-open range. The next project was to plow a firebreak. Three furrows of sod were plowed under around all the property, with an additional two furrows on the north, as that was the direction of the predominant wind which carried the greatest danger of prairie fires. Prairie fires were a real threat to loss of life and property and caused great consternation when their smoke and flames could be seen in the distance. One time, we actually had to fight one. This was done by using wet gunny sacks to beat out the flames. We were lucky in that the wind was not too high and we had been able to build a small backfire. The prairie fires left an area of blackened grassland with little volcanoes of smoke from the burning cow chips; there was a stench that permeated the buildings, clothes and hair and lasted for weeks on end. A prairie fire left a scene of devastation, sadness and evil. We always felt that the fire was suspicious in origin and was perhaps an effort to burn us out and thus get rid of us.

Of course, the big cattlemen resented the sodbusters. One morning, we awakened at daylight to find our field of foot-high corn overrun by a herd of two or three hundred hungry range cattle. It was with difficulty that we drove the ravenous beasts out of our fields. There was evidence the cattle had been deliberately driven against the fence. Also, it appeared the barbed wire had been actually cut in a couple of places. Of course, the cowboys at the line shack denied any participation, but a considerable portion of our corn crop was ruined for that year. Several years later, my brother, La Verne, told me that my brother, Earl, had in retaliation shot the testicles off one of the cattleman's prize bulls. Maybe so. No wonder the various cowpunchers at the line shack seemed to always keep an eye on Earl.

Travel was a rather simplified procedure - by wagon, horseback or on foot. Trips to town were always by team and wagon. I doubt that we made more than three or four trips to town per year. We always went to Pueblo, a distance of thirty-five miles, which was an all-day process. My father took me with him several times. I remember when we got to town, we would go to a livery stable where the horses would be put up and we would sleep in the hay, snug in some of Mother's handmade quilts. Generally, we took food with us. But one time, Dad and I ate at an honest to goodness restaurant which had white tablecloths and napkins. There, I slurped up roast beef and brown gravy to my heart's content. I gazed in wonder at the opulence of a fancy eating place full of well-dressed people and elegant furnishings, including a beautiful metal ceiling, stamped out in intricate designs. I was dazzled by the brightness of the electric lights.

On one trip to town in the middle of winter, my dad said I nearly froze to death. We would bundle up in heavy clothing and place quilts around our legs and feet. Inside the bundle, we would place a lighted lantern with just enough air to keep it burning. But if there was a wind, we suffered greatly and at times, would have to get out and walk to keep warm. One time, Dad felt sorry for me and let me continue to ride. I remember I gradually got the feeling I was warm and cozy and very content and I protested when my father forced me to get out and walk. He said later making me do so undoubtedly saved my life.

We searched far and wide for the carcasses of dead range cattle. We would gather the bones, pile them up back of the barn and haul them to town on our next trip, where they were worth money when converted into fertilizer. One time, Dad and I were a long way from home. We were south and west of the homestead along the banks of Squirrel Creek. It was summer and we were hot and became very thirsty as we had somehow neglected to bring water. We started for home, but our thirst became worse and worse. We were traveling up the dry bed of Squirrel Creek when we came to a spot where there was a vertical bank several feet high which made a spot of shade. Here was a patch of mud containing several cow tracks full of brownish colored, rather thick looking water. Our thirst was great. Dad went first, got down on his belly and drank. He got up, wiped his mouth with the back of his hand and motioned me down. One sip of the foul concoction, located about a foot from a pile of cow manure, was enough for me. In the future, we saw to it that we had some drinking water with us.

Along the bed of Squirrel Creek, we used to find fragments of fossilized bones. Some of the spinal column would be quite large and the cause of considerable speculation on our part, especially my father's. Obvious bone that had turned to stone puzzled him a great deal; he had only a sixth-grade education, so was not too well versed on geology and allied subjects.

Our homestead consisted of 320 acres. It was no small job just to fence the place, which was not done all at once. To begin with, maybe 40 or 50 acres would be put under cultivation and a sort of temporary two wire fence with fence posts far apart would be put up. Then as soon as possible, a permanent four-strand barbed wire fence would be installed around the entire property. Only on the south did we share a fence line; all the rest had to be done by us. The split cedar posts and the barbed wire had to be hauled from Pueblo. Dad and Earl did most of the fencing, which was hard and tedious work.

Corn, Beans and Other Crops

The main crops for Squirrel Creek were corn and beans, then later milo was grown with some success. Milo or "kaffir corn," a type of sorghum, was grown for grain and fodder as it did well in a dry region. We sometimes put it through a coffee grinder and used it as mush for a change of taste from the old standby of corn meal mush.

Corn was planted with a lister. A lister was a contrivance pulled by four horses. It had two wheels, a seat for the operator and a seed box that dispensed one corn kernel about every foot. The plow was V-shaped and made a V-shaped furrow about eight inches deep. The seeds were deposited in the bottom of this furrow, the idea being that the depression would help to collect and retain moisture. After the corn came up and was about six inches high, a harrow would be dragged over the surface of the ground, partially filling the furrow and thus giving more root surface to the plants and at the same time helping to get rid of the ever present weeds. The beans were pinto (Mexican beans). They were planted with a bean planter, pulled by horses, that placed one bean every four or five inches.

Thus, two of our main crops were corn and beans, these supplied a considerable portion of our food chain. In the spring, we would eat many roasting ears picked from the field corn; later, the mature corn would be ground up in a coffee grinder to make corn meal for johnny cake. Beans were our real staple; we often had beans three meals a day. For breakfast, Mother would mash them up with a potato masher, mold them into patties about a half inch thick and fry them like a piece of meat. But they still tasted like beans. We generally ate our beans with white or corn meal bread, but for variety, we often ate them plain with a lot of vinegar over the top. The type of beans that we grew were called Mexican or pinto beans. They were harvested in the late fall by a knife blade set at an angle on the front of a horse pulled sled that cut the bean plant roots just below the surface of the ground. The plants would then be piled in wind rows and eventually hauled to a stack yard.

On a day when the wind was just right, portions would be placed in the center of a large canvas, threshed out with the back of a pitchfork, then tossed repeatedly into the air for the wind to blow the chaff away. The beans would then be sacked ready for the market or stored for our consumption. I am sure we ate more than we sold, as beans were really what we lived on and the price for the sale was not too great. We had a milk cow so that we had milk, butter and cottage cheese part of the time. White flour was purchased in 100 lbs. bags and Mother baked all of our bread. If we ran out of white flour, we lived on corn bread, often for considerable periods of time. We ran out of sugar once for several months and how good it tasted when we got some once again.

Watermelons were planted in the cornfields, but the coyotes got more melons than we did. The coyotes would bite through the rinds in order to enjoy the sweet juicy insides of the melon.

Corn was harvested in the fields. A wagon was fixed with a backboard so that the people doing the picking could throw the corn in the general direction of the wagon. If their aim was a little high, the backboard would deflect the ears of corn into the wagon box. The corn was then hauled out of the field and piled adjacent to the barn.

Later on, we would husk the corn. To do this, one wore in the palm of the husking hand a sort of blade that was used to jab into the husk, breaking it away from the underlying corn. This blade would rip open a couple of inches of the husk, then the fingers were used to separate the rest of the husk, bend it backward over the base of the ear and break off the husk, more or less in one piece. The husks were saved for many uses: bedding for the horses, cornhusk mattresses and even for food if the animals were hungry enough.

After the corn was husked, it was stored in a room inside the barn. At first, we shelled the corn by hand which was a mean, tiresome and slow job. Later on, we used a hand-powered sheller. This was a mechanical contraption about 2x3 feet in size and 6 or 8 inches in thickness. It stood on legs. On one side was a crank turned by hand which activated a flywheel and a series of gears and mechanical apparatus that stripped the kernels off the cobs. Ears of corn were inserted in a hole in the top; kernels of corn were caught in a bucket and cobs exited on the floor or were collected in a suitable container. It took a lot of work to operate this metal monster, but it surely beat shelling by hand.

We ground some of the corn in a coffee grinder to make cornmeal which was made into a bread called johnny cake. Cornmeal was also used for breakfast as mush. In the spring, we enjoyed corn on the cob, which tasted pretty good even if it was field corn and not the usual sweet corn used for roasting ears. All in all, corn certainly helped supplement our diet of beans, beans and more beans.

Rattlesnakes

We lived in a constant, haunting fear of rattlesnakes. Not only did we have to worry while on the range, in the fields, in the barn and chicken house, but in our home. Several snakes were killed on our doorstep. In fact, my mother kept a garden hoe beside the door for that purpose and once killed a rattler within a few feet of my brother, Claude, as he played, as a baby, beside the door.

Several of our domestic animals were bitten, two horses on the nose and one milk cow on her udder. None of these animals died, but certainly suffered a great deal. My small rat terrier dog was bitten on his face. His head swelled up to the size of a basketball and we feared that he would not live. We took him into the house and nursed him for nearly a week. We kept him warm and as comfortable as possible and force fed him by prying his mouth open and pouring milk and other liquids down his throat. He finally recovered and from then on, was death on rattlesnakes. He would go out of his way to hunt them down. In fact, he seemed to spend the rest of his life hunting snakes. When he found one, he would raise a hell of a ruckus by barking, whining and growling. His trick was to circle around and around the coiled viper, taunting it to strike. When it did and was stretched out full length on the ground, he would dash in and grab the snake close to its head and shake vigorously, finally throwing it over his shoulder as far as he could. Then, before the snake could recoil, he would pounce on it again and repeat the process until nothing was left but a few lacerated shreds. He was bitten several more times, but did not suffer any severe consequences as he now seemed to have some degree of immunity.

Numerous experiences stick out in my mind. My mother tried, without much success, to raise a vegetable garden to supplement our meager diet.

Nothing seemed to grow but weeds. One day, after enduring the hot summer heat hoeing in her garden, she returned to the cook shack to prepare food. As she stepped on the stoop to go in the door, a snake struck at her, but missed as she jumped back. Needless to say, she beat both the stoop and the snake into smithereens. Some of Mother's hens preferred the barn in which to lay their eggs rather than the chicken house, which was just a sort of shed. They also laid their eggs in the horse mangers. And of course, rattlesnakes liked eggs. One day, a snake swallowed an egg in one manger then crawled through a good size knot-hole into the adjacent manger and swallowed another egg. There he was, trapped by the two eggs in his gut, when my father discovered him. Mr. Snake raised a hell of a fuss, but Dad lost no time in chopping it to pieces with a shovel, making no effort to retrieve the eggs.

My dad dug a cistern in which to store water for our livestock. We had to haul water, by wagon, in wooden barrels from the line shack of a large cattle owner one mile to the west of us where there were two windmills and a couple of water tanks. The digging of this cistern produced a large pile of moist sand about five feet in diameter and maybe two or three feet high. My brother, Earl, five years my senior, and I had a lot of fun playing in this sand pile. We made a bunch of roads, but our crowning joy was a series of complicated tunnels throughout the dome-shaped playhouse. The next day was Saturday, the Sabbath for my strict God-fearing Seventh-Day Adventist parents. On that day, no work was to be done. The time was to be spent in prayer, reading the Bible and religious contemplation. We probably did not get a bath as water was far too scarce for such foolishness, but we were forced to kind of get dressed up for the Holy Day. Dad would shave with his straight razor and even put on a white shirt and perhaps a necktie. That morning, Earl and I were ill at ease, as we impatiently endured what was to us a prolonged reading of the scriptures, in our anxiety to get back to our sand pile. Earl beat me to it and jammed his right forearm, half-way up to his elbow into one of the tunnels to clean out some corn husks that had blown in during the night. As I approached, I saw Earl get a real funny look on his face. He froze all motion and then very slowly pulled his arm from the hole. His fingertips were followed by the head of a rattlesnake with its evil forked tongue flickering to and fro. Earl continued to withdraw his hand very slowly for two or three feet, then let out a yell and jumped backward about twenty feet. One close call!

My brother, Earl, was obsessed by rattlesnakes. It was an unwritten law that we were to take the rattle of every snake we killed. These were kept in a fruit jar and counted at the end of the year. I remember one count of 108. But the rattles did not satisfy Earl. He would skin out all the ones that he could. He soon had a collection of rattlesnake belts and then started on getting enough skins to make the whole front of a vest. Earl's fervor with rattlesnakes was compounded by considerable foolhardiness. He bragged to me that he was going to get brave enough that he would get a snake to strike, then grab it by its tail and pop its head off. To my knowledge he tried it at least once. I watched as he got the tail all right, but never completed the pop.

Myself, mother and baby brother Claude. Squirrel Creek - 1917

After Earl's death, in about 1970, my younger brother, Claude, went to his trailer home located near Lytle Creek, Calif., to pick up some of his possessions. The neighbors all said that he kept a pet rattlesnake, which had supposedly bitten him a time or two, but he had seemed to be immune to its toxin.

Earl taught me a little trick. You would take a piece of string about twenty inches long and in the center, tie half a square knot between the first and second rattles, make a couple of 2 inch loops on each end and put the loops over your thumbs. Keeping the string taunt, you would rotate your thumbs in a semicircle. With practice you could really simulate a rattlesnake rattle. My mother detested the sound, so the house was off limits. One time we were invited over to Uncle Ed Lohman's to eat. After dinner, my dad was taking a nap in a homemade barrel-stave hammock on the shady side of the house. I chanced to sit down close to his head and made some honest to goodness realistic sounds. The next I knew, I was over his knee and getting a real earnest paddling with the admonition: "Don't you ever do that to me again!"

Coyotes, Skunks and Other Varmints

Along with rattlesnakes, there was an overabundance of coyotes. Several varieties of hawks abounded, which we collectively called "chicken hawks." Present were hundreds and hundreds of jack rabbits, but not too many cottontails. A prairie dog town was located in a swale that joined our homestead on the west. Antelope were rare; the largest group that we ever saw consisted of only four animals. Skunks were numerous.

We considered the coyotes to be a real menace. They killed our poultry, were not above killing or maiming calves, harassed our dog and disturbed our sleep with their never-ending howling. As night approached, there would be a lone coyote voice in the distance, soon answered by one in another direction, until we were surrounded by their mournful spine-tingling voices which seemed to come ever nearer. Often their coyote chorus ended up in our yard just outside the door. Sometimes my dad would grab a gun and blast away in the darkness; this would put only a temporary stop to their infernal racket.

We waged a constant war with coyotes; they seemed to hold their own and sometimes won. My brother, Earl, trapped them. We hunted for and dug up their dens. Digging up their dens was a lot of work as they were often as deep as six feet. We would sometimes take a piece of barbed wire, maybe eight or ten feet long, make a sort of corkscrew hook on one end and thread it down the hole, twisting and twisting until we snagged the fur of a pup and pulled it out. This would be repeated until we figured we had them all. There was a bounty on the varmints: $2 on the scalp of a pup (which had to include both ears) and $4 on the pelt of a larger animal.

One day, we went on sort of a picnic. Uncle Sam and Aunt Minnie Ness from Yuma County, Colorado, were visiting us. They had driven all the way to our homestead in a vehicle called a "Saxon Six." They had been stuck several times in the sand; it had taken them nearly all day to drive the thirty-five miles from Pueblo because of the poor roads and several flat tires. Our visitors wanted to see some of the surrounding country, so away we went in our covered wagon without the cover. Dad and Uncle Sam were in front, sitting on a plank seat, with a couple of cleats nailed on each end on the bottom side to hold it in place on the wagon sideboards. Behind them were Mother and Aunt Minnie, riding in the luxury of the spring seat. Earl, my younger brother, Claude, and I were in the bottom of the wagon box, semicomfortable on folded quilts and gunny sacks. We traveled several miles across the roadless prairie at the reckless speed of about four miles an hour. Several miles from home, we accidentally discovered a coyote den. Since we did not have any barbed wire, but had a shovel and plenty of manpower, we decided to dig it out. So we went to work. Dad took a shot with his .40-.82 Winchester rifle at the mother coyote, who watched us from a ridge a quarter of a mile away. This only caused her to scurry momentarily out of sight. While the digging process was going on, Mother and Aunt Minnie spread out some quilts on the prairie grass and gave us some sandwiches and other fixings. At the bottom of the den, nearly six feet deep, we found six several week old pups, five of which we properly dispatched. Earl and I wanted to keep one and raise it as a pet. Against my parents' wishes, the huskiest one of the litter was placed in a gunny sack and taken home. We had to handle him with great care to keep from being bitten. We finally got a collar on him and staked him out with a six-foot chain some distance from the chicken house. He never showed any indication of becoming tame and would always try to bite the hand that fed him. We kept him for several months. He grew quite rapidly and became meaner each day. He became really crafty. He would lie down next to his stake and pretend to be sound asleep, but the instant that an unsuspecting hen searching for food got within reach of his six-foot chain, she was a goner. After the loss of about three of her chickens, Mother put her foot down for the final time and his scalp joined the others of the coyote "bank" nailed to the north side of the barn.

Squirrel Creek - 1917
Cook shack and adobe sleeping quarters

Coyotes are creatures of habit. It got so we could set our watches each afternoon about 4 o'clock when a big one would appear in the distance in the southwest. He would come toward our home, then cross the road in the prairie dog town that went to the windmills and water tanks, try to catch a dog or two, then trot off to the north. We would often see him close up on our way to haul water. But if we carried a gun, he would keep his distance. One day, Dad hid down in the wagon box with his trusty .40-.82 Winchester while Earl and I drove the team. Sure enough, Mr. Coyote crossed the road a few yards ahead of us and stopped to sniff at a prairie dog hole. Dad sneaked his head up over the edge of the wagon box, took dead aim and banged away. The coyote dropped like a rock and never moved a muscle. Dad let out a whoop of glee, jumped out of the wagon and ran to pick him up. As he reached down to grab him, the coyote lunged at him and just missed biting him in the face…the bullet had broken the critter's back, but he was still mobile enough to almost do my dad in.

Somehow, my mother got her hands on a few turkey eggs. These she put under a brood hen and we soon had some turkeys. But only one survived to adulthood. It grew into an immense tom. He was an arrogant bird and would rush at me and try to knock me over with one of his wings. We were saving him for a Christmas feast, but the coyotes beat us to him. They grabbed him from right under our noses, dragged him back of the barn and had him pretty well mutilated before we could come to his aid.

The coyotes harassed the hell out of my poor little rat terrier dog, Jack. He generally slept on the doorstep, but we often would have to take him inside at night. They loved to tease him and get him to chase them. Generally, he would chase them only so far, always staying in sight of the house. Sometimes, as he headed for home, they would chase him back. One time after we had been at the homestead about two years, they teamed up on him. One coyote lured him over a hill out of sight where others were waiting. They tore him to shreds; we found his bones and part of his hide sometime later. Needless to say, I was broken-hearted as Jack was my pride and joy. He was my dog. His demise in such a cruel manner did not improve my opinion of coyotes.

Chicken hawks caused us a lot of trouble. Our chicken house and pen were located close to our house for protection from these winged predators. Dad kept a shotgun just inside the door so that he could blast away at the marauders if he was in the house or close by. We acquired a pair of guinea hens to act as sentinels. When a hawk or coyote was in the vicinity, they would set up a hell of a noise. Their raucous yells and screams could be heard from afar and served to alert us to the presence of intruders. They considered themselves to be aristocrats and were too high-toned to associate with the other fowl. They stayed by themselves. In good weather, they roosted on top of the barn; in bad, they stayed in the barn. One of my father's most prized possessions was his L.C. Smith 12-gauge double-barreled hammerless shotgun with a sliding safety on the tang, which was hard to read. To gain quick access, he hung this gun above our low-slung door. In case of invasion by four-footed beasts, winged enemies or even human intruders, it was in a perfect position; even if a voice should say: "Come to the door with your hands up." One Sabbath day, after our necessary religious obligations had been consummated, we were all taking a nap. It was a chilly fall day, but we were cozy in our adobe walled living quarters with a cow chip fire smoldering in the heating stove. All of a sudden, all hell broke loose. The guinea hens started to yell and scream. There was a furor in the chicken pen with a lot of squawking of the hens and barking of the dog. Dad jumped up, with me right behind him, and threw open the door. The air was filled with dust and feathers. Just outside our door was a giant hawk trying to carry away one of our largest hens that was protesting with loud squawks, flapping of wings and trying to dig into the dirt with her feet. Dad reached above him for the shotgun, which had somehow or other been hung up with one of its supporting nails between the double triggers. Both barrels went off with a resounding thunderous roar and the room was filled with the odor of burning gunpowder. The resulting recoil was considerable and the butt of the gun hit me right between the eyes, throwing me backward across the room and onto the bed behind me. I started to shout at the top of my voice: "I am shot! I am killed! I am dead!" After I was finally calmed down, Dad had to break the Sabbath by patching up the hole in the roof.

Skunks were another pest. They ate eggs and killed the chickens and often got caught in my brother Earl's coyote traps. One time, I was with Earl in the wagon as he tended his traps. Sure enough, there was a skunk in the trap caught by one of his hind legs. Earl shot at it with the .22 rifle, but missed a vital spot. We got sprayed, but good. We had to bury our clothes in the ground for about a week. But still the stench persisted and Mother would hardly let us in the house for a long time. The horses and wagon were likewise contaminated and continued to be a source of irritation for many days.

There were literally thousands of long-legged jack rabbits. They made actual trails, beaten down to the bare ground, in the prairie grass. Sometimes I would try to shoot them in the head with the .22 rifle so as not to mutilate the meat. But generally, I would set steel single spring traps in their pathways and catch them. In cold weather, I would gut them out, but leave the hides on and nail them by their hind legs, high up on the north side of the barn, out of reach of other varmints. Believe it or not, these carcasses were of value for food during WWI (pre-McDonald's) times. On one of his rare trips to Pueblo for supplies, my father took a load of 22 frozen jack rabbits for which I received the magnificent sum of $0.25 each. I am not sure what the money went for, but rest assured, it was not wasted. My hoard probably went to buy more .22 rifle short shells for the .22 pump action Winchester, Model 90 that shot only shorts. My parents considered rabbits as "unclean" food, but one time when they were away, Earl and I cooked a jack rabbit. We were unable to eat the tough, stringy meat as hard as we tried and as hungry as we were for meat of any kind. In early winter, with snow on the ground, rabbits infested our fields. One bright sunny day, there was about four inches of snow on the ground. I drove the team and wagon while Dad and Earl stood in the wagon box, Dad with his shotgun and Earl with the .22 rifle blasting away. In about an hour, they shot nearly thirty rabbits, mostly jack rabbits, but some cottontails, most of which eventually ended up in a Pueblo meat market.

We saw few antelope. Although it was illegal, my dad or Earl would try to shoot them to supplement our larder. One time, Earl got carried away and was gone all day on a futile hunt on horseback. He returned that evening with an empty shell belt. Shooting foolishly from horseback, he had been unable to retrieve the empty cartridge cases and Dad gave him hell. It was an unwritten law that all expended cases were to be saved. We reloaded our own brass. Dad would put a hunk of lead pipe in a container, stoke up the fire and melt it down. The melted lead would be poured into a bullet mold, the old primers knocked out, black powder measured in, everything placed in the reloading tool, screwed up tight, and we had a new cartridge ready to go. After Earl's episode, Dad had to buy a new box of shells and start all over again with the ammunition supply for the .40-.82 Winchester, meat-in-the-pot rifle. This Model 1886, octagon barrel, lever action rifle, now worth much more than the original $21 that my grandfather paid for it, and the reloading tools in the 1890s are among my most prized possessions and the rifle helps form a reading lamp in my home, beside my easy chair.

Prairie dogs were a nuisance. A gigantic dog town joined our property on the west. They, unlike cattle, could not be fenced out, so they destroyed much of our adjacent fields of corn or beans. Their

Squirrel Creek Barn

burrows were home for many rattlesnakes and were also inhabited by small, six or seven-inch tall, prairie dog owls which were rather cute birds with round heads and eyes. After my brother, Earl, left home, I was often entrusted with the .22 rifle and would spend most of an afternoon shooting the critters. Often, little skinny-legged sandpipers flitted between the prairie dog mounds and numerous meadowlarks brightened the air with their melodious songs. But even on the most pleasant days, there was always the ingrained fear of an unsuspected encounter with a rattlesnake. One never dared let his guard down!

There were many, many sparrows, especially in the winter, which we called "snowbirds." Earl and I used to shoot their heads off (otherwise there was nothing left) and put a half-dozen of their tiny breasts, about the size of the end of your thumb, in a pot of beans for flavor. It helped.

Weather

Spring and early fall were quite pleasant times on the plains, especially spring, when the entire landscape would be green and the prickly pear cacti would be in bloom. Other tiny wild flowers, including primroses, and an abundance of sunflowers bloomed around the edge of the fields. Encouraged by retained moisture from the winter snow, the crops, mostly corn and beans, would be lush and green. But when the heat of the summer came, it was a different story. The crops began to wither from lack of rain from the moisture-laden clouds that seemed to always pass around us. The heat at times became almost unbearable. The fowl would get in what shade they could, squat on the ground and spread their wings, open their beaks and pant for air. The horses and cows became listless; people suffered, too, and kept out of the sun as much as possible in an effort to beat the heat. If a hot dry wind came up, conditions became worse and everything, crops, animals and people, became desiccated and ready to blow away. The heat in our wooden cookshack was nearly intolerable, but the inside of our one room adobe living quarters was more pleasant.

In early fall, we harvested what was left of our poor crops. Then in late autumn, the wind began to blow and blew unceasingly until spring. We could see Pike's Peak fifty miles in the distance located a little north of due west. The wind blew perpetually from a direction of about fifteen degrees north of Pike's Peak. It blew all the topsoil off our plowed fields toward the southeast. Our homestead was surrounded on the north, east and west by open prairie; to the south of us were a couple of homesteads, separated from ours by a barbed wire fence. Tumble weeds from our farm would blow against the fence, and sand would lodge against the tumbleweeds so that one could soon walk right over the top of the fence. Dust and sand from farms located about five miles to the northwest of us would nearly choke us to death and sometimes we could not even see the sun at mid-day. The wind blew with great force; my father had to brace the barn with 2x6s to keep it from blowing over and away. The sand and dust storms would sometimes last for several weeks and soon everything - houses, clothes, hair and eyes was filled by grimy dirt. Sand gritted in our teeth when we chewed our food. The never-ending screeching, howling wind was depressing to both man and beast.

Winter was the worst season. The snow and wind combined to create a blizzard. The blizzards were terrible and sometimes lasted a long time. One time, Dad was unable to find the house when he tried to return from the barn after tending the animals, so we put up a wire which we could follow. We had trouble keeping warm with our cow-chip fire and had to supplement by burning corn cobs, cornstalks, or anything else we could get. No trees grew on the prairie and thirty-five miles was too far to haul coal, which we could not afford anyway.

There were a couple of things that always fascinated me. One was the aurora borealis which we saw on rare occasions on a clear cold winter night; the other was the mirages that we would see quite frequently during the simmering summer heat. It was an odd sensation to be choking with heat and suddenly see a beautiful lake, surrounded by green trees and cool grass, dancing in the distance, only to soon fade away.

Some 28 years after we left Squirrel Creek, my father, my stepmother, Maurine, and I went back to visit the old homestead. We had difficulty in finding the place, but finally located the cattle company's line shack which was one mile due west of our place. There the buildings, windmills and water tanks were much the same; only the living quarters had been considerably upgraded and a man and his wife now lived there instead of just an old batch cowpoke. Only the woman was at home and she warned us to watch out for rattlesnakes when we used the outdoor privy. The women decided that they did not really have to go. We proceeded eastward, although there was no road, fence or other landmark remaining to guide us. It was with considerable difficulty that Father was able to locate where our buildings had been. There was no evidence even of cement foundations; everything was gone, even the one solitary cottonwood tree that my mother had so diligently nursed with every drop of available water and which we heard had grown into a tree some two or three inches in diameter. Nothing remained; all had returned to the virgin prairie except for one thing. There was a circular bare spot of sandy soil about eight feet in diameter in the center of which was a thin saucer shaped piece of cement, about two feet in diameter, bearing the trowel marks of my father's handiwork when he had plastered the bottom of the seven-foot deep cistern nearly thirty years previously. Here was visual proof of the unbelievable amount of dirt that had been moved during the dust bowl years

Meandering across this bare spot of soil was the unmistakable trail of a rattlesnake!

Water

In the Squirrel Creek area, water was more valuable than gold. The entire region was known as a dry farming project, meaning that all crops relied entirely on moisture from the sky to produce their growth. It just did not happen. Rain clouds would appear, skirt around us and seldom give us a drop. Not enough rain fell to produce a decent crop. Father used to moan and groan as he said over and over how sad it was that we were "just out of the rain belt." We grew corn, beans and milo, but they were not good productive crops.

Besides the lack of water for vegetation, water was scarce for people and livestock. For a long time, we had to rely entirely on the wells at the line shack one mile west of our home. All water was hauled by wagon in wooden barrels. As I remember it, our lumber wagon would hold four barrels of about 50 gallons capacity each. The wagon and empty barrels would be driven up close to one of the large metal water tanks located beneath each of the two windmills. A bucket would then be used to fill the barrels, then a gunny sack or piece of canvas would be placed over the top of each barrel and held in place by a larger metal barrel hoop forced in place over the top of the barrel and cloth to keep the water from splashing out. Considerable time and effort were required to supply the necessary water for 6 to 8 head of livestock and 4 or 5 people. Earl was the official water hauler and I usually went with him.

Sometimes the trip turned into quite an adventure. Besides the usual visiting with the cowboys and learning their cusswords and ribald songs, there was always the chance of watching a bullfight. All of the cattle were herefords and the bulls were gigantic in size. At times, several hundred head would come in at the same time to drink at the water tanks. Then all hell was sure to break loose among the bulls, each considering himself to be king. They would bellow and roar and paw the ground before charging each other with a force that literally shook the earth. Should an encounter chance to take place next to our wagon, I was scared to death, least of all I did not want to be gored to death by a hulking bull who in his rampage might upset our wagon or cause the horses to run away.

After we had been at Squirrel Creek for a couple of years, one of the windmills was found dangling at a forty-five degree angle. Rumor was that one of the cowpunchers, who had recently acquired a new .22 Savage Hi-power rifle, had celebrated a drunken orgy by trying to shoot the windmill off the tower. It was said that he would have succeeded had he not run out of shells. The episode cost him his job, and the mill still hung at its crazy angle when we left the area.

With water produced at two wells only a mile away, it stood to reason that we could have a well also. The lack of money held us back for about two years. Finally, Dad gave in to Mother's pleading and hired a man to come and witch for water. After a lot of hocus-pocus with a couple of willow sticks, a site was picked. A sort of derrick was set up with a pulley arrangement at the top. A piece of heavy steel pipe about five inches in diameter and one-fourth inch in thickness and about two or three feet long, was suspended by a rope at the top and was worked like a churn by pulling up and down on the rope that went over the pulley. When the pipe became filled with sand, it was pulled up and the sand knocked out. It was a slow and tiresome process. Many times, the pipe would contain little or no sand. Most of the time, the sand contained enough moisture to stick in the pipe; other times, we would pour a little water down the hole to make it cling better. It took a long time to get down 100 feet when we quit because no water was found. Also, the sand became finer grained and would no longer stick to the inside of the pipe no matter what we did.

But Father would not give up. He moved the rig several hundred yards and started a new hole directly over the top of a small plant known as "water grass," as local legend said that water existed beneath such a plant. And so it did. At about 80 feet, we hit a gravel-like formation which indeed contained water, but only in limited amounts. After the well was cased in and finished off to the best of our ability, we could pump no more than three buckets every 20 minutes. Sad to say, it had somewhat of an alkali taste and was not as good as the water we hauled. But it sure as hell beat nothing, even if we did have to continue hauling water to help out. Mother brought home, from a trip to town, a finger-sized cottonwood tree sprout, which she planted close to the well. She nursed this little tree diligently and it had grown to be over an inch in diameter by the time we left. As mentioned, my dad dug an underground cistern that we could use for storage which was an advantage.

Water was and is a very precious thing. We drank with a dipper from an open water bucket. We learned not to take a drink in the dark as we might swallow a fly, a miller or even a spider. Our only bathtub was a #2 tub of the galvanized variety. Mother had to wash all our clothes by hand on a washboard, which was no small chore. She ironed with an iron heated on top of the stove. Life on a homestead was tough for everyone, but was certainly hell on women. My mother never ceased to berate father because he had built a barn for the animals but no home for his family. We had lived the first year in the barn, then Father started to build an adobe home about 40-feet square with walls a foot in thickness. It soon became evident that he had bit off more than he could chew, so he built what was really supposed to be a chicken house, a structure 16x12 feet in size with 6-inch adobe walls which became our living and sleeping quarters. We had acquired our poorly built wooden cook shack, about 10x14 ft. in size from a disgruntled homesteader who had been smart and gave up and pulled out after the first winter. He sold us his "home" for $15.

Neighbors

Neighbors were characterized by the lack of.

The Black Squirrel Creek region was one of the areas opened up for homesteading. The whole area had been utilized as gigantic cattle empires since the 1870s, but became pockmarked by homesteads like ours that disturbed the longstanding utopia of the cattle ranchers. The headquarters of a big cattle outfit were located at some springs ten miles west of our homestead, but an outpost was situated one mile west where there were a ramshackle house, two windmills and large metal water tanks.

The people we saw most frequently were the cowboys who drew duty at this line shack. As a rule, only one was stationed there at a time. But sometimes, there would be two or more. They were variable as to looks, size and disposition. Only one dressed like a cowboy with high-heeled boots, Levis and a big hat with leather cuffs at his wrists. Some of the rest looked as if they had been dragged in from some back alley adjacent to a house of ill repute in a low class city (Pueblo?). Some had long hair; others were bald. Some shaved once a week; others never. Some were neat and clean; others filthy. Clothes were generally well worn. These men came and went: some stayed a few weeks; others for as long as a year or more. Their job was to look after the many hundreds of cattle being grazed in that area of the open range. Some of these characters took considerable delight in teaching me, a kid, plenty of swear words, dirty poetry and vulgar songs. They also taught me to roll cigarettes with Prince Albert, Dukes Mixture or Bull Durham tobacco. Earl was an adept pupil, too, perhaps more than I.

Two homesteaders joined our property on the south; one lasted only a few months and sold us his "house" when he left which we put on skids and pulled over to our place to use as a place to cook and eat. The other one lasted maybe two years before pulling up stakes.

Billboard advertisement for Bull Durham tobacco, an often seen enticement to smokers to "roll your own" cigarettes. Credit Everett Dick

About three miles northeast of us were the Reeds. They lived in a dugout built in a hillside. The family consisted of a man and wife and a boy about my age. They seemed to have a little more money than most of the others, as evidenced by their home furnishings, clothes and farm equipment. Their home in the hill was mostly underground except for the front. It was small, but cozy, and they kept it neat and clean. I was fascinated by the barbed wire fence they had built around the top to keep livestock off the roof of their home.

Five miles northwest of us was a little settlement of less than half a dozen houses. This was an extended family named Drummond who by mutual agreement had taken up a group of adjoining homesteads. One time this group of people invited the whole area to a Fourth of July celebration. Dad and I were the only ones of our family who went, as Mother said that she and Claude did not have decent clothes. Earl was off celebrating somewhere else. So Dad curried and brushed the horses, shined up the harness and wagon; we dressed in our best bib overalls and took off. When we arrived at the Drummond settlement, Dad slipped a big fat nickel into my hand and cautioned me to spend it wisely. I did. It took me all day to spend it. I had a difficult time deciding between an ice cream cone and a bottle of pop. I knew what an ice cream cone tasted like, but had no idea about the pop, which came in so many different flavors and colors that I was confused and took most of the day to decide. I finally picked a red one, but it was warm and tasted insipid as I had waited so long that all the ice had melted in the galvanized cooler tub.

There were maybe 50 or more people from all over the prairie at this celebration of the glorious Fourth. The drivers of the four or five automobiles there decided to have a race. This had to be run against time as there was no road available with more than one track. A mile was measured off and the cars went one at a time. Everybody wanted to ride; the vehicles were overloaded even to the running boards and hood and I am sure no speed records were broken. The noise and the smell of the vehicles were new to me so I managed to get as close as I could, but never got invited to ride.

Eventually, a schoolhouse was built five miles west of us on Squirrel Creek, but no one lived there. The only other neighbors were at a small settlement seven miles northeast where we sometimes picked up our mail.

We did not have many visitors. The Raleigh or Watkins man came perhaps once a year selling his scanty stock of goods. Money was hard to come by so perhaps all we got was a jar of Vaseline, Mentholatum or Vicks Vaporub. One old biddy, of unknown origin to me, came by when I was deathly sick with the flu (called in those days la grippe). She talked my folks into giving me a tablespoon of sugar filled to the brim with kerosene. Oh, Gawd! I sure got well in a hurry because I was afraid of a repeat dosage!

Some strangers came by in a covered wagon filled with scrawny little kids. They had come a long way, were tired of living out of a wagon box and had a long way yet to go. So my parents took them in for a couple of days and gave them our living quarters while we slept in the barn. My mother really hit the roof after they were gone as they had infested everything with a generous crop of bedbugs. Boy, how she muttered and sweat as she directed all of us in scrubbing down all the bedsteads with soap and water and kerosene. Then she doused everything with some kind of powder that she squeezed as a spray out of a triangular shaped cardboard box. All bedding had to be hung outside, shaken and then washed. Boy, what a mess! After it was all over, Mother came up with the statement: "It was no disgrace to get bedbugs, but it sure was a crime to keep them."

Et Cetera

When my older brother, La Verne, went with Dad and Earl early on to do some of the preparatory work at the homestead, they took the wagon box with its canvas cover off the running gear of the wagon and lived in it until the barn was built. La Verne stayed on during the first summer, but in the fall he returned to Wray to finish up his last year of high school. He lived with Grandpa and Grandma Dorman during the school year so we did not see him until the following spring. When he showed up, he gave me a shiny new dime which I kept putting in my mouth. He scolded me about this, but I kept on. Finally in exasperation, he yelled: "Keep that damn dime out of your mouth before you swallow it! If you don't, you will have to crap in a bucket for a week to get it back."

He graduated from the Yuma County, Colorado, High School in the spring of 1916. He visited us at the homestead for a time then got a job as a "news butcher" on a passenger train that ran south and east out of Denver. His trip was from Colorado Springs to La Junta, Colorado, and return. He sold newspapers, magazines, candy, gum, etc. Shortly thereafter, he enlisted in the 12th

Cavalry of the United States Army, where he served on the Mexican border trying to keep Pancho Villa under control until his discharge September 24, 1919.

About a half mile to the southeast of our home was what we called a "blowout." This was a bare spot of sand in the prairie. It was like a sand dune in reverse; instead of being elevated, it was a concave depression of sand which constantly shifted its surface as the winds ebbed and flowed. This was a great place to find arrowheads and we would visit it often, especially after a windstorm. One of my jobs was to herd our small bunch of spare cattle on the open range. I would ride bareback on one of our plow horses, sometimes for a period of half a day. I had to stay on the horse as I was too small to get back on by myself. One day, I was with the cattle at the edge of the blowout and saw what I thought was an arrowhead. I rode out on the sand and sure enough, there was a beautiful arrowhead. The temptation was too great, so I slid off the horse to pick it up as I had noticed a nearby mound of sand, partially covered with vegetation, that I figured I could stand on to get back on my horse. I was barefoot and enjoyed walking around in the sand as I looked for more artifacts. Finding none, I decided to get back on my horse, so I led the animal over to the sand hummock which would be my only way of getting remounted. But the entire sand lump was covered with a luxuriant growth of sandburrs! I tried and tried to get on my horse unaided, but could not. After about a half hour of frustration, sweat and tears, I plucked by hand as many of the vines as I could off my stepstool, but the horse did not want to stand still so I was forced to step on the burrs to get on my horse. My feet were sore for a long time as it was most difficult to get all the stickers out. In the future, I insisted that I be allowed to take a saddle, as I could always pull myself up on it. Previously, my herding had been considered too mundane a task for a seven-year-old to warrant the use of our one and only saddle, which someone else more important might need anyway.

Cow chips were used for fuel, both for cooking and heat. Cow chips were nothing more than dried cow manure, sometimes called "prairie coal." The ideal way to collect good cow chips was to find a spot, sometimes in a little hollow, where a large herd of range cattle had bedded down for several nights in a row. When such a spot was located, we would watch it very carefully until the piles of manure had dried to the right consistency. The chips that were a dark brown color were the best. The large pancake type were not so good; neither were those that had a light gray color to them, as the gray indicated that they were too old to burn well. We would hunt far and wide for this fuel source, gather them in the wagon, haul them home and pile them up on the east side of our adobe residence. They would be covered with a piece of canvas to keep them dry as a wet cow chip was unburnable. It was difficult to make the best of them burn hard enough to get much heat, and it took considerable skill and patience to make them burn at all.

During WWI, my father worked in Pueblo during the winter months. He unloaded 100 lb. sacks of cement from boxcars for some war effort project. His salary was $3.00 for a ten-hour day. He said his breakfast consisted of a large bowl of oatmeal plus toast for 25 cents. His work supplied funds for food and other family necessities that helped to keep us alive during those lean years. Of course, Mother and we kids were alone at the homestead while Father was gone for several months at a time.

We planted watermelons at scattered areas in our large cornfield. The idea was that perhaps the melons would do better in the semishade of the corn; also, the melons would be out of sight. But it was a poor idea; the worst melon thieves were the coyotes. We kept a sharp eye on the bigger melons, waiting for them to get ripe. Just as sure as we thought one would be ready the next day, the coyotes would beat us to it. They would bite through the rind to get to the inside meat and leave a very mutilated melon for us to gaze at in disgust. This problem happened several times in a row, but there was one very special large melon that we were watching daily that the varmints so far had left alone. One morning, Dad and I went to check on it as we were sure it might be ready that day. Utter devastation greeted our eyes; the fruit was broken open, the beautiful red meat was gone and there were bite marks all over the rind a la coyote style. But they were human bite marks and the tracks in the dirt were not coyote, but human. My brother, Earl, had been unable to withstand the temptation in his greed and had attempted to disguise the act. Dad gave him a good lecture about sharing the good things in life with others.

Earl had other problems, too. He smoked cigarettes a good deal of the time, but Dad made a deal with him. If he would not smoke any more, he could have as his very own a young beautiful colt that one of our mares had produced. Things went nicely for many months, then Dad caught him with a cigarette in his mouth, scolded him severely and told him that the colt was no longer his. The next morning, Earl was gone. He took with him our only decent saddle horse and saddle. He was not quite fifteen years of age. This episode happened about six months prior to the time that we were to "prove up" on our homestead. Both of my parents were heart broken. Dad rode bare back several days looking for him, without success. We did not see Earl again for over four years until he showed up where we lived in Greeley, Colorado. He told us then that Dad had passed within a few yards of him as he lay in a ditch close to the small town of Fountain many miles to the west of us.

My parents taught me to read and write at home. One fall, it was decided that Earl and I were to go to school. A new schoolhouse had been built on the banks of Squirrel Creek, five miles to the west of us, so off we went, with Earl in the saddle and me hanging on behind for a butt-jarring five miles. The school consisted of a one-room building with a stove in the center of the room, his and her outdoor privies and a small shed to protect the horses that everyone used to get to school, either by horseback or by some sort of horse-drawn vehicle. The teacher was a tiny wind-blown female who looked decidedly unhappy and was probably about 18 years of age. At most, a dozen students of all sizes, ages and looks attended. Earl was the oldest and biggest one there. He threw his weight around during the noon hour by riding our saddle horse across the school grounds at breakneck speed, to display his skill as a "ruff" and "tuff" cowboy. I remember that our school lunches often consisted of homemade bread, spread with Crisco, as Mother sometimes had no jam, jellies or at times even butter, if the cow was dry. We went to school only about two months that fall until the weather turned bad with a lot of wind and snow. Our parents were afraid to let us continue, for fear that we would become lost or even freeze to death in a terrible prairie blizzard.

One of the few items we got in the mail was a Henry Field seed and garden catalog. One spring they had a promotion on. Customers selling so many packages of seeds would be eligible for certain prizes. One of these prizes was a Daisy BB gun. I soon had a whole slew of seeds to sell, but few people for a sales audience. The Reeds bought one package of flower seeds. The neighbors to the south had moved away. After my folks had bought all that they could afford, many packets remained unsold and it looked as if I was going to be stuck with a lot of seeds and no BB gun. One day, I talked my mother into letting me go over to the Drummond settlement. A horse was saddled and I was bundled up for the five-mile ride. I was in luck for a sewing bee was being held at one of the houses which, by chance, I hit first. The old gals there thought they were being visited by some kind of a being from outer space. They took me in as a poor little desert waif, mothered me by unwrapping my many layers of outer clothing, made hot chocolate for me and bought all my seeds, although they did seem to have to dig into their stocking tops and bosoms to find the money! I got my BB gun, which never did work properly.

Sometime before Earl ran away from home, our one and only good milk cow turned up missing. Both Dad and Earl spent many days in the saddle looking for her. Rumor had it that she had been stolen and sold by one of the cowboys at the line shack. He showed up soon after with a new saddle, boots and hat. Later on, this person became famous as a world champion bronc rider at the Cheyenne Frontier Days and other rodeo events.

There was one thing that I disliked most of all. That was getting my hair cut by my father. He had no clippers or barber shears, so he used one of my mothers larger sewing scissors. I am sure that he hated the procedure as much or more than I did. First of all, Mother would have to nag at him for a month or two to get him to go ahead and if he was not in an ill humor when he started, he certainly was before he finished. I would be placed on a high kitchen stool, a dishtowel tied around my neck, told to shut up and sit still. Dad would be closely supervised by Mother, who often remarked that she could probably do a better job. Dad would throw down his shears and tell her to go ahead, which she was never willing to do. Dad always threatened to "use a soup bowl next time" for a pattern to cut around, but thank goodness next time would be at least six months or more in the future. I think my little brother, Claude, enjoyed the home barber shop about as much as I did. I can still see him wiggling in protest.

Exit Homestead

At last the required three years were up. Three years of fighting the elements; too much cold in the winter, too much heat in the summer, combined with the cursed wind that blew all the time. Three years of fighting the coyotes, the rattlesnakes, the prairie fires and the drought. Three years of hunger for proper food, living conditions and companionship. Three years of dashed hopes and ambitions. Three years in the prison of poverty, not only of the body, but of one's very soul. These are but a few of the things that my parents went through-life's dreams shipwrecked on the sagebrush and cactus of Squirrel Creek.

My father had to take care of all the legal procedures necessary to "prove up" on our 320 acres. Then he had much difficulty in trying to dispose of the property. Virtually all of the nearby homesteaders had given up and moved away before their required time had been put in. The Reeds hung on and managed to sell their ground to the predominant cattleman in the area for $5.50 per acre. The Drummond crowd had decided to try and stick it out for a while. We could not stay on and starve to death, yet we could not go any place until we obtained money from the sale of our homestead. Dad made numerous trips to try and sell to the local cattle baron. As mentioned, this man lived 10 miles to the west of us and balked at paying us $6 an acre when he had bought Reeds at $5.50. But Father stuck to his asking price and after a month or two, a deal was finally consummated, probably because our place was the last remaining homestead, giving the cattleman control over the vast grazing area that had been his prior to the time all the homesteads had been taken up.

It took many trips and a lot of work to get all our possessions moved to Pueblo by horse and wagon, which was a full day's journey. I made several trips with Dad and remember a terrible rainstorm we were caught in without protection, which resulted in everything including us getting totally drenched. I remember my father worried about his Winchester .40-.82 rifle stashed upright in the front left-hand corner of the wagon.

My parents had spent much time planning where they would locate when they left Squirrel Creek. They had considered a place in Wyoming, Paonia, Colorado, and Greeley, Colorado. They finally picked Greeley, possibly because Grandma Dorman, Uncle Sam and Aunt Minnie Ness lived there, as did Aunt Edythe, my dad's youngest sister.

Mother, Claude and I came on a passenger train to Greeley, leaving Dad to follow in a boxcar with the livestock and household goods. I do not remember much about the trip except that the train was filled with soldiers. We stayed at Grandma Dorman's where at my re-entry into civilization, I got my hind-end wet when I first used an overly vigorous flush toilet.

Mother did not lose much time in beginning to seek a new home. She took me with her the next day and we started walking and looking. We stopped at a "For Sale" sign or two, but she did not find anything of interest until we got on West 5th Street, where there was a four-room house with a small barn, a chicken house and a large garden plot. She talked with the people who wanted to sell the property for $1000. The place at 1904 5th Street seemed to please her and she soon made arrangements to purchase it. This home was put in her name as the money for it was a legacy from her mother, Emma Hammond, who soon came to live with us. Dad arrived eventually with all the family belongings and purchased a plot of ground about three blocks to the west with the proceeds from the homestead sale, which was always referred to as the five acres.

Carpenters were called in and a beautiful bay window was constructed on the east side of the kitchen and a back porch was built on the south side of the house. A new water well was drilled deep enough to avoid the contaminated superficial strata. The hand-powered pump was located in the southeast corner of the porch, with a screened-in bedroom for Claude and me to the west. The central portion contained some cupboards, a hand-powered washing machine that had to be worked 500 strokes per batch and a cream separator, also hand turned.

So began a new lifestyle for the Dormans at Greeley, Colorado, considerably different from what we had been used to at Squirrel Creek because we now had plenty of water to drink for man and beast in addition to all the water we wanted to irrigate our crops. I had to adjust to civilization and not use all the cuss words that I was accustomed to with the cowboy ranch hands. I had to learn to get along with kids; in one fight, I used the supposedly devastating solar plexus punch only to get the hell beat out of me by a fellow who had never heard of it.

Although I was nearly nine years old, I started in the first grade in school. But in a couple of months, I was promoted to the third grade. Claude started to school early and was my nemesis in our one-room Seventh Day Adventist church school because if there was a spelling or mathematical contest, he would always beat me. We had a variety of teachers, some male some female. Each school year, we were furnished one new pair of bib overalls and Mother made each of us two new blue chambray shirts on her foot powered sewing machine. For my ninth birthday, I was given a youth-sized ax so I could help Dad chop wood as that is how he made part of his living - chopping down some of the immense overgrown cottonwood trees that lined the streets of Greeley. For

Christmas, I got a bicycle and a pair of clamp on ice skates, so things were sure a lot better that I had been used to at Squirrel Creek. All in all, most things were different. But there was always that taint of being different because you were Seventh-Day Adventist and went to church on Saturday instead of Sunday.

And so life went on at our new home in Greeley, Colorado.

Greeley, Colorado

Our lifestyle in Greeley was much improved over Squirrel Creek, but still there were problems, mainly because of our poverty. Having expended most of their money on the two properties, my parents were hard pressed to put food on the table. In the winter months, my father would chop down the overgrown cottonwood trees that had become a hazard on the streets of the town. He did this for the wood. After the trees were cut, he would haul the huge logs home by team and wagon. Then I would supply part of the power for a two-man saw to cut the logs into about fourteen-inch lengths for burning in the kitchen stove. It was my job to split the cut logs into proper size to fit the stove. This I did before and after school and on Sundays. If I worked faithfully until noon on Sunday, I would be permitted to go ice skating for a few hours in the afternoon. The prepared wood was racked up in our back yard and occasionally, my father sold some, but mostly it was used in our home. Early on, the wood was very green and had to be dried out on the oven door before it would burn well in the kitchen stove. Once a year, Dad would drive the team and wagon about twenty-five miles to get a load of coal. This type of slate, sold as coal, was used primarily in our heating stove, located in the living room, which heated the house proper. Our home had only two bedrooms, one of which was occupied by Grandmother Hammond. My brother, Claude, and I slept on the back porch, enclosed only by wire screen and canvas, with temperatures sometimes as low as 44 degrees below zero. Our beds were warmed by pieces of soapstone, kept on the kitchen stove, then wrapped in fragments of old blankets at bedtime.

We had a team of horses and a jersey milk cow. Mother kept several dozen Rhode Island red chickens. Our getting up time was 5 a.m., summer or winter, rain or shine. In the winter, Dad would get up first, rebuild or shake the fires and milk the cow. Claude and I always dressed and undressed behind the coal stove in the living room in cold weather. Breakfast was at 6 a.m., leaving little time for chopping wood or other work before school. The morning milk was for family use; also, there was a frequent order from a neighbor down the road for a five-cent quart that was delivered in a small uncovered bucket with the caution: "Don't spill a drop." Mother churned butter and made cottage cheese. At night, it was my job to get in the wood and coal and milk the cow. The evening milk was run through a separator and the resulting cream would be sold, along with some of Mother's eggs, as a source of income.

In spring, summer and fall, the work really piled up. Dad put in about two acres of sugar beets and over an acre of alfalfa. The rest of the five acres was planted to vegetables and melons. The sugar beets were hell for my younger brother, Claude, and me. Beets, in those days, were planted as solid rows. When they were about two inches high, they would have to be blocked and thinned. Dad would block with a hoe, leaving a small clump of perhaps a dozen plants about every ten or twelve inches. Then Claude and I, crawling on our hands and knees, would pluck out all the plants except the most vigorous one, which was left in place to grow into a sugar beet. It was slow tedious work, hard on backs, knees and fingers. Soon the knees of our overalls were worn through and our bare knees became grime encrusted and tough. The work was hard on fingers, too, so that they nearly reached the bleeding point. The first year we were in the beet business, Claude was four years old and I was nine. We hated the wearisome job and would sneak off when we could to go swimming in the large irrigation ditch that was located at the upper end of our property. When the tiresome job was finished, we got our reward. Dad would hitch up the horses and we would drive across town and squander twenty-five cents for a 100 lb. block of ice. Then we would make a gallon of homemade ice cream in the wooden ice cream maker, taking turns at the crank, arguing over who would get to lick the paddle when it was removed from the metal container.

Dad grew vegetables to sell to the public. We planted radishes of several varieties, onion sets for green onions, yellow and green string beans, peas, leaf lettuce, spinach, cabbage, sweet corn and tomatoes. This took a lot of work; the ground had to be prepared, the crops planted, weeded, cultivated, irrigated and harvested. Radishes and onions were the first things ready for market. We would be in the fields at dawn, then prepare the radishes and onions at home by washing and tying them in bunches. All the produce would be loaded into the wagon and Dad would drive to the more prosperous part of town, then the three of us would go from door to door, with the handle of a large wicker basket over our arm, selling the fresh garden products. This was done Monday, Wednesday and Friday of each week. Claude and I would often sell as much as $2 per day, rarely $3. It took an awful lot of radishes or green onions at a "nickel a bunch or three for a dime" to count up. Dad was good to us; he would give us one-fourth of what we sold. We hoarded the money in a fruit jar, counting it frequently as we saved it to be used for necessities such as clothing, a new pair of shoes or maybe a box of .22 shells. An occasional nickel was frittered away on a Hershey bar, the only candy bar available in those days. We paid a faithful tithe on our earnings.

We grew several kinds of watermelons, Greeley wonder muskmelons, cantaloupe and honeydews. This posed a problem since our melon patch was close to town so it was convenient for the town kids and young adults to help themselves. The farm was three blocks from home. Dad put up a tent in the middle of the melon patch and would sleep there on a cot at night with his 12-gauge double-barreled shotgun loaded with rock salt instead of lead shot. When I was twelve or thirteen years old, I used to spell him off. The melon thieves were too smart for me. One trick they had was to drive past the field in the darkness, going very slowly, with the car lights off. They would drop one or two people off and drive away. When I had gone back to bed, they would return and pick up their companions along with a few melons, which had been sneaked to the road. Another scheme they fooled me with was to sneak one or two pranksters into the patch who would very quietly pick a half dozen melons and float them down the irrigation ditch adjacent to our field where the loot could be picked up down stream by their gloating buddies. In all honesty, I need to reveal a couple of episodes that have never been told before. One morning just after dawn, as I prepared to walk the three blocks home for breakfast, I saw a magnificent cock pheasant in front of my tent about fifty feet away. I succumbed to the illegal temptation and pulled the trigger on my 12-gauge blunderbuss the blast of which rocked the entire country. The rock salt load, being of light weight, did not travel very far and did no damage to the bird. The noise of the gun, besides the cackling and squawking of the rooster as he cussed me in pheasantese when he flew away, made a terrible racket. I feared that the combined noise had aroused the nearby town and expected the city cops to show up on their bicycles any moment. One time, I enticed a neighborhood girl to visit me in my tent early one moonlit evening. Before our adolescent hormones could start to function, her mother raised the tent flap door and called her home!

In the early 1920s, to make a few dollars, Dad hired out to a friend to help cut Christmas trees for sale. They took Dad's team and wagon and went about twenty miles to Ft. Collins Canyon. On the way home, loaded down with trees and in the dark, the wagon overturned on the treacherous icy mountain road, breaking both of Dad's arms at the wrists. He was in the hospital for a few days and then came home with both arms in casts. I can remember being kept out of school one day a week to care for him while Mother worked, doing housework at thirty-five cents an hour, to help with the family finances. Dad was pretty helpless, being unable to even feed himself. This meant that Claude and I had to do all the physical work around the place for a long time. It took him several months to recover from his injuries. The local Salvation Army sent a 100 lb. sack of flour to help us out. Dad sent it back with the remark, "We are not going to accept charity from anyone!" Dad was left with a permanent deformity to his right wrist, which hampered him the rest of his life.

I started to school the fall I turned nine years of age in December. The Seventh-Day Adventist church school at Greeley was somewhat primitive, at best. It was a one-room wooden structure located in a sparsely settled area on the southwest outskirts of Greeley, at the approximate location where the Weld County Hospital now stands. It stood nearly alone, with two adjacent houses on the south and another one nearly a block away on the north. Fields were to the east and west. There was no running water in the building, only a cold water tap in front. Boys and girls outhouses were located at a distance back of the building. The school was heated by a potbellied stove in the center of the oblong room that housed about twenty-four pupils. The desks were of several sizes and shapes. Grades one to eight were taught, by one teacher, sometimes female, sometimes male.

To begin with, there was no playground equipment for the kids to play on. After a year or two, a couple of old telephone poles were set up for a double swing and a plank was balanced for a teeter-totter. At recess and noon, "andy-over" was played with a ball tossed over the roof. Everyone brought lunches which were eaten, under supervision of the teacher, at our desks. In good weather, the boys, for want of something to do, would dig caves in the ground some distance away from the schoolhouse, complete with a fireplace and makeshift roof.

It took me some time to adjust to city life and going to school and associating with people after the isolation at Squirrel Creek. I got in trouble if I cussed too much or told dirty stories that the cowboys had taught me. We kids who went to the dilapidated SDA church school were semi-looked down upon by many of the other children in town, with their nice brick school buildings, as being sort of queer. They would pick on me as I went to and from school and frequently slap me around. At times, I would carry a ball bat on my shoulder if on foot, or avoid them if I could on my bicycle. Still there were times when I got roughed up. Often, it seemed better to run rather than fight.

If the teacher was a woman, I would have to go to school early in cold weather to build a fire and have the schoolroom warm when it was time for school to start. When the kindling pile was depleted, the problem was finding enough wood to start a fire. The ax had disappeared so I was trying to break up some 2x4 size wood by dropping the end of the telephone pole on the wood propped up on a block. The wood did not break and the end of the telephone pole bounced up and broke my nose. Many years later, in medical school, I had it straightened out. I was also selected at times to be the school janitor, although generally the teacher was responsible for keeping the place clean. Other things were new to me. I made periodic visits to a barber shop where I could get my hair cut for thirty-five cents, including generous squirts from a long-necked green bottle of Lucky Tiger hair tonic rubbed into my scalp. I made my first trip to a dentist, where a burly man with huge hands and long black hair on his arms took care of my neglected teeth. He filled my mouth with handfuls of silver amalgam, all of which later had to be removed, along with several teeth. He was a poor dentist, but the best my parents could afford. I remember the flu epidemic of 1918-19. Before the epidemic ended, about 20 million Americans sickened and more than 500,000 died. We were given one-inch size cloth packets of asafetida to wear around our necks. This malodorous concoction did not keep the flu bug away, but certainly made it easy to avoid people. Luckily, these bags of obnoxious stench were easy to lose. No one in our immediate family became seriously ill.

We went to church all morning and again at 3 p.m. on Saturdays. Prayer meeting was held at the church on Wednesday evening. In the summer, I frequently mowed the church lawn and often helped out with the janitor work, as my parents felt that such was part of my religious obligation. Sometimes Greeley was proselytized by Mormon missionaries who would attend the

Adventist church; once we invited them into our home for a Sabbath dinner. I even changed my hair style to a part in the middle after the pattern of one of the Saints. There was no resident minister for our church. About once a month, an itinerant preacher would make the rounds; otherwise, it was up to the locals to preach a sermon on Saturdays. My father was a frequent speaker. One time, he really let go about the evils that went on in the local parks under cover of darkness among the trees and beneath the bushes. Several of the brothers and sisters got a little upset about his talk, supposedly out of my earshot. Maybe he had been a little too explicit in his description of his version of the clandestine sexual activity that he feared was taking place in our small town as he stressed the dire consequences of breaking the seventh commandment, perhaps a bit too vividly.

We had to get dressed up to go to church. To me, this meant black stockings and knee pants that had been previously worn by my older brothers, Earl or La Verne. I hated the discomfort of a buttoned up shirt, tight necktie and uncomfortable semishined shoes. Time, sitting in hard pews, went slowly in church.

Long winter evenings were spent in various ways. Dad disgruntedly half-soled his, Claude's and my shoes in front of the kitchen stove. He had a cobbler's last with several metal patterns for different sized shoes. He would put the shoe nails in his mouth and pick them out, one at a time, with the thumb and forefinger of his left hand while he used a hammer in his right hand to drive the nails. He did not have a proper cobbler's hammer, so had to use a more cumbersome 16 oz. claw hammer. There were times when he would inadvertently clobber the thumb and forefinger of his left hand, which would cause him to spew out a mouth full of nails and mumble to himself. The leather he used was about one-fourth inch in thickness and had been cut from a big sheet of sole leather. He would use the old pried off shoe sole for a pattern for the new one if possible; otherwise, he would cut a new one from scratch. After a new one was roughened out, he would soak it in water to make it more pliable in order to mold it to the bottom of the shoe. It was obvious that he did not enjoy the job.

Besides the routine church magazines, we subscribed to, when finances permitted, The Farm Journal and The American Boy. Dad would read to us aloud the stories in The American Boy. Claude and I would lie on the floor and Mother would be in her rocking chair with her crocheting. Dad was a good reader and we all would be sorry when the magazine was finished. I can faintly recall some of the stories about Connie May, Mark Tidd and James Willard Schultz'

Sioux Indian stories. It was against the rules for us to read the stories ahead of time, but when I got so I could read pretty well, I would snitch the magazine as soon as it came. This in no way lessened my enjoyment of Dad's reading as I perhaps got more out of it on the second rendition.

When he was five years old, my brother, Claude, followed me to school one day without our parents' knowledge. He was permitted to stay. Claude put me to shame several times. When there was a spelling or arithmetic contest for all the grades, he would frequently outperform me. He was smart!

I discovered the Greeley Public Library and read with great pleasure the animal stories by Thornton Burgess about Reddy Fox, Jimmy Skunk, Bobby Coon and Buster Bear. I graduated to western stories. B.M. Bower and "Chip of the Flying U" was okay, but my parents were a little skeptical about the likes of Zane Gray or O. Henry, so some reading had to be done under the covers at night, sometimes by flashlight. Claude read everything I did. Our sex education was augmented by the Montgomery Ward and Sears and Roebuck catalogs. These twice a year thick volumes could be perused surreptitiously in the house or more at leisure in the privacy of the outdoor privy, showing scandalous pictures of females in their corsets, panties and brassieres.

We ate very little meat. Father consumed no meat at all. The rest of us ate no pork or other "unclean meat." Mother would sometimes sacrifice one of her chickens to the pot. About once a year, she would buy a slab of beef roundsteak which she would beat like hell to tenderize before cooking. At Thanksgiving, we were sometimes invited out to eat, generally to Uncle Will and Aunt Ida's where we had turkey and all the fixings; Claude and I would really stuff ourselves. Even though Dad ate no meat, he loved the gravy, which led, on occasion, to his being teased with the expression: "You might as well eat the devil as to drink his broth." He would only grin, half-embrassed, and wipe up more gravy with a crust of bread.

In about 1922, Dad bought a well-used Model T Ford. It was a single seater that had been converted to a pickup. The price was $220, with $100 down and payments of $10 per month for a year, which Dad managed to pay off sooner, as he hated to be in debt. It had a folding top which we soon discarded because it was in poor shape. Dad had a problem in learning to drive and nearly had an accident downtown when he reared back on the steering wheel and yelled "Whoa" when he wanted to stop instead of applying the brake. The operation of the old "Tin Lizzie" was by three pedals on the floor, to be manipulated by the driver's feet, besides a tall left-hand lever for neutral and high. The left pedal controlled clutch and low, the middle pedal was pushed in for reverse and the right was the brake. Oddly enough, the gear ratio was lower in reverse than in low gear so if a real steep hill was encountered, it was backed up. He kept his team of horses for farm work.

There was no foot-feed for gas. On each side of the steering column was a hand operated lever on the right for gas; a left lever controlled the spark. Starting the engine was done by hand crank. One learned not to wrap his thumb around the crank handle as the engine might backfire and break a wrist. Freezing weather posed a real problem in starting the car. Anti-freeze solutions such as Prestone were unknown. A brass petcock at the bottom of the engine was opened, which drained the water out at night. The next morning, the drain valve was closed. A little lukewarm water was poured in to avoid breaking the block. The radiator was then filled up with hot water from the teakettle and maybe the car would start. Sometimes, one rear wheel was jacked up as the engine was cranked, which for some reason known only to Henry Ford, seemed to help.

One summer, Dad, Claude and I decided to drive to Denver, some fifty miles away, to attend the Adventist camp meeting that was being held there. We started out at daybreak. Our early model car did not have demountable rims, so we could not carry a spare tire. When we got a flat, we jacked up the wheel, got the tire irons out and soon had the inner tube out of the casing and patched the tube with a tire-patching kit that contained several sizes of rubber patches. The offending hole in the inner tube would be located, the adjacent area abraded, the correct amount of rubber cement applied with a finger, the right size patch applied with pressure, tube and casing reinstalled on the wheel, then the tire pumped up by hand. We became experts that day; on the hundred mile round trip we had fifteen flat tires!

My mother, being a very devout God-fearing person, was determined that I be educated to become a Seventh-Day Adventist minister. Even when I was a tiny child, she always told everyone what my calling was to be. But one thing that I did not want to be was a preacher. I secretly detested the very thought, but was afraid to speak up. One day at church, she was proclaiming to everyone that I was going to be educated to be a minister and said: "Isn't that right, Eldon, dear?" I surprised myself and said: "No, I am going to be a doctor." She was flabbergasted, but had to acquiesce as her stepfather was a physician and she considered a doctor as being perhaps one step higher up the social ladder than a minister. I had no real idea what being a doctor entailed, but said what I did to get her off her preacher kick. I was in about the seventh grade at the time.

In 1924, I graduated, by skipping a grade or two, from the eighth grade at the Adventist church school in Greeley. My parents wanted me to continue school at Campion Academy, an Adventist boarding school for grades nine through twelve, located three miles south of Loveland, Colorado, twenty miles away. That summer, I was lucky to get a job four miles away from home for a short time. I was paid three dollars a day for "sticking cabbage." I bent over all day making a hole in the ground with a dibble (a metal pointed stick) putting a five-inch cabbage plant from an apron on my belt into the hole, then closing the hole with the dibble. All the time I was working fast to keep ahead of the stream of irrigation water that was already running down the furrow to soak the just-planted cabbage. I made enough money to buy a pair of much desired long pants, a pullover sweater and my first pair of oxfords. I ordered all of these things from Sears and Roebuck and had enough money left over to make a down payment on tuition, room and board. That fall, I started school at Campion Academy.

On The Road

Having just finished my junior high school year at Campion Academy, a friend and I decided to make some money for the next school year. In late May, the day after school was out, we hopped a freight train going toward Denver on our way to the harvest fields of Oklahoma. The year was 1927; I was 17 years old.

In those days, the wheat-growing states of Oklahoma, Kansas, Nebraska, the Dakotas and even southern Canada were all harvested by itinerant workers who supplied the muscle to do the work that is now done in a fraction of the time by combines. The harvest would start early in Oklahoma and proceed northward as the season progressed, ending in Canada about September.

We had planned this journey for a few weeks, keeping our idea secret from our parents as we knew they would not give permission for our harebrained adventure. We had each purchased a WWI backpack in which we carried our meager belongings with a rolled up blanket on top.

We managed to get through Denver, Colorado Springs and Pueblo, part of the time on freight trains and part time hitchhiking. Then we started across the great plains of eastern Colorado toward Rocky Ford, La Junta, Las Animas and Lamar. The railroad and highway followed the course of the Arkansas River. We were menaced by husky looking brakemen, shaking their brake sticks in our direction, so we did not ride the rails. The highway was mostly unpaved with stretches that were not even graveled. Worst of all, it started to rain – a constant drizzle, day and night. We were hard put to keep dry since we had no raincoats or slickers. We tried draping our bodies with our blankets, but they only absorbed the moisture and made us more miserable. We huddled under trees or by buildings adjacent to the highway. Most of the rides we got were short ones, only a few miles. We invaded a barn's dry haymow after the family had gone to bed only to be sent on our way at dawn by a farmer who motioned us on with a manure covered pitchfork. It took us two days to get to Lamar, a distance of about 150 miles from Pueblo. It was a Saturday afternoon when we got to Lamar and the town was filled with farmers doing their weekly shopping. People were more friendly here and we spent most of the afternoon in a tolerant pool hall. It was still raining and the usual eastern Colorado wind had started to blow.

Lamar was a weather-minded small town. The sidewalks in front of the stores on main street were covered by wooden or metal-roofed canopies which extended out to the curb. At the outer edge of this protection were rolled up canvas curtains, which could be let down in inclement weather, forming a sheltered tunnel in front of the buildings. My friend and I were kicked out of the pool hall about midnight. Around 1 a.m., the town marshal got tired of chasing us from one bench to another in the protected area and invited us to spend the rest of the night in the local jail, so we enjoyed the night in the luxury of a warm building with clean and comfortable beds.

By the next morning, the wind had blown the rain away and we went on our journey under better circumstances. We eventually reached my friend's uncle's farm in extreme northern Oklahoma. Instead of the prosperous farm that had been indicated to me, we found a dilapidated two story home located in a treeless yard. My friend's relatives were obvious sharecroppers, bordering on poverty. We arrived just as the family members had finished their evening meal.

We were unmistakably as welcome as a couple of skunks at a Sunday School picnic! It seemed for a time that we were not even going to be offered any food. But finally, the disgruntled housewife prepared a scant greasy meal. We were told in a resolute manner that because of the overabundant rain in that area, the harvest would not start for maybe two weeks. It was hinted that perhaps we should try farther south, where possibly the work would begin sooner. We were put to bed upstairs in a tiny dingy room with a lumpy uncomfortable bed.

The following day, my friend decided to stay, but I thought it best to move on. After a revolting breakfast, even to my hungry stomach, I walked away, now on my own. I soon came to a north-south running railroad. There was a short freight train parked on a siding next to a section house. The man there saw me hanging around, came over and talked to me and helped me into an open boxcar, with the advice that the train was a slow one, but would be going south pretty soon. The train stopped at every siding and whistle stop. In my snug boxcar Pullman, I did notice that the wind blew like hell during the night – in fact, hard enough that the freight car rocked back and forth. Just before dawn, I heard a lot of loud excited talk going on and assumed that the end of the line had been reached. I crawled out of the boxcar and walked away from the rail yard. When it became fully daylight, a scene of utter devastation met my eyes. I was in a town that was completely destroyed. Most of the buildings were down and the streets were filled with debris. People were wandering around looking with disbelief at the wanton destruction. I could not believe what I saw, so asked a man what had happened. He said that shortly after midnight, a terrible tornado had destroyed the town of Enid, Oklahoma.

I walked right back to the rail yard and climbed into the same boxcar which was now headed north. Toward evening, I ended up at the same section house that I had left the day before. I stayed in my accommodations overnight. The next morning, my section hand friend invited me into his home and his wife cooked me a sumptuous breakfast of hot cakes and eggs, the first real meal I had in many days. He told me because of scattered tornado damage the train was going to stay right where it was. I thanked the couple for their great kindness, threw my pack on my back and started walking toward Kansas. I did not know exactly what to do. I finally thought of a teacher friend of mine back at the academy who had mentioned to me that his parents lived at Otis, Kansas, and had a wheat farm there. But to get there, I had to travel most of the way across Kansas. I spent the last nickel of my funds at a crossroads cafe for a cup of coffee, which I filled with multiple spoonfuls of sugar and a lot of cream. The owner was kind to me and tossed me a dried-up doughnut, which tasted good. He also let me sleep on a cot in a woodshed behind his place of business.

A little later, I became bogged down in a small Kansas town because of torrential rains that came down in bucketfuls for a couple of days. All roads were nothing but mud, so any travel was out of the question. I went into a pool hall to get out of the weather; this was also a good place to get information about jobs. I was flat broke and desperate for work. I let it be known that I would do any kind of work at a minimal wage. The general discussion was mainly about the excessive rain, how it was slowing up the harvest, the muddy roads and so on. There was a man there who claimed to be the boss in charge of a small carnival that was mired down because of the weather. He heard me asking about work and volunteered that he could give me a job with his carnival. He bought me a two-bit bowl of stew and gave me a sales pitch, claiming that I could make more money with the carnival than I could in the harvest fields. He explained to me that the carnival had 8 or 10 tents or booths consisting of a shooting gallery, several games of chance, a freak show or two plus a very active hootchy-kootchy – striptease bunch of females. He hinted that there were a couple of available tents where the girls would do more than take off their clothes for the edification of the country bumpkins. I was too naive to realize at the time that his carnival was really a modified whorehouse on wheels! He wanted to sign me up right away to work for him. I told him that I would have to think it over. He agreed and told me that because of the bad weather, he had a room in the hotel upstairs where I could stay, since he would have to be out at the carnival grounds that night. He gave me the skeleton key to his room and said he would see me in the morning. The first thing I did was scrub the dirty ring out of the bathtub located down the hall and take a long, luxurious hot bath. Then I went to bed, clad only in my last clean shirt; I was soon asleep. But not for long; I was rudely awakened by my so-called benefactor, very vigorous in his craven urge to commit sodomy. I had to fight the bastard off and made my escape by the skin of my teeth from the locked room with my scanty belongings. It did not take me long to realize, as I huddled in a damp doorway until dawn, that I had been "set up" by this man's devious plan to get me alone and at his mercy.

Tornado funnel - E. Dick photo

By daylight, the rain had stopped and I walked on my way northward. In a couple of days of hitchhiking, begging food and shelter in return for offered work, I arrived at Otis, Kansas. Needless to say, the parents of my teacher friend back at Campion Academy had never heard of me. After considerable hesitation, they took me in. I stayed at their place for about a week. I tried to pay for my board and room by milking cows, chopping wood and shoveling manure. I helped haul a couple of wagon loads of last year's wheat to the elevator at Otis, a couple of miles away.

One evening, the sky was filled with terrible looking clouds that seethed back and forth in the western sky. A funnel cloud formed and came in our direction. We descended into a cyclone cellar and stayed there all night, our only illumination being a smoky kerosene lantern. The next morning, it was discovered that a neighbor's big red barn had been moved about two feet off its foundation; otherwise, no real damage was done. Many of the farmers in this tornado belt had an underground, heavily reinforced cellar that contained food, water and cots. Here, they could seek shelter in event of a tornado. I did not have sense enough to be afraid in the same degree as my hosts.

The opportunity for a job opened up a few miles away and I was hired to work in a "header barge." This was a contraption built much like a hayrack, except that the frame was lower on the right-hand side with a higher back on the left, all lined with a wire netting to retain the heads of wheat. It was pulled by two horses alongside the "header," which was a huge machine, pulled by four or six

Header, showing elevator loading wheat heads into "Header Barge" - Kansas Historical Society

horses, that cut the heads off the wheat and then loaded the grain by means of an elevator. This was a rotating endless belt with cleats, throwing the severed heads of grain into the header barge with considerable force. My job was, with a pitchfork, to shift the wheat heads evenly on the wagon for a full load to be hauled to a stackyard for future final work by a threshing machine. The pitchfork used was larger than usual, with more tines which had an increased curve. At first, I was unable to manipulate this tool to get a good forkful of material. One had to stick the fork into the loose heads with an up and down twisting motion to gain an acceptable load. Not only did I have to keep the load level tromped down as the wagon filled up, but I had to have the horses guided straight and at the right speed so that the elevator put the stuff in the wagon and not on the ground. Then too, when the wagon ahead was full, I had to manipulate my wagon by whipping up the horses, so that the transition of one wagon to the other was made in such a manner that no precious grain was lost from the header that kept going at full tilt.

It was hot. The relentless Kansas sun bore down unmercifully. It was a dirty and dusty job and I was soon covered with a salty sweat and sometimes could hardly see because of the dust thrown in my face by the machinery; a breeze was a blessing if not blowing the wrong way. When my wagon was filled to the brim, I drove to the stackyard and pitched the load off to a man who stacked it. As the stacks got higher, the grain had to be pitched up, which was real work for a 103 lb. skinny kid.

My employer was a Seventh-Day Adventist German man, whose family refused to speak English most of the time. The children certainly knew English, but seemed determined not to speak it unless they had to. I went to church one Saturday, but all the services were conducted in German, so I did not go any more. And I was also ashamed of my bedraggled clothing, especially with everyone else dressed in suits, white shirts and ties.

We worked six days a week. The work started well before daylight. The horses had to be harnessed. Breakfast was served predawn and the wagons and other equipment were in the fields shortly after sun up. There was an hour off at noon, during which time the work animals were watered and fed before the workers. The food was ample and then some, but I did have to point my finger at what I wanted as all conversation was in German. Often, I would be forced to say the German word for what I wanted, so I did learn a few necessary words at the table as well as in the fields. We quit work about sunset, unharnessed, curried, watered and fed the horses, then quickly washed our face and hands in order not to be late at the supper table. I was allowed to sleep in the barn and take a bath in the house once a week.

My wages were $5 per day, which were the universal wages in Kansas that summer for field hands. I had worked at this place for a little over two weeks when I ran a wheat beard into the palm of my right hand. A wheat beard is an inch and a half long slender splinter-like projection that grows alongside the grains of some types of wheat. They are sharp pointed and have little barbs on their shafts, not unlike a miniature porcupine quill. I tried to pull the offending splinter out, but it broke off beneath the skin. I picked at it with my pocket knife, with no luck. I continued to work for a day or two and finally showed my hand, which by this time was swollen and painful, to my boss. It was obvious that I could no longer work, so he paid me off, explaining that the harvest was about over anyway. I was told that there was no doctor available in the immediate area. I did not know what to do, so I walked the five or six miles to my friends at Otis. There, I sent a money order of $60.00 to my parents in Greeley, Colorado, keeping back a few dollars. I went to a drugstore for advice about my hand; the druggist sold me a jar of "Denver Mud" for a poultice. The next day, my hand was more swollen and painful, so toward evening I started for home. I got to the main line of the Missouri Pacific Railroad, called "MoP" by bindle stiffs (so-called bums on the R.R.) who had warned me to watch out for the "Bulls" (brakemen) who would take pleasure in throwing one off the train. I found a small town with a water tank, where the locomotives would have to stop to take on water. I had to stay away from the immediate vicinity of the tank, as there was too much activity there and I would be seen trying to get aboard. So I walked down the tracks a short distance.

Just about dark, a freight train stopped and I was waiting when it pulled out. But it was going too fast when it got to me. I was hampered by my backpack and was not running fast enough when I grabbed the front end of a boxcar. (If a train was going fast, one always caught the front end of a car; otherwise, the forward momentum of the train would, instead of slapping you up against the side of the car, throw you between the cars, so if you lost your grip, you would fall beneath the wheels.) Anyway, I made the mistake of grabbing too hard with my right hand. The pain in my injured hand was so excruciating that I let go and tumbled apple over apple cart on the cinders and ties beside the roadbed, down into a ditch. It took me a while to recover and my hand hurt like hell. In desperation, I got brave and moved closer to the water tank. I soon succeeded in grabbing a boxcar, crawled up on top where, fighting the lurching of the train, I went several car lengths, finally locating a flatcar loaded with heavy machinery. I huddled down at the base of this equipment. Just at daylight, I was disturbed by two bums who shook me down for money. I had a silver dollar and some change in my pockets. They took the dollar, but left me the balance. They jokingly thanked me for their breakfast. They did not find the $12 I had in my boot top. They told me that Pueblo, the town we were approaching, was a tough place and if one got caught as a bum in the railroad yards, the penalty for vagrancy was 30 or 60 days on a road gang. So I hopped off the train when they did, before the yard was reached. Once again, I went head over heels as the train had not as yet slowed enough. I had to walk quite a distance into town. I was walking on the sidewalk in a poor section of town when I met a woman with two or three small children. Much to my surprise, she pulled the kids aside for me to pass. I sneaked into the restroom of a service station and looked into a mirror, where I saw the reason for her concern. I could not believe my eyes; my face and entire body were filthy dirty. The cinders and smoke from the train were on my face and clothing to the point that I hardly recognized my disreputable self. I cleaned up the best I could and was soon thumbing a ride. I was lucky and reached Campion Academy that night, where I was welcomed by one of my former teachers, Joshua Turner, who was in charge of the school farm. There were only a few students staying in the men's dormitory as they worked at the school during the summer months, so I moved into one of the empty rooms. I took a long soaking bath to get rid of my accumulated grime. I gratefully got into some clean clothes, loaned by my friend, Dow Brown. All the time, my hand was giving me much pain; the onceconvex palm of my right hand was now a dome of purple colored flesh which throbbed incessantly. Although exhausted, I walked the floor most of the night because of the extreme pain.

Dow Brown took me, in Mr. Turner's car, to Loveland, where I went to the office of William P. Gasser, M.D. It was early in the morning, his waiting room was full, but his secretary took one look at my hand and I was immediately taken into the office. Under local anesthesia, Dr. Gasser made an inch long incision and got about an ounce of greenish-yellow pus and part of the causative wheat beard. There was immediate relief of pain. I saw the doctor several times in the next two weeks. I was very grateful to him, especially when he asked me what I was going to do when I grew up and I told him I was going to be a doctor. He told me, in that instance, there would be no charge for his services. In those days, the practice of medicine was a profession and not a business. He could tell that I was a poor kid and he was generous and kind enough to help me out. His good deed inspired me, later on, to do the same in my practice.

While my hand was healing, I had the opportunity to hitchhike to Greeley to visit my parents and younger brother, Claude, for a few days. Since there was no prospect of a paying job there, I went back to see my doctor, leaving poor Claude to help Dad on our small farm. I was given a job at the academy irrigating spuds on the farm. The wages were about $2 per day, to be applied to my tuition in the fall. This work I could do, using the irrigating shovel pretty much with one hand. My friendship with Dow Brown increased and soon we were planning to take part in the late summer grain harvest that would begin in the irrigated area west of Longmont, Colorado.

When my hand was ready for hard work, we hired out to a threshing crew. Things were done in an entirely different manner from the dry land farms of Kansas. A man by the name of Etzel owned a complete threshing outfit. It consisted of a big steam tractor, a water wagon, a coal wagon and a cook shack on wheels. All this equipment would be spotted in a strategic region adjacent to several grain fields. All grain was cut with a binder that deposited the bundles on the ground, which were then put into shocks by hand. My job was to drive one of the large hayracklike wagons to the shocked grain, which would be pitched on the wagon by a man on the ground. Then I would, with a pitchfork, properly load the wagon as high as possible, drive the team to the steam-powered threshing machine and pitch the bundles into its open mouth. If the bundles were thrown too fast, it would clog the machine and I got hell; if too slow, I was lazy. We worked more than a twelve-hour day by the time we tended the horses, morning, noon and night. Dow and I were the youngest on the crew; most were tough, worldly wise, grizzled men who followed the harvest from state to state. Sometimes, Dow and I were lucky and could snitch a few apples from an adjacent orchard to help last us until the next meal. Dow was ahead of his time; he had a portable battery operated radio with earphones that we could listen to at night by stringing up a long copper wire. But generally, we were too tired after getting bedded down in a haymow or straw stack.

It was an interesting event when all the equipment had to be moved to a new location. The big black steam tractor would be in the lead, spouting smoke and steam, towing the threshing machine, the water and fuel wagons besides the large cook shack at the end. The speed was about three miles per hour. This gave us a chance to rest a bit. Meals in the cook shack were an adventure. Men were hungry and we had to fight to get our share of fresh baked biscuits, as that plate was always empty. But in general, the food was plentiful and good. There was a fat female cook who had a rather good-looking young gal named Esther helping her. Dow was attracted to her and called her "Queen Esther." I noticed a couple of times he cautiously patted her butt; but I was usually too interested in food to get very excited.

Steam tractor that powered threshing machine
Utah State Historical Society

Our wages were $3 a day and all we could eat. There was a bonus of $0.25 if we threshed over 1,000 bushels per day. We made this goal several times. We would go to Dow's home in Longmont for weekends, where we could get a good bath and some clean clothes for the following week. We worked at this job for about a month, which gave us a pretty nice nest egg for school starting shortly after the first of September.

Some summer!!!

On To School

I graduated from the twelfth grade at Campion Academy as president of my class in 1928. I went to college for three years at Union College in Lincoln, Nebraska. For two years, I worked in the home of a wealthy woman as combination butler, chauffeur, gardener and general flunky. The third year, I was an assistant teacher in the chemistry department and made a few dollars on the side as a tutor. In 1931, I entered medical school at Loma Linda, California.

There, I worked part-time as a hospital orderly for one year and another year as an assistant in a doctor's office taking X-rays and doing laboratory work. The last two years, I worked as a laboratory technician in the poliomyelitis ward of the Los Angeles County General Hospital and helped a doctor there in his research on poliomyelitis. This job deprived me of sleep as I went to work at 6 p.m., got off at 2 a.m. and had to be in school at 7 a.m. A sympathetic doctor gave me one of his discarded suits so that I might have a dark suit for graduation, but I had to spend $2 to have it altered to fit my 117 lb. body.

Scholarships were virtually unknown in those days. I borrowed $300 at the beginning of medical school. My brother, La Verne, sent me $25 per month for four years and my parents sent me a few dollars when they could. At the beginning of my senior year, I married a nurse, Nettie Baerg, and her salary of $75 a month helped out. At graduation, I had to borrow $260 from my Colorado friend, Dow Brown, in order to get my diploma. I interned at the Santa Barbara General Hospital, where my salary was $20 per month, including uniforms. I do not deplore the difficulties; I am grateful I had the chance. I think it made me a better doctor.

I practiced at Consumers, Sweets and National from January 3, 1937 until the fall of 1939, almost three years. The Blue Blaze Coal Company at Consumers closed down. There was hardly enough work in the area to support a full-time doctor. I decided to go back to school to specialize so I went to Takoma Park, Maryland, where I was a resident in eye, ear, nose and throat for a year at the Washington Sanitarium and Hospital. I then enrolled in the Graduate School of Medicine at the University of Pennsylvania for a year in that specialty. I picked this specialty because, as a general practitioner, the field of E.E.N.T. was a challenge about which I knew little and the public need was great. In those pre-antibiotic days, sinusitis, throat infections and mastoiditis were real problems.

After these two years of study, I was offered a job with a clinic in Los Angeles, where I worked for a few months. But I had developed a severe allergy for Bermuda grass, so flipped a coin to see if I would stay in California or return to Utah where I knew I was allergy free. I had to toss the coin twice to make it come up Utah. I began my practice of eye, ear, nose and throat at Price in September of 1941, the only specialist, in any field of medicine, in all of Utah east of the Wasatch Front. After two years of school, I was in poor financial condition. I borrowed on my car and life insurance for a down payment on office equipment.

How A "Stay At Home" Doctor Fought World War II In Carbon County

On Pearl Harbor Day, December 7, 1941, I was conducting a clinic at Moab, Utah, when news came over the radio concerning the Japanese attack on Pearl Harbor. I listened to the radio all the way home to Price from Moab, unable to believe what I was hearing.

I was perhaps overendowed with patriotism and immediately started trying to get into the service. While in Philadelphia in 1940, I was encouraged, along with the other doctors in my class, to join the Army Reserve because of Hitler's actions in Europe. But the Army was pretty picky. I was turned down because I was four pounds underweight. It was suggested that I eat a bunch of bananas to bring up my weight. So I gorged myself on about ten pounds of bananas, reapplied again, but still was underweight by about a pound or two and was once more rejected.

Because I was the only E.E.N.T. doctor in all of southeastern Utah, I was declared essential by Dr. Cyril A. Callister, Utah director of Medical Selective Service and Procurement. I was told emphatically that I was needed where I was and to forget about anything else.

So the Civil Air Patrol offered a means for me to help out with the war effort. We eventually had a good-sized group as members of C.A.P. Our group was referred to as the Price Flight of the Utah Wing of the Civil Air Patrol.

Joe Bergen, manager of the Salt Lake Airport, was commander of the Utah Wing with the rank of colonel. Other high ranking officials I remember from the Salt Lake area were Sherman Falkenrath, chief of detectives of the Salt Lake Police Department, and Roy Jensen of Salt Lake City. As might be expected, when it came to officers, the Wasatch Front area supplied most of the "brass," so there was none left over for me as commander of the Price Flight. I was made a warrant officer, which is a stage or two below 2nd lieutenant, but was later promoted to a 2nd lieutenant.

I had started taking flying lessons in 1942; I was apparently not a very good student, as I did not get my private pilot's license until September of 1944. In the meantime, I managed to crack up a Piper J4. I had my solo permit and went flying on a gusty, windy day. I had the plane all stalled out for a landing about five feet above the ground when a gust hit me and raised me up about twenty feet. I did not know enough to get the nose down so the plane pancaked in, washing out the prop and landing gear. I had a parachute on and the harness took the hide off my shoulders. They told me to get in another plane and fly again right away, but I chickened out for several days. On the way back to town, I threw up.

The Taylorcraft Airplane (N.C.# 24089) chiefly used by the Civil Air Patrol at Price was owned by a club of about five people. It was also used occasionally for instruction purposes by the airport operator Laurence Jorgensen. At times during the war, it was the only plane located at the Carbon County Airport. Part of the time, I was about the only person with a private pilot's license who flew it.

It was a black, side by side two-seater covered with fabric. It was a high wing monoplane with conventional (tailwheel) landing gear. It was powered by a 65 hp Continental engine. There were a minimum of instruments: compass, ball and bank, altimeter and R.P.M. indicator, throttle, carburetor heat and air speed. There was no radio. It did not have a starter, so had to be hand propped. The propeller was wood with metal facing, which could give a fatal haircut if caution was not used when hand propping. It was easy to stick a thumb through the fabric on the wings of the plane, so it was covered by a multitude of patches. The brakes sometimes worked. The gas tank was located behind the cowling toward the engine in front of the pilot. The gas gauge was incorporated in the gas cap consisting of a cork float in the gas tank. It was attached to a stiff $^{1}/_{16}$ wire with a little $^{1}/_{2}$ inch red ball on top as an indicator which stuck up through a hole in the gas cap - so the higher the ball stuck up, the more gas you had and vice versa.

Loops were a no-no, but we did them anyway. As part of our training, we were taught how to recover from spins, but were not supposed to do loops. To loop the Taylorcraft, you had to pick up all the speed you could by a steep dive and then pull her up and over. One time, I didn't get quite enough speed so I almost came to a stop at the top of the loop and about a quart of gas ran out of the gas cap - but luckily, no fire!

Sooner or later, all fledgling pilots had to buzz their hometown. I, too, enjoyed the forbidden fruit and got quite a kick out of watching little kids as they ran out onto the lawns or streets to watch my amateurish antics in the sky. Warren Brown told me that his small children came running into the house one day screaming: "Daddy, come outside quick and look! There is a P38 flying in formation!" All kids in those war years knew the names of planes, even if they did not always identify them properly.

Toward the end of the war, an interesting thing happened at the Price Airport. On a Saturday afternoon, I was at the airport and was surprised toward evening to have a P51 fighter plane come in from the south and land. The pilot was ferrying this plane from someplace in Texas to the air base at Mountain Home, Idaho. The weather was marginal and he had become lost in the vast deserts of the Four Corners area and was just about out of gas. He was overjoyed to locate the Price Airport, which had a runway long enough on which to land his plane.

The pilot crawled out of the cockpit and told me that this particular P51 was an experimental plane and one of a kind. It was a super-secret aircraft and must be guarded with great care. It was too big and cumbersome to get into the hangar, but I posted a Civil Air Patrol guard to keep the public away. I can still see Gene Averill, one of our older members, in his spiffy Civil Air Patrol uniform with a .45 pistol slung on his hip as he strode up and down around the plane. He and other Civil Air Patrol members guarded the plane all night and into the next day.

I took the pilot into town, where he could stay overnight and also explain his situation to higher-ups via telephone. The next day, a DC4 tanker plane flew in with a load of proper aviation fuel for the P51. Of course, the pilot buzzed the field when he left, as he was sure as hell glad to be on his way again.

This particular P51 had an experimental reversible prop. The pilot claimed it was the only one in existence at that time. He explained to me that in aerial warfare, such a prop might be of great value. In a dogfight with an enemy on his tail, a pilot in the P51 could throw on a brake by throwing the P51 prop into reverse pitch, the enemy would go scooting by and the P51 would then be on his tail and in position to shoot him down.

Probably this plane was never used in that way, as jet fighters soon came into existence, making propeller driven fighters passé.

Early on, I had trouble getting aviation gas for our plane. Doctors could get all the gasoline they needed for their practice, but the general public was on a severe gas rationing program, even with a speed limit of 35 mph..

Gomer Peacock was in charge of the gas rationing situation for this area. Mr. Peacock managed the Price Trading Department Store, where you could buy anything from groceries (delivered to your door) to a suit, a saddle or a pair of spurs. I approached him about gas for our plane. He quickly told me no gas was available for such foolishness. I showed him an order from the C.A.P. and Army saying that we could get all the gas we needed. He told me that this order did not mean anything to him. But when I threatened to cancel my account at his store, he quickly capitulated and we got all the aviation gas we needed. After all, one needs to be practical!

The higher-up powers kept trying to whip us into shape as a military unit. We went to school to study such things as theory of flight, navigation, military courtesy, aircraft recognition, etc. We used the classrooms at Carbon College and the hangar at the airport, meeting as frequently as twice a week in the evenings. We used as a text a handbook put out by the C.A.P. which was an excellent reference. We were eventually supplied with uniforms which were beautiful, nicely tailored. The winter ones were made of a magnificent woolen cloth, with a three-bladed propeller on the shiny silver buttons. At first, we had red shoulder epaulets to set us apart from regular service personnel; the red epaulets were later done away with because some C.A.P. people felt they were somehow a badge of inferiority.

A great campaign was launched by the higher-ups to improve our military status. All units were to practice military drill and become a spit and polish military organization. Since none of us knew anything about this fancy military stuff, we were lucky when "Young Bill" Lines returned home from fighting the war in New Guinea.

Bill was one of the very first men from Carbon County to go into the service. He had been in Australia and later New Guinea, where he had contracted a severe recurrent malignant type of malaria, so he had been given a medical discharge. On his return, he served on the Utah Highway Patrol and later as chief of police of Price City. He had been a 2nd lieutenant in the service, so I appointed him as drill sergeant for our Civil Air Patrol unit. He soon whipped our non-descript outfit into a precision military marching machine by barking orders as we practiced hour after hour.

A statewide C.A.P. marching contest was held in Provo to determine the best unit in Utah. The Price Flight took 1st place. An article and pictures ran in the Salt Lake Tribune, showing several of the more glamorous gals from the Salt Lake area in their elegant uniforms. The last two lines of the newspaper article mentioned, almost as an afterthought, that the Price Flight had won the statewide marching contest!

After the war was over, the Price Civil Air Patrol became more or less inactive as a quasi-military unit. I had many leftover uniforms, both summer and winter types, in all sizes and descriptions stored in my basement. A patient and friend of mine, the late George Schade, had 17 children (two sets of twins). George had had one eye blown out and other injuries in a dynamite explosion while helping build the road to the Horse Canyon Mine. At times, he was hard put to feed his family, let alone clothe them. I asked him if he could use some of the spare uniforms and apologized for their numerous and varied sizes. He eagerly took them as he said: "Don't worry Doc, I've got the kids to fit 'em!" Early on, all doctors participated in preinduction physicals. On those days, several hundred Carbon and Emery County young men were herded into the Price City gym. There, naked as jaybirds, they suffered the indignities of a physical exam to see if they were eligible to serve as cannon fodder for their country. I can still see them in endless lines, some sweating, some shivering, trying to hide their nakedness, standing first on one foot and then the other, as they slowly proceeded to their final destiny. I issued the ultimate word on the eye, ear, nose and throat situation.

One young man was sent to me because he said he was deaf. He had already flunked a couple of hearing tests elsewhere and was referred to me for a final evaluation. After a considerable hassle in attempted conversation and in writing because of his alleged poor hearing, I made it known to him that he was to sit with his back to me with his eyes closed and repeat after me whatever I said. We went into my quiet hearing testing room, accompanied by my secretary. I stood behind him about ten feet away and talked in a normal and then a loud voice. No response. Finally, I walked up within about two feet behind his back and shouted several times at the top of my voice. Still no reaction; then I dropped my voice very low to almost a whisper and in an exasperated manner said, "What the hell is the matter with you, Pete? Don't you hear me?" he replied: "No, Doc, I never heard a word you said." Eureka! I will never forget the look on his face when he realized what he had done.

We were told to fly and "observe the country" as much as possible. We were not told anything specific to watch for, but to report anything "unusual." We did not know it until later, but one of the "unusual" things we were supposed to be looking for were bomb carrying balloons which the Japanese were sending over! One was supposedly found by a sheepherder near the Colorado border.

One of my favorite flights, which started at daylight so I could get back to my office, was from the Price Airport to Hanksville and return. I enjoyed the rugged scenic beauty of flying along the east side of the San Rafael Reef. Also, I discovered rather large herds of wild horses in the area west of Goblin Valley, known as Wild Horse Mesa and Little Wild Horse Mesa. I enjoyed flying rather low over Goblin Valley and then sort of pouncing up on top of several hundred head of the horses, each of which would run in a different direction as they had been chased from the air before into traps by Jimmy Lund and others.

One day, I discovered several herds so I spent more time than usual chasing them all over the southern end of the San Rafael Swell. All at once, I discovered I had to go "potty." So, I started looking for the used quart pasteboard milk container that we always kept in the plane just for such emergency use. But alas, no container could be found. Since it was early in the morning, I decided to fly to nearby Hanksville, land on the abandoned CCC strip south of town, relieve my bladder, hop in the plane again and be on my way. But there was no windsock on the strip, so I circled over town a time or two to find a smoking chimney for indication of wind direction. But when I started to land at the so-called abandoned airstrip, the entire population of Hanksville was waiting "to see the airplane!" So I had to "hold it" until I could fly all the way back to Price. It took several weeks before my overdistended bladder returned to normal.

As the war in Europe and the South Pacific heated up, I became increasingly anxious to get into the service. But repeated inquiries to both the Army and Air Force were met with a terse: "No, you are classified by the Selective Service and Procurement director as being essential where you are. If there are any changes, we will be the first to let you know."

However, a doctor friend of mine suggested I try the Navy, about which I was somewhat less than enthusiastic because I knew of my tendency for extreme seasickness. He, Dr. Laville H. Merrill, also declared essential to Carbon County because of his coal camp coverage of the mines in the

Standardville and Spring Canyon area, had met with approval on his application to the Navy. So I applied to the Navy, sent in all the necessary papers, including my birth certificate which was not easy to get because the courthouse in Yuma County, Colorado, where I was born had burned down. But in due time, I showed up in Salt Lake City for a preinduction physical. The doctor who examined me, a gynecologist in civilian life, said everything was fine except that I had a perforated eardrum on one side. After I protested, he looked again and said, "Sorry, but there is a perforation" and bid me goodbye. I was certain that I did not have a perforated eardrum so I started a long stream of correspondence with the Navy. The powers that be finally consented to have me re-examined. For this purpose, a special doctor was flown into Salt Lake City from San Francisco to make the final decision. It so happened that Doctor Merrill had also been recalled for a final answer by this same doctor because of a questionable cardiac situation. As I got off the elevator in the old Federal Building upstairs above the post office in Salt Lake City, I met Dr. Merrill. He had a big grin on his face and said that he had passed with flying colors. He also told me that the doctor, who had been flown in from the West Coast just to examine the two of us, was extremely drunk and that "anybody can pass him."

I was ushered into the examining room by a Navy medical corpsman. On a cot in one corner of the room was a man, obviously out like a light. On a chair back next to the couch was hung a uniform coat, while on the seat of the chair rested a Navy cap. Both were covered with enough gold braid to sink a battleship. The Navy corpsman aroused this officer, spoke a few words to him, placed an otoscope in his hand and assisted him to my side. He finally located my ear, nearly pushed the instrument through my head, grunted and staggered back, with help, to his bed and waved me out. I asked his assistant what his answer was and he said: "He says you are turned down because you have a perforated eardrum. That is one thing the Navy does not accept."

Of course, I was now more frustrated and angry than ever. There ensued a long stream of correspondence with the Navy medical personnel. I was finally told that, if I could get affidavits from two civilian otologists, I would be reconsidered. In a few weeks, I got such a statement from James Cleary, M.D., in Salt Lake City stating that there was a piece of wax on the ear drum and not a perforation. To get the second statement, I decided that Maurine and I would fly the Taylorcraft to Grand Junction to see Dr. James P.

Rigg, another qualified otologist. This I did and got a similar affidavit from him. Flying back to Price, paralleling the highway along about Woodside, I suddenly noticed that the vehicles on the highway were passing me up in the air. When there was a real strong head wind, the ol' Taylorcraft didn't make much progress!

There was another extended correspondence with the Navy. About two years later, one week after the surrender of Japan, I received my commission as a lieutenant commander in the Navy, which of course, I promptly sent back.

This ended my experience of trying to get into the service in World War II.

Others declared essential besides the doctors were most coal miners, farmers, sheepmen and stockmen whose work was considered necessary for the war effort.

Most ethnic peoples in Carbon County considered themselves Americans. I felt that the Italians, Greeks, Austrians and even the Japanese all willingly did their bit for their country. Their names were like an Ellis Island roll call. Helen Papanikolas says that 125 Utah Greeks served in the armed forces; seven of whom were killed. At the College of Eastern Utah, there is a plaque listing 39 names of former students of Carbon College (the predecessor of CEU) who were killed in World War II. There are 13 names with an ethnic lineage such as Amador, Angotti, Nogulich, Bikakis, Protopappas and Kochevar. Carbon County had a total of 87 men who did not return from World War II; one-third of these had ethnic names.

I do not remember that there were many serious labor or ethnic problems with the coal miners during the war. There were numerous short-term wildcat strikes, which generally lasted only a few days. The miners at Royal went on strike a day or two on several occasions because they wanted the American flag to fly over the portal of the mine instead of above the company office. After the war, there was a prolonged and bitter strike.

The civilian practice of medicine during the war years was no bed of roses. We had a good 70+ bed hospital operated by Price City. We were shorthanded; at times the hospital administrator had to double as laboratory and X-ray technician. All doctors read their own X-rays. All doctors in the area were general practitioners but me. My specialty of eye, ear, nose and throat met some resistance to begin with. For example, there were hundreds of tonsillectomies done in those years in Carbon and Emery counties, all by the individual general practitioner. Being a specialist, I cut into the general practitioners' source of income in the tonsil business. But that resentment did not last too long when the G.P.'s found out they could call on me when they got in trouble, which they frequently did. During the summer months, the hospital set up two days a week for wholesale T & As. Since some of the G.P.'s were not too adept at the procedure, I spent considerable time, generally at night, stopping "bleeders."

Coal production more than doubled during the war years, with a jump in the number of miners from 2,600 to 3,800. Because of the tremendous rush to get more coal, the mines often worked six days a week with lots of overtime. This caused a considerable increase in accidents. I saw many severe eye, head and facial injuries as a result of this mad effort to mine more coal at all costs.

In those days, infectious diseases were a real problem. Sulfanilamide became available in 1937, followed by other sulfa drugs. All of these were helpful, but caused, at times, many serious side effects. Penicillin, a real miracle drug, came on the scene in 1942.

Penicillin was in great demand, but in short supply. Almost all penicillin was consigned to the armed forces and the civilian supply was very meager. In my field, it was very helpful in cases of tonsillitis, sinusitis and otitis media and prevented many instances of mastoiditis. I remember one local doctor somehow got his hands on a few vials and the whole town flocked to his office to get a shot, whether they needed it or not. One time, in a hurry to get to the next patient, he broke off a two-inch needle in the buttocks of a prominent attorney. The needle was never recovered, in spite of a surgical excavation the size of the Grand Canyon in the patient's rear end. This particular doctor was also somewhat of a problem in that he perpetuated himself, through clever political manipulation, as chief of staff at the hospital from 1935, all during the war years, to about 1949 before he was finally dethroned.

Not all of the doctors in the area shared my (perhaps misplaced) desire to get into the service. Several did volunteer, some were declared essential and others were drafted. All in all, the doctors who stayed home worked hard. We all worked six days a week, often had evening office hours and made house calls day and night. But it was whispered in medical circles that at least one, and possibly three doctors, had taken medication to make their hearts go haywire so that they would not have to go into the service. Many of them made a great deal of money for their hard work; two later got in trouble with the IRS. One of these openly boasted that he kept two sets of books. But when he took a quick "vacation" trip to Mexico and deposited $50,000 in a bank there, he was soon in real trouble with the income tax people. I certainly did not get rich. In the practice of medicine, I have always felt that the welfare of the patient was more important than money so I put many thousands of uncollectible dollars "on the books," which I charged off as my contribution to the war effort. But I do have hanging on my office wall a certificate signed by the great (?) F.D.R. thanking me for my several years of donated work as an examiner for Selective Service in World War II.

From Allan Kent Powell, Utah Remembers World War II (Logan: Utah State University Press, 1991, pp. 132-37).

Warren S. Peacock
1881-1949

Warren S. Peacock

Warren S. Peacock was my wife's father. He was a giant of a man, six-foot-six inches tall with broad shoulders, long arms and capable hands that snatched many a lawbreaker from his lair.

I married his daughter, Maurine, in 1943 when he was chief deputy to Carbon County Sheriff Marion Bliss. He had also served previously as Price City marshal.

Barber Shop Saloon

Warren Peacock used to tell me stories about some of his escapades as a young man shortly after the dawn of the 20th century. He would talk about when he and his brother, Gomer, worked at the gilsonite mines in the Uintah Basin at the present day ghost town of Dragon, Utah. He supplemented his wages from the mine by running a combination barber shop by day and a saloon by night, housed in a large tent. He said he bought most of his whiskey in 55-gallon wooden barrels, which he would place against the back of the tent behind the crude makeshift bar, which consisted of two heavy planks, supported on each end by empty barrels. Each barrel that contained an alcoholic beverage would have a small hand pump on top from which to draw the booze. It was against the law, of course, to sell liquor to the Indians from the nearby Ute reservation. He did not sell it direct; instead, an Indian would come into the saloon tent, give Warren a silver dollar, then proceed around back of the tent located on the edge of a deep wash. A rubber hose was inserted into the top of a barrel bung hole and run beneath the edge of the tent into the gully behind. Mr. Indian would get one or two gulps through the hose, then the tube would be clamped off. The process would be repeated by numerous Indians until a lot of yipping and ky-ying in the back of the tent would get too boisterous. When the sounds approached the war-whoop stage, the rubber tube would be clamped off for the night.

One time, he received a 30-gallon wooden keg of near beer which he could not sell because everyone wanted the real stuff. Near beer tasted like real beer, but contained no alcohol. The mining camp was visited by a Ute chief and his group of Indians on one of their periodic jaunts into the wilderness of the reservation. They had stopped at Dragon for supplies and approached the saloon owner in an effort to get some booze. He, of course, shook his head and said "no way." But the chief persisted and kept coming back, assuring him that they would take the liquor with them on their journey before consuming it so that no fuss would be made close to the whites. Then Warren thought of his small barrel of near beer which was of no value to him. He finally showed the keg to the chief, pointing out the word "beer" on the insignia NEAR BEER stamped into the keg. Apparently, the word "beer" meant something to the Indian, but he questioned the word "near" with a pointed finger. Warren assured him it meant good. He wanted a sample to drink, but was told that such was not possible. He pulled the wooden plug out of the bung hole and sniffed the contents. He introduced a grimy finger into the opening to lick for a taste. This produced a glint in his eyes and a couple of appreciative grunts. After more haggling, the sale was consummated for a few silver dollars, with the assurance that the beer would be taken far away from camp before it was consumed. So the keg was loaded on top of a pack horse and the Indians took off over a hill with great anticipation and jubilation.

Tents at Dragon Camp.
Credit F. A. Kennedy photo,
V. L. McCoy collection

Several weeks later, the Utes again showed up in Dragon. The chief immediately looked Warren up, shook his fist in his face and said: "You lie! You lie! Stuff no make 'em drunk, only make 'em sick— much puke. You lie! you lie!"

Flat Wheel

One Sunday, for want of something to do, Warren, Bill Lines and two or three other fellows jumped a train on the Uintah RR and rode up to the summit, where there was a saloon. One of the men was a fellow called "Flat Wheel" because of a bad limp in one leg caused by a gunshot wound. This man was a disreputable character, considered to be a semi-reformed outlaw. He was an inveterate gambler who raised hell in general. No one trusted him.

After having a few drinks, Flat Wheel inveigled Bill Lines into a crap game. They rolled their dice on a blanket on the saloon floor. Bill soon cleaned Flat Wheel out of about a hundred dollars and left him flat broke. While they waited for the return train to Dragon, they whiled away their time pistol shooting at the knots on the wooden walls of an outdoor privy. Their shooting was somewhat aimless. Bill would stand close to the outhouse, calling the shots. Warren said that suddenly he saw an evil, cunning look in Flat Wheels eyes and felt that he was about to shoot Bill and call it an accident. He placed his hand on the butt of the pistol in his shoulder holster, making sure that Flat Wheel noticed him. Flat Wheel saw at once that he had a problem in his devious plan. He became more surly and disgruntled about his gambling loss to Bill and finally challenged him to a one-shot shooting match, with $100 to go to the winner. If Bill was the loser, Flat Wheel was to get $100 in cash; if Flat Wheel was the loser, Bill was to get an IOU. A paper target was placed on the outhouse door with a nail in the center for a bull's-eye. Flat Wheel insisted that Bill shoot first, which he did, driving the nail head bull's-eye completely out of sight. Flat Wheel threw his hands in the air, cussed and gave up in despair at Bill's unbeatable shot.

About that time, the train whistled and they were on their way home, everyone good-natured and happy except the disappointed arrogant Flat Wheel.

About a week later—the following Saturday morning —Flat Wheel showed up at Warren's tent barber shop emporium for his weekly shave. In those days, shaving with a straight razor was a real chore and task for men. Mr. Gillette had not as yet come on the market with his safety razor and electric razors were undreamed of. The city dudes in larger towns often had a daily shave by a barber where the clients own private mug and brush were kept on a shelf. But in rural areas or mining camps, things were not so civilized. Many men put up with a shave by a straight razor once or twice a week, generally doing the disagreeable job themselves. So a shave in a barber shop was often a once a week luxury. Warren's barber chair was a primitive contraption consisting of a tall high-backed sturdy wooden affair, which Warren would lean back against a support when shaving a person.

While he waited his turn, Flat Wheel made numerous uncouth remarks about Bill Lines, the dice game and the target shooting of the previous Sunday. About halfway through his shave, he suddenly reared up and complained that Warren`s razor was dull and he thought that his ear had been nicked. Warren grabbed his heavy thatch of hair, banged his head back in place and said, in a quiet, but commanding voice, at the same time brandishing the razor in front of his customer's throat: " Don't you move or I might cut more than your ear." Flat Wheel never twitched a muscle, got up, paid his bill and stomped out. Shortly thereafter, he left the community, to everyone's delight.

Ghost

The gilsonite miners had to work hard. It was inevitable that some of them, to make their work less tedious and liven up their day, would play practical jokes. Men working in one section of the mine concocted a prank on a group working in an adjacent area. They started talking about ghosts. One man said he had seen something, garbed in white, which looked like a person in shrouds. Another said he had seen a white wolf that had chased him. Others mentioned hideous moans and groans, accompanied by clanking sounds. And so the build up went on for days, with all sorts of weird stories. The men worked with carbide lamps, which at best gave a poor flickering light. Underground, everything was black — even the men became covered with the grayish-black gilsonite dust.

There was an immense black mule that went from one section of the mine to the other to pull the ore cars. This well-trained animal would go from one area to another at the sound of a whistle, generally rewarded by a bite of apple, a little sugar or best of all by a secondhand chew of tobacco. On one night shift, at just about time to go off duty, the perpetrators whitewashed the big dark mule from the tip of his ears to the bottom of his hooves. They waited for the whistle that would call the beast to the other part of the mine. They then let go with a bunch of loud moans and groans and sent the white-painted mule pell-mell down the drift, augmented with a generous dose of turpentine and strings of buckets and tin cans tied to his tail!

That ended the ghosts in the Dragon mine.

(Reference: 1, 2)

The White House Saloon

Warren and Gomer Peacock owned and operated the White House Saloon in Price in the mid-nineteen-teens. It was located on west Main Street in Price at the approximate location where the new Carbon County Jail now stands. I asked Warren once how he and Gomer got into the saloon business. He said: "Well, Gomer and I had been working at the gilsonite mines in the Uintah Basin and we had made quite a bit of money and were looking for a way to invest it. A whiskey drummer (salesman) came to town and we spent the evening with him. When we came to the next morning, we discovered we had bought a carload of whiskey so we decided that we had better open a saloon!"

He said that Matt Warner was one of their best customers. Matt had been a member of Butch Cassidy's famous "Wild Bunch" and had served time in prison. He loved to play poker and would often play all night or sometimes even into the next day, depending on the stakes. One time, Matt had played the night through and was getting started on the day shift when his wife showed up, scolded him and told him flatly that it was time for him to come home. Matt berated her, letting her know that he was the boss and would come home when he "damned well pleased" and she was to go home where she belonged! She left and Matt crowed to the saloon crowd that he was the boss in his house. In short order, Mrs. Warner returned and, walking over to Matt's side quietly said, " Matt, come home right now." Matt immediately threw down his cards and trailed her out the door. Matt was not seen in the saloon for some time. When he did come in, he was teased no end by the saloon habitués as a coward and being chicken and a mama's boy for so meekly leaving the joint at his wife's summons. Matt simply replied: "Fellows, you do not understand. When she returned, she held my six-shooter under her apron!"

Warren told me a couple of other stories about Matt Warner. These happened at a later date, during prohibition times.

Matt had a pool hall in a basement close to where the Sun Advocate now is. Of course, the pool hall was a front for a "speak-easy" and if you knew the correct password, you could get some moonshine. One time, a couple of federal revenuers came in to Matt's place and lured him into giving them a drink. They took their drinks and poured them into some large test tubes which they had in their pockets, laughed at Matt and said they would see him in court. The next thing they knew, they were looking down the barrel of Matt's pistol as he ordered them to drink the evidence — which they hastily did!

Another time, Matt was hauled into court for some minor infraction of the law and was given 30 days in the calaboose. But some sanctimonious citizens complained to the sheriff because Matt was wandering the streets at night. The sheriff, a good friend of Matt's, replied that the judge had given him 30 days in jail all right, but had not said anything about nights in jail!

Warren said they kept dice on the bar in the saloon which a customer could roll to see if the house would pay for the drinks. He said the patron would nearly always lose unless some smart ass would drop the cubes in a glass of water, where they would always come up the same way because they were loaded. Then the bartender would have to cough up.

The Volstead Act eventually put them out of business. Warren and Gomer converted to farming and sheep raising on upper Miller Creek. But soon, Gomer got involved with the Price Trading Company and Warren took up law enforcement, first as Price City marshal, but later on as chief deputy sheriff under Carbon County Sheriffs Deming, Bliss and Dudler.

Sheriff Marion Bliss

Warren told me many stories about his exploits and adventures as a law enforcement officer.

Prohibition Days In Carbon County
Jubilant officials celebrate finding of giant still and are from left to right Sam Woodhead, county comm. from Kenilworth; Warren S. Peacock, deputy sheriff; Judge J.W. Hammond, Sr.; Sheriff S. Marion Bliss who held office from 1927 until his tragic death in 1945; Judge John Potter; George W. Collingham, deputy sheriff; unidentified; and Arthur E. Gibson, deputy sheriff, seated by mammoth copper still. Credit Edna Bliss Mahleres

One time, he and Sheriff Bliss were looking for a one-armed Greek sheepherder who had supposedly murdered his partner. This was in the Range Creek area which, in those days, was dotted with numerous homestead cabins. They had hunted the fugitive for a day or two and Sheriff Bliss had to return to town on other urgent business. He left Warren there to continue the search, with the promise that he would return toward evening of the next day. So he was alone and afoot. At dusk, Warren chanced on a cabin in a little clearing. He could see no one around, but thought that he detected a wisp of smoke from the chimney. So he watched all night, nearly freezing in the frigid Range Creek air. Just before dawn, he quietly approached the cabin. It was a small two-room affair with a kitchen in one end and a bed-living room in front. The blinds were pulled on the front room, but one was partially raised in the kitchen. The back door was locked from the inside. So he went to the window and, taking a long time, finally quietly raised it enough so he could crawl in. He tiptoed to the door leading into the other room, which was as dark as the ace of spades. When he entered the door, with pistol in hand, he heard the unmistakable sound of the action on a rifle being worked to inject a shell from the magazine into the chamber. He shouted at the top of his voice: "Drop that gun or I will blow your guts out!" He said that after what seemed about a month, the rifle clattered to the floor. Warren said he was thankful that he was dealing with a one-armed man because that slowed up the pumping of a shell into the barrel, thus probably saving his life.

Later, the rifle was given to him by Judge Wood as a reward, so to speak, for bringing the fugitive in. He gave the gun to his son, Lloyd. It was an old beat-up Model 94 Winchester .30-.30 carbine. Lloyd later traded it to me for a .30-.06 Springfield. I took it to a gunsmith, Bennett Ray Gunderson, who reblued and fitted it with a beautiful checked stock and fore-end. My son, Dory, now has this rifle in his possession.

Another time, Warren was looking for a colored man at the Castle Gate mine who had allegedly committed mayhem, searching for him among some big boulders adjacent to the town. He saw the man about ten feet away pointing a sawed off shotgun at him from the top of a big rock. He talked quietly to the man and said that if he were shot, it would only make things worse and the thing to do was to give the gun up and face the consequences, which would be a lot better than shooting him. The man hesitated a long time, but finally gave him the gun and went meekly to jail.

More bootleg - S. Marion Bliss, sheriff
Warren S. Peacock, deputy; & A.E. Gibson, deputy
Credit Edna Bliss Mahleres

Warren had an obsession to obtain possession, if possible, of any weapon that had threatened his life. I have in my collection two pistols which he gave me. One is a double-action .41-caliber Colt, the so-called Billy the Kid special; the other is a .32-caliber large framed double action Colt. The stories connected with these guns are too vague in my mind to repeat with accuracy.

Sometimes things came a little easier for the lawmen, but not often. One time, two prisoners had escaped from the Utah State Prison and were believed to possibly be in the Carbon County area on their way to Colorado. They were supposed to be armed and dangerous. On a hunch, Sheriff Bliss and

Warren drove out to Wellington. They had a good description of the men and sure enough, spotted them hitchhiking on the east side of town. The officers, in civilian clothes, were in their large, two-seated, unmarked sheriff's car with the top down. Bliss was driving with Warren in the passenger seat with a double-barreled sawed off 12-gauge shotgun cradled in his lap. Sheriff Bliss stopped the car within a few feet of them on Warren's side of the car. The men were delighted at the prospect of a ride and asked for a lift, saying they were on their way to a wedding in Grand Junction. Warren casually asked if they were going to a shotgun wedding. They replied, "No, just a regular wedding." Whereupon, Warren poked the menacing barrel of the shotgun over the top of the car door into their faces and said: "No, boys, this is a real shotgun wedding." He held the gun on them while Sheriff Bliss confiscated two pistols, handcuffed them and invited them to share the bachelor suite of the Carbon County Jail for a few days. Years later, when anyone would happen to mention the term shotgun wedding, Warren would laugh and tell the story.

Bill Lines

Through Warren, I got to know the Bill Lines family. There were two people named Bill Lines: "Old" Bill and his son, "Young" Bill. Old Bill, like Warren, carried a lawman's badge much of his life. When I first knew the family, Young Bill, one of the first young men to join the army from Carbon County in WWll, had just returned home from the fighting in New Guinea. The Lines family,

Another Still about 1928, 29 or 30? Bill Lines on left with sheriff Marion Bliss. Credit: Edna Bliss Mahleres

including Old Bill's wife, Jaquetta, used to visit my wife, Maurine, and me on Saturday evenings after doing their weekly shopping in town. We had a good visit one Saturday night, including several of the cups that cheer. About nine o'clock, they left with Young Bill, yet unmarried, for their home in Sunnyside. Between Price and Wellington, Old Bill had to empty his bladder as he felt he would never make it home and his hind teeth were floating. Jaquetta and Young Bill chided him to no end and told him that he would have to wait until they got home as there was no place that he could go. But Bill was in great distress and insisted they pull the car off to the side of the road. As no cars were coming on the main highway, Bill stood by the front fender and proceeded to get relief. But suddenly, a car approached from a side road and its headlights struck Bill head on! So he pulled up his zipper with great force and haste. Now a critical portion of his anatomy was over-endowed with a more than generous foreskin, which was suddenly enmeshed in his zipper, firmly welding them together.

Warren was just getting ready to leave our home when there was a great commotion on our front porch. Old Bill, his black overcoat flapping in the wintery breeze and his high-peaked Stetson hat pulled down over his ears, was standing all spraddle-legged, making noises like a bleating ewe, begging me, as a doctor, for help. He entered the house with great care, walking slowly and very deliberately, one leg at a time. After a hasty explanation of the problem, I went to work. Because of his distress, Bill was unable to cooperate. Young Bill, Warren and I finally had to spread-eagle him onto a bed. Jaquetta and Maurine gave much giggling advice through the bedroom door, Jaquetta cautioning to be careful with the foreskin, simpering that maybe that was "all there was left." Any effort to move the offending zipper was met with loud groans, squeals and not so muffled cuss words. Pliers, wire cutters, scissors and a file finally freed the victim, with a minimum loss of blood and skin. Bill was most grateful for my zipper surgery; he asked to use the bathroom before leaving.

A couple of years later, Old Bill decided to take up farming and purchased a farm west of Cleveland. He was enthusiastic about the progress he was making and invited Maurine and me out to show off his ability as a farmer. We went one weekend; Maurine stayed at the house to visit with the women folk while Bill and I took a walk to the fields. It was a beautiful spring day; we were in our shirt-sleeves. He proudly showed me his freshly plowed and planted fields. We decided to take a shortcut back to the house. Our route took us across a shallow, but broad wash filled with head high brush. We kept scaring up multiple cottontail rabbits. I remarked that I wished I had my .22-caliber rifle with me so I could shoot some of them. Bill said: "Do you want a rabbit?" I said "Yeah," and suddenly there was a loud bang. I almost jumped out of my skin. Bill was holding his smoking six-shooter in his hand and a cottontail was kicking the dust, shot through the head! I nearly wet my pants as I had no idea that Bill was carrying a gun. He nonchalantly tucked the .38-caliber six-gun down inside the loose fitting waistband of his trousers, held up by suspenders, into its holster strapped to his leg. I had heard a great deal about Bill's prowess with a pistol; now I was a believer!

Judge Fred W. Keller

Judge Keller was another person I became acquainted with through Warren. After he was released from service in WWl, he located a homestead, which he developed into a ranch, in the Monticello area and eventually was appointed a district judge, with headquarters in Price. He was known as the "Cowboy Judge" and was famous throughout southeastern Utah for his legendary song, "Blue Mountain."

Judge Fred W. Keller -"The Cowboy Judge"
Credit: Pearl Oliver, CEU Prehistoric Museum

Fred was a great storyteller. He invented a fictional character called "Hard-Twist." Hard-Twist had many escapades, which Fred would relate with great glee. Many stories had to do with the Blue Goose saloon in Monticello. I deeply regret that I can remember but a few of these wonderful tales.

Hard-Twist was a scrawny, bleary-eyed cowpuncher who worked for one of the large cattle outfits in the area. On payday, he would show up at the Blue Goose saloon to raise hell as long as his meager wages lasted. He would proceed to get drunk as soon as possible. One Saturday night, he really whooped it up, but shortly after midnight decided to leave as he had promised to be back at his cow camp the next morning. He was very inebriated and had to be helped onto his horse. In the meantime, someone had turned the saddle around so that it faced backward. So, Fred said, "He ended up going north toward Moab instead of south toward Blanding." Another time, Fred said that a bunch of sanctimonious old biddies in Moab decided to clean up the town. They forced the law officers to close up all the houses of ill repute and herd all the soiled doves to a spot some 25 miles west of Moab. There, they were placed across a narrow neck of land, onto a small island, surrounded by 1,000-foot cliffs. The escape route was barricaded. Soon, Hard-Twist and his buddies missed their prostitute friends and a search was begun. Finally, they found them, all dead. So, Fred said: "That is how Dead 'Hors' Point got its name!"

Hard-Twist showed up early one Saturday afternoon in Monticello. He had numerous mandatory drinks at the Blue Goose and then proceeded to shoot up the town, proving his ability with a six-gun as his bullets repeatedly rang the big brass bell hanging in the church steeple. Soon, the town marshal locked him up in the calaboose, but he was kicked out at daylight the next morning. In spite of his terrible hangover, he was starved and made his way to a restaurant. Being known there, he was greeted in a not too friendly manner. He demanded bacon and eggs - lottsa eggs. He was told that they were out of eggs. Hard-Twist pointed to a bowl back of the counter that contained several eggs, saying that he had to have some eggs as they were a scarce article of diet at his cow camp. The proprietor explained that the eggs were pretty old, but Hard-Twist insisted. The eggs were old, all right; in fact, they were rotten. But the owner, holding his nose, scrambled them anyway. Hard-Twist mumbled and grumbled, but finally choked his breakfast down. As he paid his bill, the cook got up enough nerve to ask him how he had liked his food. Hard-Twist picked his nose, belched a couple of times and said: "Well, I could tell that the damn skunks had been screwing the chickens again!"

One of Fred's best stories did not involve Hard-Twist. As a judge, it became his duty to preside at a paternity suit in Sanpete County. A farmer claimed that a certain young man was the father of his unmarried daughter's child. In court, the young man admitted that he and the girl had been friendly. In fact, he acknowledged that on a certain spring evening he and the girl were pitching a little woo on the soft green grass of a ditch bank that ran through her father's pasture. Yes, he and the girl were lying down and he was on top of the girl. Maybe he was the father of the child, but it was the girl's father who was responsible for the pregnancy. He, again, claimed that there would have been no pregnancy if it had not been for her father. When he was asked to explain, he said he was in the proper position all right and repeated that nothing would have happened if it were not for the father. Questioned further, he said that there would have been no real penetration or ejaculation had not the father hit him on the butt with great force by an irrigating shovel right at the critical moment, causing him to do what he had not really intended to do. So the father, not he, was to blame for the child!

I cooked up an excuse one time to visit Judge Keller in his chambers in the old Carbon County Courthouse. I wanted to see the fireplace Warren had told me about. It seems that in bootleg days, the officers would frequently deposit the confiscated loot, later to be used as evidence, behind the iron doors of the judges unused fireplace. We chatted for a moment or two; the judge offered me a chew of tobacco and I quizzed him about the fireplace that had been the safety deposit box for the illicit booze. He laughed and confirmed Warren's story, admitting that on occasion, the liquid evidence would practically disappear before the case came to trial. He grinned, licked his lips, slapped his leg and mentioned that in the dry climate of Carbon County, the evaporation rate was very high.

The following are three events of Carbon County history in which Warren S. Peacock was involved.

Lynching In Carbon County

I have in my possession a document, rescued from the burn barrel at Castle Gate during a 1960s house cleaning at the mine office. It has two titles: 1.The Killing of City Marshal Burns by Robert Marshall, negro, at Castle Gate and 2. Lynching of Marshall, by mob, at Price. It is dated June 1925. This record contains carbon copies of fifteen telegrams, sent by mine officials at Castle Gate to the Utah Fuel office in Salt Lake City, detailing the murder of Castle Gate City Marshal Milton Burns by Robert Marshall and the eventual capture and lynching of Marshall. There are also more than a score of newspaper clippings, mostly from the Salt Lake Tribune, but some from two local papers, the News Advocate and the Price Sun.

I am reproducing several of the Castle Gate papers because they represent an on-site drama of what happened as it happened.

COPIES OF TELEGRAMS HERE:

CGGOHO Castle Gate June 16, 1925.

C. B. H.

A. C. W.....Salt Lake

About two weeks ago Robert Marshall,

colored, was seen by Burns looking around the post- office with a gun strapped on him. Burns did not know what his intentions were and consequently took the gun away from him. Apparently Marshall has harbored a grudge against Burns for his action in taking the gun. He drew his time Saturday evening and Joe paid him off about 3 o'clock yesterday afternoon. Marshall stationed himself by the store last evening about 6:30 PM, apparently awaiting for Burns to make the rounds with the clock. Burns started at the amusement hall, then to No-1 fan and No-1 bath house and then to No-1 barn. In the meantime, Marshall stationed himself on wagon bridge leading to the barn and on Burns return from Barn and in crossing bridge, Marshall began to shoot. One bullet took effect in Burns abdomen, in each thigh,one in calf of leg and other in either the right or left side. His intestines are riddled and torn quite badly, which made an operation necessary Burns seems to be resting easy this morning, which is attributed to the drug acting as a stimulant. No one is allowed to see him this morning and will have to wait until Doctor McDermid arises before we can get his true condition. Might also add that Marshall beat Burns over head with a gun after he had shot him and also took Burns gun after he was down. Marshall took to the hills behind house 259. It is reported by East that he came off hills about 4AM this morning as Deputy Sheriff

Olson who was stationed on the tracks in
the vicinity of Heiner and had gun battle
with him at that time, but due to it being
dark, he was soon lost sight of.

EEJ.....1105

CGGOHO Castle GatemJune 16, 1925.

C. B.H.

A. C. W.

Burns still alive. However, in talking
to Doctor McDermid at 230 this morning, he
stated Milt's chance for recovery is very
slim. A posse of about forty men are
still out
securing the hills, but so far they have
not apprehended him.

JP.....905A

CGGOHO Castle Gate June 17, 1925.

CBH

ACW...Salt Lake

Mr. Burns passed away at 10 PM last
night. This confirms phone conversation
with Mr. Watts. Negro still at large.

J.P....905A

CGGOHO Castle Gate June 18, 1925.

C.B.H.

A.C.W.

F.Ericksen.....Salt Lake

At about 9AM, a colored fellow by name
Grey came to the office and advised me
that Marshall who killed Burns had wandered
into his batch during the night. Of
course, Marshall had been staying with Grey

previous to the crime. The shack where Marshall was found is located a couple of doors east of the Coffee House. I immediately called East into the office to xxxxxx dicuss plans for his capture. East decided that we would take eight or nine men to the shack for the purpose of surrounding it and then he and Daskalakis would go in and grab Marshall who was laying on a bed. This plan worked perfectly we were able to capture him without any resistance although he was arid. He was taken by posse, surprised. Immediately started to Price with the prisoner to deliver him to the sheriff. However, when we got to the courthouse, there had been a mob gather there and they took the prisoner in charge and drove out on the Sunnyside road for about two miles and lynched him.

EEJ.....155P

Arrest warrants were issued June 20, 1925 for Morgan King, Price electrician; George O'Niel, Price barber; Charley Atwood, Price barber; Henry East, Castle Gate special officer and deputy sheriff; and Joseph Richard Golding, Golding Brothers Vulcanizing Works. The next day, warrants were served on E.E. Jones, superintendent of Utah Fuel Co. at Castle Gate; Joseph Parmley, chief clerk, Utah Fuel at Castle Gate; T. Davis, store manager at Castle Gate; John Daskalakis, night watchman at Castle Gate; Warren Peacock, Price City marshal; and Joseph E. Caldwell, employee of Utah Fuel at Castle Gate.

The eleven men were confined in the Carbon County Jail. They were jailed, but not in the usual sense. They were visited by family, friends and the general public who brought in tubs of soft drinks, ice cream, cakes, cookies and candies. No wonder that a telegram was sent from Castle Gate to the Utah Fuel office in Salt Lake saying "Boys treated royally at Price." Six of the eleven men were from Castle Gate. Evelyn Jones-Patterick (daughter of E.E.Jones) says (1994), "The reason the officials were visited by friends and given gifts was because of their love and respect and a belief in their non-involvement in the lynching."

Newspapers of the day are fairly consistent in their reporting of the melee. The men who took Marshall to the courthouse in Price were overpowered by a mob of armed men and the negro was hanged from a huge cottonwood tree two miles south of Price. After he had hung for nine minutes, officers arrived on the scene. Deputy Sheriff S. E. Garrett cut him down and Price City Marshal Warren Peacock removed the noose from his neck and the officers started to put him in their car. Showing some feeble signs of life, the victim was seized from the law officers and again strung up. After the lapse of about half an hour, the sheriff's men were allowed to take possession of the body and it was taken to Flynn's Mortuary in Price. Not long after, pictures showing the negro dangling from the rope were sold on the streets of Price. It was estimated that a crowd of 800 to 1,000 men, women and children viewed the lynching. District Attorney Fred W. Keller was incensed with the poor cooperation of Sheriff Ray Deming and demanded his resignation. Governor George H. Dern was visited by a delegation of black people who, while admitting the brutality of Marshall, deplored the lawless lynching. On June 30, the defendants were released on bonds of $7,500 each. A grand jury was selected on July 28th. A total of over 125 witnesses were called, none of whom could remember the names of the people involved. A typical witness would say that he was present at the lynching, but would deny seeing who the participants were, prevented he said, by the vast crowd that obscured his vision. All men were eventually turned free, to the disgust of District Attorney Keller, because of "lack of evidence."

The following is a quotation, which, in a way, explains the complexity of the situation:

"It is asked just what do you understand by a mob? Usually, one associates this word with a crowd of strangers — disorderly, violent, undesirables, bent on committing acts from which the decent folks of the community withdraw and which are disparaged by all reputable citizens.

"But had one glanced over the assembly whose members took by force the negro slayer of Castle Gate city marshal from the arresting officers as they arrived at the county jail yesterday, you would have seen your neighbors, your friends, the townspeople with whom you are to barter day by day, public employees, folks prominent in church and social circles and your real conception of a mob might have undergone a radical turnover."

The Sun, June 19, 1925

It is interesting to interview some of the people who remember the incident. Mona Livingston-Marsing was 15 years old at the time. She recalls being in the Price Trading store with her mother when several men came in, in a great rush, leaving their car engines running at the curb, to purchase a rope. Evelyn Jones-Patterick and her sister, Fern Jones-Boyack, were the daughters of E.E. Jones, superintendent of Utah Fuel at Castle Gate. At that time, Evelyn was 13 and her sister was 11 years old when Marshall shot Burns. Evelyn says that she and her sister, Darlene, were playing in front of their house that evening when two men carried Burns to the hospital next door. She vividly remembers (as he was carried within a few feet of her) that his face was all bloody and mutilated from being pistol whipped and kicked by the negro.

Both Evelyn and Fern are high in their praise of Marshal Milton Burns. They say he was well liked by everyone in Castle Gate who respected and admired him in his work as a law enforcement officer. He was especially liked by the children, with whom he would visit and joke as he made his rounds. One might postulate that this admiration, respect and love for Burns might be one reason that six of the eleven accused were from Castle Gate. Also, Burns' wife was an aunt to Warren Peacock. Thus, at least seven people had perhaps more than a usual concern about the murder of Burns because of their love for him; possibly, that is why they were regarded with suspicion.

Most Utah historians consider that the Ku Klux Klan was involved in the lynching. There had been many recent cross burnings throughout the state and Carbon County. Larry R. Gerlach, in his book Blazing Crosses in Zion, says: "Although the Klan as an organization was not responsible for the illegal execution, it was common knowledge that Burns and virtually all of the men charged with the lynching were Klansmen." Both Evelyn and Fern vehemently deny that their father, E.E. Jones, was a Klansman. They say that he was greatly upset when they lived at Hiawatha and a cross, illuminated by carbide lights, was burned on the hillside there. They also mention his friendship with the negro, Grey, at Castle Gate, whom they often invited to eat at their table, as an indication of their father's tolerance of all nationalities, white or black. He was a Mason, yes, but a Klansman, no.

The hanging of the negro Robert Marshall was the last of five recorded lynchings in Utah. It was a black mark on Carbon County, but hardly compares in outright ferocity with the lynching of a colored man in the City of Zion who, too, had killed a peace officer. His body was dragged up and down Main Street by a howling mob in August of 1883.

Nowadays, you can get your guts blown out by a couple of pistol wielding teen-age gang members if you attempt to use a pay phone against their wishes!

Carbon County Jailbreak

The following, under the headline of "PAIR CHARGED WITH SHOOTING OF SHERIFF S. M. BLISS CAPTURED," is a newspaper article published in the Price Sun November 5, 1931.

"Lee Diamenti, 24, of Helper and Frank Smith, 23, of Salt Lake City, who shot and seriously wounded Sheriff S. M. Bliss early Monday morning, were returned to Price Tuesday evening after their dramatic capture that morning near Cortez, Colo. Deputy A. E. Gibson, who was on duty the night of the shooting, was severely beaten about the head by (the) desperadoes in their attempt to get the keys to the main block of cells.

"The intention of the pair was to secure the release of Ruggerio Gargula, who was being held for trial in the district court on a charge of robbery.

"The search for the desperadoes after their flight from Price extended to four states, Colorado, New Mexico, Arizona and Utah. The entire west was aroused by the brutal attack made on the officers, and escape for Smith and Diamenti was almost impossible in view of the wide publicity given to the inc dent.

"To the list of crimes with which Diamenti and Smith were already charged are added assault with intent to commit murder and assault with a deadly weapon. Complaints charging each with both offenses were filed Tuesday immediately after news of their capture was received here.

"By a strange whim of fate, the capture of Smith and Diamenti was accomplished by a brother-in-law of Sheriff Bliss, William Haller, who runs a service station east of Cortez. They were apprehended after they abandoned the automobile in which they left Monticello... The car which Smith and Diamenti had abandoned near Cortez contained several bombs, a small arsenal and some provisions.

"They obtained a ride with a tourist who drove into the Haller service station. Haller, recognizing the men as the fugitives, covered them with a pistol and held them until the authorities from Cortez arrived. No resistance to arrest was offered by either Smith or Diamenti; nor did they cause any trouble on the ride back to Price..."

The Sun account continues:

"The pair walked into the sheriff's office about 2 o'clock a.m. Monday morning. Diamenti went into the bedroom where Gibson was sleeping, threw a blanket over his head and slugged him with a heavy revolver. Diamenti then demanded the keys to the cell and when the request was refused, he continued to batter Gibson severely about the face and head. The living quarters of the sheriff are on the same floor as the jail and Mrs. Bliss heard the commotion. She roused her husband the sheriff and he, thinking that the noise was from some drunken men, walked into the main office unarmed.

"He switched on the lights, but before he could do anything, Diamenti covered him with a revolver on one side and Smith... covered him on the other side with a sawed-off shotgun. They ordered the sheriff to give up the keys to the cells, and he advised them not to become excited. Suddenly, Smith fired at Bliss who had started to raise his hands and the desperadoes fled without seeking further for the keys. The sheriff's action in lifting up his arms was responsible for his life being saved, as his right arm was directly over his heart and received almost the full force of the shot..."

Sheriff Bliss was hospitalized for the amputation of his right arm just below the elbow. He was back on the job in less than a month, continuing to live in his courthouse basement apartment, adjacent to the jail.

Smith and Diamenti were jailed in lieu of $20,000 bond. In late December, Ciperano Comargo smuggled hack-saw blades and other tools to Diamenti. According to subsequent court testimony, Diamenti threatened an inmate of the jail, who was a trustee, to "slit his throat from ear to ear" if he did not bring him a hack-saw frame. Being forewarned, Sheriff Bliss was able to foil an attempted escape effort when he surprised the prisoners sawing a hole in the main cell section. Separate trials were held in January 1932. The jury took forty-five minutes to find Smith guilty and two and one-half hours to convict Diamenti of attempted murder. They were committed to the Utah State Penitentiary for five years to life in February of 1932.

Deputy Sheriff Warren Peacock is mentioned as directing the manhunt from Price and being in charge while Bliss was incapacitated.

Death Of Sheriff Marion Bliss
April 23, 1945

Sheriff S. Marion Bliss
Credit: Edna Bliss Mahleres

About 10 a.m. on the morning of April 23, 1945, Price Mayor J. Bracken Lee dashed into my office in great excitement. He told me that Verdell Pace had been murdered the previous day and that the suspect, Angus Robb, had hidden out on his farm in the Carbonville area and was being sought by law officers. He wanted me to fly him over the area in the hope of spotting the fugitive. The only plane available at the airport was one I had never flown before, so I had a little problem with the controls. Also, it was a gusty spring day and the air was very rough. Brack wanted me to fly low over the area in order to give him a better chance at locating Robb who, he had been told, was concealed in a dry irrigation canal. On our first pass, Brack became violently air sick and threw up all over the plane, himself and me. Brack was incapacitated and I was too busy flying the plane to see anything, so we returned to the airport. My pilot's log for that day indicates that we were in the air for 20 minutes!

I hurried home, got my .257 scope mounted deer rifle and drove two miles north on the Helper highway to a place called Maxwell siding on the railroad that paralleled the automobile road. I found a wild scene: highway patrolmen, police officers from Price and Helper, deputy sheriffs and special officers from the Denver & Rio Grande Western Railroad besides a conglomeration of citizens, all armed to the teeth, mostly with hunting rifles. All were shielding themselves behind cars, trees, houses and outbuildings as they faced the combat area to the east. Most of the law enforcement officers were patients and friends of mine. I immediately ran into Highway Patrolman Jack Sullivan, who filled me in on the circumstances. He said that on the previous day, Verdell Pace, while driving his small herd of cattle toward their summer range, had possibly been murdered by Angus Robb, probably in an argument over trespassing. In any event, Pace had been shot twice through the chest and in both arms; several empty .30-.30 cartridge cases had been found adjacent to his body. The evidence had pointed to Robb; consequently, that morning Jack had stopped at Robb's farm to question him. No one answered the door, so Jack walked to the back yard. He saw Robb working in his corral a short distance away and called to him, saying: " I need to talk with you." The reply was two sudden rifle shots at him by Robb, one bullet hitting a tree just a few inches from Jack's head. That pretty well clinched for sure who Pace's murderer was and the manhunt was on. Robb had retreated, with his rifle, into a maze of dry canals, irrigation ditches and washes, all surrounded by a jungle of tall willows, brush and other foliage with large cottonwood trees and roots lining the canal banks. Deputy Sheriff Hugh Taylor seemed to be in charge, although everyone there, especially the hangers-on, had ideas about what should be done. Hugh said he thought that Sheriff Marion Bliss and Chief Deputy Warren Peacock were on the other side of Robb, trying to sneak up on him from that direction. He wanted to contact Sheriff Bliss for orders and to work out a plan for the capture of the fugitive. Hugh, Highway Patrolman Lyle Hyatt, T. Migliori and I made a wide circle to the north through a network of semidry alkali washes and approached the area where Bliss and Peacock were supposed to be. Shouting contact was made, and Hugh asked Lyle and me to cover while he and Migliori went to confer with the other two men. In our anxiety to do a good job of protection, Lyle and I exposed our heads and shoulders only to have bullets whistle by, one of which passed between our heads close enough that we could feel its "breath." The shots could have been from Robb, but were more likely fired by some of the trigger-happy manhunters. Hugh, Lyle and I returned to the west side of the canal; Migliori stayed in the region where Bliss and Peacock were. The plan decided upon was that the Utah Highway Patrol in Salt Lake City be telephoned to bring down a supply of tear gas that could be lobbed into the canal where Robb was concealed and thus flush him out. Robb was in an almost impregnable fortress. He was in the dry bed of the Price canal, which was three or four feet deep and eight or ten feet wide as it coursed its way on the lower reaches of the western flank of Wood Hill. The canal had a dogleg in it which enabled Robb to move back and forth, so that he could shoot from different locations and thus confuse the posse as to his exact location.

I perched myself on the sloping roof of a chicken house, which gave me a vantage point to observe the proceedings. Joe Arnold of the highway patrol crawled to the top of Robb's house, his body protected by the brick chimney, as he scanned the area with his scope mounted rifle. He shouted: "I believe I can see his head. Shall I shoot him?" He said that he had Bliss and Peacock in view. I asked him if he could see Migliori and he said no, so he did not pull the trigger for fear of shooting the wrong person.

The collection of police cars and the gun-toting group of manhunters attracted a multitude of cars on the highway; even a passing school bus stopped so that the kids could watch the mass confusion. A WW II veteran showed up and borrowed an automatic M I carbine from one of the officers and started crawling toward the fugitive through the ground infested willows and other brush. He soon retreated when Robb put a couple of bullets close to him.

Cars continued to come and go, frequently bringing armed men eager to join the melee. Periodic gunfire punctuated the day, mostly by the so-called posse, but some by Robb when he thought he was overly threatened. In late afternoon, the tear gas from Salt Lake City arrived and several canisters were shot into the dry canal where it was thought Robb was located. Shooting increased, aimed at anything that moved. Lyle Hyatt and Walter Westbrook, special officer of the D&RGW, were to the left of me. Westbrook fired several shots and suddenly shouted: "I rolled him over!" Sure enough, we walked the scant 100 yards to the canal and Robb was there with the top of his head blown off. His .30-.30 carbine was nearby, with a half box of loaded .30-.30 shells in his coat pocket and more than $1,100 in greenbacks.

I immediately left to go to the hospital to visit my neglected patients. I did not know until later that evening that Sheriff Bliss had been killed. For a time, it was believed that he had been killed by Robb. However, the two bullets removed from his body did not match those from Robb's gun, but were indeed from the M I carbine which had been used by several law enforcement officers at various times that day. It was apparent that Sheriff Marion Bliss had been accidentally shot, being mistaken for Robb by one of the posse. The entire episode might well have ended differently if Sheriff Bliss had not been pinned down so that he could not direct the proceedings. It was a miracle that more people were not injured or killed. Robb could have shot many people, but tended to hold his fire unless threatened. The real danger was from the indiscriminate shooting by the trigger-happy mob.

As chief deputy sheriff, it was up to Warren Peacock to conduct the investigation into the chaos that had resulted in the deaths of three men. This he did with great thoroughness by conducting coroners juries, calling expert ballistic witnesses and anything else needed. His inquiry revealed that Robb was a sullen man, hostile to his neighbors and had, at one time, been committed to the mental hospital in Provo. Also, it was established that Bliss had been shot accidentally, not feloniously, about half an hour before Robb met his demise around 5 p.m.

It was assumed by most of the community that Warren Peacock would be appointed sheriff to take the place of Bliss. But that was not to be. The county commissioners, all of whom were Democrats, appointed Joe Dudler to fill out the term of Bliss, who had been elected for many terms as a Republican. Peacock was retained as chief deputy. Warren Peacock was greatly hurt. He maintained that he did not really want the job, but it would have been nice if he had at least been offered the position.

Personal Notes-Warren Peacock

Warren Peacock was born at Molen, Emery County, Utah, August 12, 1881. His early life was spent as a farm boy in Emery County. He told me once that as a youth he worked one summer at a sawmill in Joes Valley making shingles. He said that he worked hard all that summer, under primitive conditions, at the mill located on the west side of Middle Mountain below Red Pine Ridge. His pay at the end was a pair of new bib overalls and a pair of clodhopper boots!

He remembers a diphtheria epidemic that hit the community. Diphtheria in those days was a terrible scourge and often wiped out nearly all the children of one family in those pre-antitoxin days. Warren said that the whole family, including numerous children, was quarantined and all were forbidden to go out the door. Two children died in one night and their bodies were passed through a window instead of the door to friends for burial. These children were buried in the Molen cemetery, with tiny headstones to mark their graves.

Part of the time, the Peacock family lived in Orangeville. The women used to save eggs and make butter to take to Price to trade for groceries and other essentials. As a rule, a whole day would be allowed to journey to Price and back because of poor roads and unreliable transportation. Warren was driving a Model T Ford when the machine ran out of oil at Washboard Flats. They had no spare oil; the engine became red hot and froze up. They were in a quandary. Then someone thought of the supply of homemade butter. Several pounds were manipulated and squeezed into the engine, the vehicle cranked up and they drove to Price, thankful for the "cow grease."

Model T. Ford getting a drink of water by Bill Lines as Amy Katherine looks on

As a young man, Warren went to the Uintah Basin to work in the booming turn of the century gilsonite mines. Gilsonite is a hydrocarbon, found in vertical veins or fissures exclusively in the Utah's Uintah Basin. It was in great demand as an ingredient in paints, varnishes and similar products. As mentioned before, he supplemented his miner wages by operating a combination barber shop and barroom. Later, he and his brother, Gomer, owned the White House saloon in Price. They then operated a farm and sheep ranch in Miller Creek for a time. Shortly thereafter, Warren took up law enforcement as a career, starting out as Price City marshal in 1921, then progressing to chief deputy sheriff under Carbon County Sheriff Ray Deming in 1926. Marion Bliss was elected sheriff of Carbon County in 1927 and Warren served under him as chief deputy. He continued as chief deputy for Joe Dudler, who was appointed following the accidental shooting death of Sheriff Bliss in 1945.

Warren's wife, Elvira Mott-Peacock, died December 22, 1928 following surgery at age 37, leaving him a widower with four of his five children living at home. The three younger children, Lloyd, age 4; Maurine, 10; and Arlien, 12; were sent to live with relatives. Lenar, 19, remained at home with his father. After one year, Warren was terribly unhappy about having the family separated and arranged for his wife's sister, Aunt Lutie, to keep house and care for the younger children for the next year. Tragedy hit again December 16, 1931 with the death of his oldest daughter, Leora.

Complications arose during the bitter Carbon County coal strike of 1933. Being a law enforcement officer, Warren received many threats to him and his family. For protection, the children would be sent to friends' or relatives' homes to sleep at night when Warren was on duty because he feared for their safety.

In late 1945, Warren Peacock was feted by the peace officers of Carbon County at a surprise birthday banquet which also marked his 25th year as an law enforcement officer. He continued to work until his retirement in early 1948. Not being appointed sheriff following the death of Bliss preyed on his mind; neither could he accept the idea of retirement, since being a peace officer had been such a consuming and important part of his life, with seldom time off for a vacation. He was now hard put to occupy his time. His hurt increased and he died a broken man June 12, 1949.

Warren S. Peacock was a MAN loved, admired and respected by all who knew him. Judge Fred W. Keller spoke at his funeral, concluding with these words: "Weep no more. Hold your heads high. Be glad and proud that you knew this man."

Delon Olsen
1899-1983

Delon Olsen was one of the most remarkable men I ever knew. As was said at his funeral, "When God made Delon, He threw the mold away." He was unpredictable — a man of contrasts; one moment, he could cuss an obstinate horse; the next, get tears in his eyes from the beauty of a tiny wildflower. He could ride a bucking horse, castrate a calf, gut a bull elk, chase a mountain lion or bake the best flap-jacks or scones in the county, together with homemade bread and a cake or pie for dessert following a venison roast or bear steak; then play the piano to entertain his guests.

Delon S. Olsen on Teka 1965

Nothing daunted him; he took everything in stride, whether it was a joyous Saturday night dance or cleaning the manure out of his barn. The last few years of his life, he was a full-time farmer and stockman. In his younger years, he had been a general laborer, camp manager, sheepherder, carpenters helper, teamster, sawmill worker, cook, hotel manager, surveyors assistant and coal miner, to name a few.

Delon was characterized by his unbounded generosity; what was his was yours. His place was a haven for homeless kids, rehabilitating alcoholics or other people down on their luck and in need of bed and board. It became a tradition that no one passed his ranch without lighting down, sitting a spell and partaking of the sumptuous food he would serve up meanwhile.

But his one great love was his ranch in Joes Valley that his father, Abinadi (Nad), had acquired as a 160-acre homestead in about 1915. I accidently met Delon while on an elk hunt in 1942; this chance acquaintance grew into a lifetime companionship that influenced the lives of my entire family.

In 1974, Maurine Dorman penned a tribute to Delon: "My personal observation is that his entire personality is expressed in his hands. They are large, work worn, capable, creative, warm and at times delicate —depending on whether he is behind an irrigating shovel, branding calves, turning the pages of a book, playing the piano, kneading dough, flipping pancakes, offering a firm handshake or picking a fragile flower."

Delon Olsen and Argene Vance were married in 1943. They have two sons, Arthur D. and Henning J., each of whom have five children.

Delon departed this world in June 1983. Over 40 years of understanding friendship have left a host of treasured memories.

The following stories will help illustrate that friendship.

OL' SMOKEY

In about 1945, Maurine and I made arrangements with Delon Olsen to take over an old partially finished cabin south of his main lodge in Joes Valley. The first summer was spent in trying to straighten up the old cabin, get it square, put a roof on it, put a floor in and make it livable with the installation of windows and doors.

In about 1946 or perhaps 1947, I decided that since I was living in Joes Valley part time I ought to have a horse and thus keep up with the other people in the area. I was inherently afraid of horses, but thought that I could learn to use one and enjoy it and thus increase my status symbol in the community.

I therefore started looking for a horse to purchase. Delon referred me to a Mr. Ezra Branch of Price who had an emasculated black horse which he wanted to sell. I consulted Mr. Branch at great length about this horse because I wanted a gentle animal. Mr. Branch assured me that this horse was indeed very gentle and that his grandchildren rode him. He said his grandchildren ran around the horse at all times and would crawl under his belly and play around its feet and that it was indeed a very gentle horse.

I bought the horse from Ezra Branch for the sum of $50. Then I had to borrow a horse trailer to take it to Joes Valley. When we arrived, Delon suggested we put the horse in the field and let it stay there overnight and adjust to the community a little bit. When we put it in the field, Delon also suggested that maybe we ought to put hobbles on the horse so that we could catch it easily the next day and then I could ride it. However, the next day, the horse was not very easy to catch. In fact, Delon and two or three other people on horse back chased the horse all over Delon's field and were virtually unable to catch it because it could run faster with the hobbles on than their unencumbered saddle horses could. However, the horse was finally caught and put in Delon's calf-loading chute in order to saddle him because he was indeed very frisky and cantankerous and didn't want to have anything to do with people and didn't want to be bridled or saddled. Eventually, it was saddled and Delon rode it without too great difficulty, although the horse was certainly far from gentle the way Mr. Branch had described it to me. Delon told me that he would ride this horse during the summer months and get the kinks taken out of it so that when hunting season came in the fall, it would be completely gentled down and I would have no problems with it.

Later on in the summer, Delon rode the horse which, since it was black we had named Smokey, up into Black Canyon. On his return out of Black Canyon toward his ranch in lower Joes Valley, at one of the worst spots on the trail on a slick side hill, the horse started to buck and bucked Delon off amidst a bunch of boulders and sagebrush. Delon told me the first thing he thought of after he was bucked off, realizing he had lost his glasses, was that probably the glasses were broken. However, he looked around and discovered his glasses lying there in the sagebrush. He was very thankful they were not broken and seemed in good condition. He put his glasses on and since he had a mouthful of dirt he had acquired during this episode of being bucked off the horse, he walked a few feet down to the Black Canyon Creek, took his false teeth out and rinsed them off thoroughly in the water. As he started to put them back in, he dropped his upper plate on a rock and it broke right through the middle. Delon, of course, was fit to be tied; there he was afoot some 3$^1/_2$ miles from his ranch house. He had on a new pair of cowboy boots that were so tight he could hardly stand in them, let alone walk. Although his glasses were intact, he had broken the upper plate of his false teeth.

However, he walked home and I received in the mail a day or two later, his upper plate with a request to take his false teeth to Dr. Lyman Kofford and have them repaired. In the meantime, of course, Delon would be toothless and would have to live on soup and get along as best he could without being able to chew properly. I took the teeth to Dr. Kofford and he told me it would take him a few days to get them fixed.

While I was there, I conceived an idea and asked Dr. Kofford if he didn't have an extra upper plate I could send to Delon as a loaner while his teeth were being repaired. Dr. K. fell in with the idea and we went into his back room. He literally had a couple of bushel baskets full of discarded false teeth. We naturally looked for the worst and ugliest pair we could find. Finally, we settled on an upper plate that was a real beaut. Instead of pearly white teeth and healthy pink gums, the whole plate was a dull mancus shale grey, which looked as if it were trying to grow some sort of moss or fungus. Three-fourths of one central incisor tooth was missing, while the other had one corner broken off. The lateral incisors and canines were chipped and jagged. The previous owner had obviously been a copious tobacco chewer, as all the gum margins had a deeply pigmented line of dark brown calcified tobacco juice staining their edges.

Since it would be some time before I could get to Joes Valley, I put the dentures in the mail with a notation on the inner sealed package that the enclosed teeth were "loaners" which Dr. K. would give to him for use until his own teeth could be repaired. Needless to say, Delon was delighted when he received the package from me in the mail, thinking that it was certainly good service on the part of Dr. Kofford and myself. However, when he opened the package, he took one look at the revolting china clippers and lost his cookies.

Subsequently, Delon really put the spurs to Ol' Smokey for the rest of the summer in order to get him into shape for me to ride during the coming deer hunt. By spending so much time with Smokey, he neglected the riding and training of his other horses, which he and his dude deer hunters would use.

We were all saddled up at dawn on the frosty October morning on opening day of the deer hunt. Ol' Smokey was as tame and docile as a lamb. With rifle in scabbard and the leather straps of binoculars and camera on the saddle horn, I got into the saddle with no trouble and watched with no little amusement the hassle that Delon was having in getting his California dudes mounted up. Some tried to get on their mounts from the wrong side. Others were hopping around with one foot in the stirrup and the other on the ground. All the horses, except Smokey, were pretty nervous and jumpy, snorting, tossing their heads and stamping around on the frozen ground.

Finally, Delon got the dudes all mounted up, showed them how to hold their feet in the stirrups and gave them other advice. When he grabbed the bridled reins of his horse and tried to mount, it acted up. He was carrying his 30-30 rifle in one hand, as he had given his own saddle scabbard to one of the dudes, and planned to carry his rifle in front of him in the saddle. Trying to get on a frisky horse with a rifle in one hand was cumbersome, to say the least, so he asked me to hold his gun until he could get squared around. At the same time, he gave me a couple pair of binoculars and a camera or two belonging to some of the dudes who didn't seem to know where or how to carry them. I could see that Delon anticipated considerable trouble with his horse. But after talking to his animal with a few well chosen aphorisms, he swung into the saddle with only a minimal problem of crow hopping from the frisky beast. The already mounted riders were sort of milling around, waiting for Delon to lead off. He surveyed the crowd with great pride at getting them all ready to go without anyone getting bucked off. He said: "Black Canyon, here we come" and let out a whoop.

You guessed it. Ol' Smokey put his head between his front legs, arched his back and bucked me ten feet in the air along with a conglomeration of guns, binoculars and cameras.

The next spring, I traded Ol' Smokey with $25 to boot to a cowpoke named Cliff Brown for a little tan-colored mare called "Squaw."

Squaw was much smaller than Smokey with a fine small head and nice slender legs, considerably different from the crude "plow horse" look of Ol' Smokey. Squaw was a fine animal, mild mannered and easy to catch and ride. She was tame, loved to be petted and would follow me all over the ranch for an apple or a lump of sugar. Things were looking up in the horse business, so I invested in a fancy new saddle and pair of chaps and new cowboy boots at Price Commission. I rode the little mare quite a lot that summer and during the deer hunt that fall with no real problems.

I was lucky and drew out for a bull elk permit in November. Delon had several other elk hunters at his lodge. We planned a trip into Reeder Canyon and up onto Reeder Ridge to the high country, where the elk were supposed to be located. It was mid-November and very cold. There was only a skiff of snow in the valley, but the higher mountains were pretty well covered.

The extreme cold weather slowed us up on opening day and we did not get away until about 9 o'clock. We rode slowly across Delon's field toward the mouth of Reeder Canyon. It was a bright sunny day, but there was a bitter cold wind in our faces. We rode all bundled and humped up, trying to keep warm. I was bringing up the rear, almost wishing that I was back in my snug cabin. One of the lead horses broke off a small piece of sagebrush and a sudden harder gust of wind whipped it across in front of Squaw and she let go. I went about two feet in the air and landed back on the saddle horn with a certain very delicate portion of my anatomy. That ended the elk hunt for me and I spent the remainder of the week in my cabin in considerable pain and barely able to get around.

A few weeks later, Cliff Brown showed up and wanted to buy Squaw back as he was "tired of that big black brute called Smokey," so I sold Squaw back to him for the original purchase price and thanked my lucky stars. I told him about my episode with the mare. He chided me to no end about being a poor horseman, that Squaw had never given him any trouble, what a fine gentle horse she was and how glad he was to get her back.

About a year later, I was making rounds at the hospital. I heard a kind of weak voice call my name as I passed a room, so I went in. There, flat on his back was Cliff Brown with one leg suspended in a cast from toe to hip.

Yes, Squaw had bucked him off.

This ended my adventures with horses and my life as a "drugstore cowboy!"

I was put to shame several years later when my older brother, LaVerne, showed up to spend his summers in Joes Valley. He had served in WWI for three years in the cavalry on the Mexican border. He was a real horseman. He soon had some of the wild ones, including "Teka," eating out of his hand and coming to his whistle. Later on, he tended "Sugar Foot" for Chris Diamanti. He seemed to "know" horses and they would do most anything for him. But personally, I had no desire to ever mount one again! Shanks ponies were best for me until I got a Jeep.

Potato Whisky

During the years of WWII, the hunting situation slowed up at Delon Olsen's Joes Valley dude ranch. Many able-bodied men were off fighting the wars with Germany and Japan. Others were working overtime in the coal mines, on the farm or cattle ranches or tending sheep. There was not much time for recreation and not many could afford the luxury of a dude ranch, so they hunted on their own. Ammunition was in short supply for hunting rifles. In fact, .30-.30 shells, which sold in those days for about three bucks a box of 20 if available in stores, were being bootlegged in beer joints all over the state for a dollar each shell. One October deer season, the only ones at the ranch were Delon, "Father" Jewkes, Maurine, me and our guests, Joe and Clyda Hammond. Joe was home on a short furlough from the Army and he wanted to spend some of his time hunting deer.

Father Jewkes was an ancient Mormon patriarch, well in his 80s. Delon always called him Father out of respect for his age and longtime friendship. He loved to come up to Delon's cabin for the deer hunt. He had brought an old beat-up rifle, but no shells as he hoped that someone would have a few spare .30-.30s. Of course, the deer hunt for him would consist of telling stories and reminiscing in front of Delon's fireplace. His stories were great; he used both hands to illustrate his tales as he turned his head back and forth and up and down, squinting through his half-inch thick post-operative cataract glasses.

It was decided to have a private hunt in order to give Joe a chance to get a buck. Maurine, Clyda and Father Jewkes stayed in camp, while Delon, Joe and I saddled up horses and took off. We rode up the west side of Middle Mountain and ended up around noon in an area known as Shoo Fly. We had our lunch and were getting ready to start out again when someone spotted a magnificent four-point buck poised on a little point about 200 yards away. Since Joe was the guest of honor, he was given the chance to shoot the buck, which he did with one shot through the heart. Of course, Delon and I both had our sights on the deer in case he missed, but he didn't so we pounded him on the back in congratulation, cleaned the deer out and packed the animal back to camp where the two girls and Father Jewkes had supper ready for us. Father Jewkes was especially pleased with Joe's trophy and made up a poem about the event in Joe's honor and then entertained us richly well into the night with deer hunting stories and experiences of his own regarding his early years in Emery County. Also, with Delon at the piano, we sang songs — best of all, "Home on the Range."

At elk season, things picked up. In those years, the elk hunt was held in November, which is a much better time than the mid-October season as now decreed by the fish and game.

Anyway, a group of five men arranged with Delon for the elk hunt. I went up to Joes Valley on the weekend of the opening of the hunt and he introduced them to me as the "Potato Whiskey drinking guys from Sanpete County." Now, it seems that some of the cheaper brands of booze, in order to conserve grain for food during the war effort, were being made of fermented potatoes instead of grain. Liquor was rationed like gasoline, tires, sugar, meat and a lot of other things. Undoubtedly, these "Sanpeters" had saved up or purloined from their church-going friends a plentiful supply of liquor stamps because they had brought with them a considerable supply of the cup that cheers. I was there on a Sunday afternoon and their main goal seemed to be, besides rejoicing that they did not have to attend church that day, to consume as much booze as possible as soon as possible because for the opening two days of the hunt, they had not yet been out of camp. I went home that evening after trying to help them out in their project. But later on, I got the details from Delon about the remaining eight days of the hunt.

It seems that they finally got into a nice herd of elk and managed to shoot five fine animals. But there was a problem: they shot five cow elk, but held permits for bulls only! Now this indeed was a dilemma. Meat was scarce and rationed because of the war. It must not go to waste. These Sanpeters had counted on the meat to feed their families during the coming winter, so even if of the wrong sex, it must be preserved at all costs.

What a problem-lots of good meat, but the wrong kind. But the Sanpeters were undaunted. In those days, there was only one full-time Fish & Game enforcement officer in all of Carbon and Emery counties. His name was Fred Larsen, Sr. He had an eagle eye and the stamina of a billy goat. He probably did more honest-to-goodness game law enforcement than the multiple officers now do. I barely escaped by the skin of my teeth one time when I shot a spike buck with horns an inch shorter than the legal limit. Fred was the nemesis of many a poacher; he would frequently sleep out in his car, with only a loaf of bakers bread for food. On rare occasions, he would stop in at my cabin for a cup of coffee shortly after daylight.

During the deer and elk seasons in Joes Valley, he would be augmented by hirelings, camped out in a tent for a checking station at the bottom of Straight Canyon. These guys, possibly picked up at a pool hall in Castle Dale, anxious to make a paltry dollar, stayed for the entire hunting season living under primitive conditions, sleeping on the ground and preparing their meals on a Coleman stove or campfire. Their work was tiresome; they had to check every passing car, day or night.

The Sanpeters were resourceful; perhaps with the aid of a few more sips of their "potato whiskey," they conceived a magnificent plan- not only would they get to keep the meat, they would also outwit the powers that be. On the living room wall of Delon's cabin hung a beautiful mounted bull elk head, with seven points on one side and six on the other, with a spread of forty-six inches. This trophy elk head was removed from the wall, placed in the back of Delon's pickup truck, partially covered with canvas, old blankets and gunny sacks; then the carcass of a cow elk, with head removed, placed adjacent to it, and down the canyon they went. Delon would take a different man with him each time and arrange to hit the checking station toward evening, always being in a big hurry to get to the meat processing locker plant before it closed. Of course, on the return trip, the elk head would be well covered with the canvas and maybe a saddle or box of groceries. Five trips were made on different days, being careful each time to expose different parts of the mounted bull elk head. Delon said that they were even congratulated more than once for the fine bull elk. He also said, with a boisterous laugh, that they damn near wore out his trophy hauling it back and forth. But it hangs today back in his lodge, albeit a wee bit scarred from its multiple pickup truck journeys.

Thus the power of potato whiskey. I am still uncertain if any of it changed hands at the checking station.

Fred Larsen never knew about the above episode; he was far too busy trying to keep track of his several checking stations to be every place at once. He was a challenge to overanxious pheasant hunters, too. One fall, a friend of mine, Scotty Messenger, who lived on a farm over the hills east of Price, invited me out for a little pre-season reconnaissance. We were walking in a broad deep wash when a beautiful cock pheasant took wing. Somehow, my trigger finger slipped and down came the bird. Shortly thereafter, Scotty pointed out to me a figure of a man silhouetted on the hill west of us, obviously watching us with binoculars. The illegal bird was quickly stashed under a bush. Fred was waiting for us at my car. Luckily, I was able to show a cottontail rabbit to his unmistakable skeptical countenance. Scotty, of course, later retrieved the rooster for his family's evening meal.

Ol' Lucy At Her Best

Shortly after the end of WWII, Delon's Joes Valley ranch was deluged with deer and elk hunters from the Hollywood area. This was possibly due to the influence of the Brandon brothers, Hugh and Clyde, longtime Emery County friends. Hugh operated a motel in Kanab and Hollywood people stayed there while on location in that region. Clyde was employed at one of the major studios in the movie capital.

Most of the hunters who came to Delon's were employed by the movie industry, but some big time actors were interested, too. In fact, Gary Cooper made arrangements for a deer hunt, but was unable to come at the last moment. As sort of a consolation prize, he sent Delon a glass framed life-sized picture of himself inscribed: "To Delon, regards of Gary Cooper." This photo hangs today in Delon's Joes Valley lodge.

In general, the Hollywood hunters were pleasant and easy to get along with. They had plenty of money, good equipment, and some were expert hunters. Several of them made repeat visits because they enjoyed Joes Valley so much.

One was a fellow named Joe, last name long forgotten. He had made two or three deer hunting trips and returned for an elk hunt one November. Since he had learned the area fairly well, Delon had no worry about letting him take a couple of companions and going horseback up into Black Canyon, where the elusive elk were supposed to be located.

Joe had good luck and shot a nice two-point bull near the top of Buck Basin, which is on the south side of Black Canyon. It was getting late in the day and a storm was threatening, so they gutted out the animal and got home about dark, with the intention of going back the next day to pack out the meat, taking along a packhorse especially for that purpose.

I was in the valley, but did not have an elk permit that year. The intended trip sounded like a lot of fun, so I decided to go along. It had snowed during the night; the new day dawned bright and clear but cold, well below freezing.

Four or five people decided to go, including of course Delon and his faithful pack animal, Ol' Lucy. Now, Ol' Lucy was his favorite packhorse and he bragged about her with pride, in spite of her known faults. She loved to rub one side of her pack against a tree in an effort to get rid of her unwelcome cargo; if that did not work, she was a real expert at finding two quakie trees just far enough apart to admit her body, but not the packs. With a couple of well-executed forward lunges, she could soon rid herself of the offending luggage.

It was a beautiful ride up into Black Canyon. The sun was out bright and there was not a cloud in the sky. It was cold, but we were well-clothed and greatly enjoyed the beautiful scenery produced by the previous night's snowfall. It was indeed a beautiful and carefree world!

We had a little trouble in finding Joe's elk and chided him unmercifully that maybe he had just dreamed he had shot an elk and was taking us on a wild goose chase. However, we finally located his kill on a little terrace or shelf near the top of Buck Basin. It took a little time to quarter out the animal and we goofed off a lot, remarking how our breath showed up in the cold air at an altitude well over 9,000 feet. We tried to snowball each other, but could not as the snow was too powdery and fluffy to pack. We were eventually ready for our trip home. The elk's front quarters were pretty well shot up, so it was decided to take only the hind quarters and the horns. This left room on the packhorse to relieve us of our numerous cameras, binoculars, extra coats and a pistol or two.

Ol' Lucy was very docile and seemed half asleep while being packed. She only half-heartedly expanded her belly as Delon tightened up the cinches on the pack saddle. He gave the pack a final inspection and suggested we head for home, where delicious food was awaiting our hungry return. Since Joe in hunting for his downed elk had not guided us on the proper trail into Buck Basin, Delon suggested, because he knew the "good" trail down into the bottom of Black Canyon, that he would go ahead, leading the packhorse and that the rest of us would follow him down the steep and somewhat precarious trail. Before we mounted up, Delon said he would turn Ol' Lucy around because she was headed in the wrong direction and we would be on our way.

Delon picked up the end of Ol' Lucy's 15-ft. lead rope, let out a yell and gave the rope a vigorous jerk. Ol' Lucy let go! She bucked, jumped and kicked, squealed and snorted. She climaxed her magnificent performance with a series of contemptuous horsey farts that blasted the frigid mountain air and sounded for all the world like multiple .45 caliber pistol shots*** (see footnote). Elk meat, horns, cameras, binoculars, guns and everything else went flying in 50 different directions and the empty pack saddle came to rest half under her belly. I was standing off to one side of Lucy and facing Delon. His eyes bulged and his mouth opened about a foot. There were split second spasmodic contractions of his lower jaw - up and down. A very loud noise came out of his mouth, but no words. The sound was indescribable-sort of a combination yell associated with a great whoosh, not unlike the imagined gasp of a bloated dinosaur. He stood there for a fraction of a second, with his frosted breath pulsing two or three feet in front of him. Then he made a convulsive leap forward several feet, grabbed in the deep snow with both hands for the upper and lower plates of his false teeth, which had been propelled out of his mouth with explosive force at his heated attempt to remind Lucy of her ancestry. Once his china clippers had been secured, he stuck them, along with a handful of snow, into his mouth. He then let go with some well-chosen expletives that would have made a mule skinner jealous.

Ol' Lucy now stood quietly, perked her ears and twitched her tail contentedly at the sound of the familiar endearing words of her master. On the way home, she only tried a couple of times to dislodge her pack.

*** Delon delighted in jokingly calling his bean-eating friends at his ranch "pistol asses." In the mountains, if no females were present, he would use both the first and last names. But in town, across the street, at social functions or at the movies, he would shout the one word: "Pistol!" Should he chance to meet one of his flatulent friends in church, he would modulate his voice to a hoarse whisper which could be heard at least 50 feet. He classified his legume-eating buddies according to their abilities into three categories: .22, .38 and .45 caliber. Only the most talented were entitled to the entire triple classification.

Teeth for Two

Delon Olsen and Hugh Brandon were two codgers of the old school. Either one could ride a horse, throw a steer, gut a bull elk or chase a mountain lion. Delon did have a minor problem or two; he was scared to death of a mouse and had a very "sensitive" stomach. Hugh had been subjected to matrimony once, but it did not take. Delon was married, but his wife did not like the primitive conditions in the mountains and held down a job in town. So the two old boys were on their own at Delon's ranch in Joes Valley, enjoying the freedom of their pseudo-bachelorhood.

They started the summer by investing in some new false teeth. This was deemed necessary for several reasons. The "old" ones were really old; their gums had receded to the point that there was trouble in keeping their teeth in place for proper chewing or even talking. There were numerous chips and dents from cracking pine nuts or hitting gravel in their beans. Many years of hard use and occasional cuss words had seared and smoked the enamel. So they decided to go the whole way and buy new ones. This they did, although the cost was almost prohibitive. Delon was especially proud of his "tailor-mades" as the lower plate had an unusual off-set dogleg on one side to accommodate the deformity of an old fractured lower jaw.

To protect their investment, Hugh, on a trip to town, purchased two china containers in which to soak their teeth at night. Hugh's was blue with violets; Delon's was pink with roses. To begin with, Hugh had trouble in breaking Delon's age-old habit of putting his teeth under his pillow when he retired. But they soon developed a smooth routine of putting their new china clippers to bed with a teaspoon of salt or soda in warm water in the pretty containers. They took great pride in their new teeth and never ceased to smile at each other or visitors who showed up in the valley.

Their new teeth even seemed to improve their personalities. Normally, at times, they tended to be cross and grumpy with fits of temper tantrums and genuine ill humor, with frequent outbursts of favorite epigrams. Now they were all smiles and everything was serene and pleasant. The ranch work went smoothly and they took their turns at irrigating, chasing the cows, tending the horses, cooking and grubbing out the cabin. They went out of their way to be amiable and do little favors for each other.

This state of semiconnubial bliss continued for a couple of weeks or more. One morning, Hugh awakened first. He had the fire built and the bacon and eggs cooking while Delon was still in bed. He slyly exchanged the two sets of false teeth from one bowl to the other, so that his teeth were in Delon's pink soaker and vice versa. He had the food on the table when Delon appeared in the kitchen door. Delon was starved, so he dashed to the cupboard, plucked the teeth out of the pink bowl and proceeded to put them in his mouth. That is, he tried to put them in his mouth. But they would not go. The more he gagged and sputtered, moaned and groaned, the less success he had. He opened his mouth wider, pushed harder and tried again. Still no luck. So he started all over and even tried to put them in upside down. Nothing worked.

By this time, Hugh was fit to be tied and nearly fell to the floor with a fit of convulsive laughter. It took Delon a moment to catch on that he had really been trying to put Hugh's teeth in his mouth instead of his own. The terrible thought that he had actually had someone else's teeth in his mouth sickened him to the point that he threw up.

For a few hours thereafter, the friendly smiles faded and things returned to the usual dour routine of previous years. Delon would not even put his own teeth in his mouth for the rest of the day.

But by the next morning, he had mellowed and could see the funny side and would laugh uproariously along with Hugh. But when he would describe to others how hard he had tried to get the alien dentures in, he would once more begin to gag and get a little green around the gills.

But laugh he did, albeit with more than just a hint of apprehension in his eyes!

Progress

Shortly after the end of WWII, Delon invested in several war surplus items. He bought three immense coal-fired kitchen stoves, two of which are still in use. He also purchased a beautiful Kohler electric light plant. This was a four cylinder job which is still in use, after several rehauls, at his dude ranch in Joes Valley. Previously, he had electric lights, after a fashion, in his main lodge from a small generator operated by an eight-foot high wooden water wheel that was turned by the outflow of water from a large spring on his property. The lights from the water-powered generator were poor at best and fluctuated bright and dim, according to the whim of the creaky wheel as it rumbled on its groaning unsteady overburdened axle.

Delon was overjoyed with the new electric light plant. He procured a nice building for it in Castle Valley. Ted Brown, Lenar Peacock and I set it up for him and rewired his cabin for 110 volt power, also running a power line down to my cabin. We all felt that the new power plant would open up a new lifestyle in that remote mountain area. This would mean the pleasure and functional use of electric lights, electric coffee makers, electric vacuum cleaners, radios and more. But what pleased Delon most was that now he could have an electric washing machine, which would relieve the drudgery of hand washing or saving up all the dirty clothes to wash in town.

Delon started looking for a good used electric washing machine. One weekend, he showed up with a nice-looking washer in the back of his pickup. We admired its shiny white appearance, complete with power wringer and white metal skirt that reached nearly to the ground. Delon was overjoyed; he told us that he had haggled with a very good friend and purchased the machine "as is" for the bargain sum of $20. He could hardly wait until morning to try it out. He was up bright and early the next day, carrying water in buckets from the creek to galvanized tubs on his kitchen range to heat. We started up the electric plant, but as the water was not yet hot enough, he told Maurine to go ahead and run the vacuum cleaner down at our cabin and let him know when she was through, as it was doubtful if there was enough power to run two appliances at once.

When she was finished, we all gathered to participate in the virginal operation of an honest-to-goodness electric washing machine in Joes Valley — the first time ever. The washer had been set up outdoors adjacent to a power outlet. Delon was all smiles and beaming as he loaded dirty Levis and work shirts into the steaming water-filled tub of the machine. He poked the clothes down with a broom handle into the soapy scalding water and yelled: "Turn her on!" I had already plugged the electric cord into a receptacle and started looking for a switch on the machine. I pushed two or three levers and nothing happened. I rechecked the electric connection and found it okay, so again pushed and pulled at anything that looked like an operating control. But still no action. Finally, I got down on my hands and knees and looked under the metal skirt of the washer, only to discover that the electric motor had been previously removed by his so-called trusted friend!

Dynamite

In about 1965, Delon was overcrowded with deer hunters at his lodge in Joes Valley. Overcrowded, in fact, to the point where a couple of the hunters were without beds and had to put their sleeping bags on the living room floor in front of the fireplace.

That was also the time that a big, frisky, arrogant pack rat raised particular hell for several nights in a row, keeping the whole place awake, but being especially obnoxious to the floor sleepers - knocking things off shelves and cupboards and even crawling over their bodies and faces. Every effort was made to catch the rat, but it avoided all traps and poison bait. Each night, its noisy activity seemed to increase and it appeared to enjoy having shoes and boots and other things thrown at it by the disturbed sleepers as they followed it with flashlights from their beds on the floor.

One of the men finally blasted the rat to smithereens with his .30-.30 deer rifle, barely missing the bottom of Delon's piano, and the bullet buried itself in the bottom part of the stairway. Of course, the terrific explosion of the.30-.30 rifle in a closed cabin awakened the whole camp, but everyone rejoiced that the rat was gone and Delon's piano, by a miracle, was intact.

Subsequent visitors to Delon's were often shown the bullet hole and told about the guy who shot the pack rat with his deer rifle and just missed the piano.

In July of 1983, Art Olsen, Delon's oldest son, found himself without mantles for his Coleman lantern. He was certain that he had some, possibly in the storage area beneath the stair. At first, his search was futile, but he kept on digging and digging as he was certain that there were some mantles there. Finally, he got way back in the depths of the closet and into a tiny storage area beneath the lower steps.

He didn't find any Coleman lantern mantles, but he did find 15 sticks of well-hidden dynamite, located immediately adjacent to the "pack rat bullet hole." The dynamite was well crystallized, with the nitroglycerine oozing out and bearing the date of 1956.

Delon passed away June 1, 1983. Henning Olsen, Delon's other son, is now convinced beyond all doubt of ESP and that Delon got time off from wrangling horses for the angel dudes in Heaven to somehow get the message back to earth about the location of the dynamite!

Amen!

P.S. Where are the blasting caps???

Joe Walker

Joe Walker was an outlaw.

Authors Pearl Baker and Charles Kelly say he hit the Price area of eastern Utah in the early 1890s. Pearl describes him as "small, but all man, rather good looking and dark, a silent man as a rule, and one given to traveling alone most of the time."

Charles Kelly postulates that maybe Walker had married a Whitmore girl at one time, which aroused the enmity of the entire Whitmore family. Pearl Baker says he came into this area via the Dandy crossing on the Colorado River to try to collect a Whitmore debt owed his mother by the Whitmores.

In any event, Joe Walker and the Whitmores did not get along. The Whitmores were a well-to-do prominent Price family. They were in the cattle business and raised blooded horses. J. M. Whitmore was a banker. Joe Walker liked the Whitmore horses and managed to steal their horses and cattle every chance he got.

The kind of a man Joe Walker was depends on who you talk to. He was a kind, friendly and helpful man if you talk to the McPhersons, the Downards and several others. Relatives of the Whitmores and descendants of the posse, of course, say the opposite. They depict him as a wild and woolly, cruel outlaw, quick on the trigger and merciless, given to fighting and raising hell, in general, and a cattle and horse thief.

Jim McPherson (Don Wilcox's granddad) had a ranch in an isolated area on the east side of the Green River at the mouth of Florence Creek, which flows into the Green River from the east. He and Joe Walker were good friends. Walker would show up at Florence Creek, often unannounced, stay a few days or weeks. He made himself useful, helping to put up hay, irrigating, giving a hand with the cattle, branding calves or other tasks. When McPherson mentioned that he needed a plow, Joe packed one in by muleback. He had swiped it from a Mormon farmer in Castle Valley. Jim McPherson was trying to build dams for ponds needed for stock watering and irrigation and needed a scraper. Joe took the wheels and axle from a large scraper parked near the railroad at Woodside, packed the stuff over a treacherous thirty miles of roadless area, got it across the Green River and delivered it to the McPherson ranch with great pride. (The Wilcoxes still have this machinery, now at their ranch in Green River.) However, Joe did not live long enough to deliver the metal scoop for the scraper.

1897 was a busy year for outlaws in eastern Utah. About a month before the famous payroll robbery at Castle Gate on April 21, 1897 in which Butch Cassidy and Elza Lay got away with $8,000 in gold, Joe Walker absconded with several of the Whitmore's prize horses. This resulted in a posse being formed, led by Sheriff Tuttle of Emery County. The posse caught up with Walker, who was camped out alone at Mexican Bend, where the San Rafael river winds around Mexican Mountain in the rugged San Rafael Swell of eastern Utah. There was a shoot-out in which Walker shot the rifle out of the hands of a former friend, but now arch enemy, "Gunplay" Maxwell. He also shot Sheriff Tuttle in the hip. The posse deserted Sheriff Tuttle and went back to Castle Valley for "help" and a doctor. One legend has it that Walker took water to Tuttle and made him as comfortable as possible before escaping during the night. The sheriff was eventually transported back to civilization, a murderous thirty plus miles by buckboard. Walker, a few weeks later, undoubtedly participated, one way or another, in the Castle Gate robbery.

During late April in the following year of 1898, Joe Walker really stirred up the community, especially the Whitmores. He raided one of the Whitmore cow camps, scared Bud Whitmore (a mere youth) and beat the hell out of Billy McGuire with his gun belt. He then threw McGuire's gun and boots into the river and ran off the cattle and all the horses, leaving them high and dry and afoot in an area of sagebrush, cactus and sharp rocks.

After this aggravated insult, the Whitmores saw to it that a posse was formed and a reward offered for Walker, dead or alive.

The posse, led by Sheriff Charles W. Allred of Price, consisted of J.M. Whitmore, George Whitmore, J.W. Warf, Pete Anderson, Jack Gentry and Jack Wilson. They went to lower crossing (Woodside) and then to Range Valley, where the group was augmented by Joe Bush, deputy U.S. marshal of Salt Lake City; Jim Inglefield; Billy McGuire, and a man named Coleman.

They left Range Valley and headed for Florence Creek on what they believed was Joe Walker's trail. About halfway between Range Valley and Florence Creek, they met Jim McPherson and because the posse knew that McPherson and Walker were friends, forced him at gunpoint to accompany them. Jim McPherson was on his way out of his remote ranch to get married. He had left a young fellow to care for the ranch and had told him under no circumstances was he to take the boat from the east to the west side of the Green

River to ferry anyone across. The kid was apparently already lonesome because when the posse members yelled across the river to him, he immediately rowed the boat over. He was surprised to find Jim McPherson with the posse and hung his head in shame when Jim glared at him. The posse crossed the river, probably making more than one trip, swimming their horses behind the boat.

The posse prepared their evening meal at the Florence Creek ranch, keeping a sharp eye on Jim McPherson and the boy to prevent their escape to warn Walker. After they had eaten, "Uncle Lou" Benton, who was building fence for Jim Mcpherson, showed up. Probably "sweet talked" by posse members and having visions of the reward money of $500, he said that he had lunch with Walker and his friends at noon that day.

With Benton as guide and Jim McPherson still forced to go with them, they rode the nine miles by poor trail at night up to the top of Florence Creek, over the divide east to beyond McPherson Spring. They surrounded the Walker camp while it was yet dark and then at dawn, shot Joe Walker and John Herring in their bedrolls at the campsite under the west side of "Walker Rock." Jim McPherson says that Walker raised up in his bedroll and got off a couple of shots with his six-shooter before being killed.

(I thought I had the brass shell casing of Joe Walker's last shot, found by Don and Jeanette at Walker Rock, which I lost, much to my disgust and chagrin.)

Apparently, Joe Walker was alone when he passed the Florence Creek ranch on his way out of the country a day or two ahead of the posse. He probably joined up with three more wandering cowboys shortly thereafter. These were Johnny Herring, Mizzoo Schultz and Sang Thompson.

According to Don Wilcox, Jim McPherson objected when some of the posse wanted to cut off Herring's head, who they thought was Butch Cassidy. McPherson was told to shut up or his body would be packed out over a saddle along with the two dead "outlaws" the forty miles to the railroad at Thompson.

The entire party, with the two dead men, entrained at Thompson for Price. The bodies were put on exhibition in Price and great was the jubilation as the second dead man was further identified as being Butch Cassidy. Both Walker and "Cassidy" were buried outside the Price cemetery. There was enough doubt in the minds of some people, however, so that the body of Herring was exhumed and pronounced by several authorities not to be Cassidy.

A Journey Back Into Time

On September 11, 1987, My wife, Maurine, and I went to the Tavaputs Plateau Ranch, an internationally known dude ranch located in the high country of eastern Utah, as the guests of Don and Jeanette Wilcox. Don showed up in my office Friday afternoon with the proposition that we do something on the spur of the moment that we had been wanting to do for several years: to wit, visit the site where Joe Walker and Johnny Herring had been shot in their bedrolls by a sheriff's posse at dawn on the morning of Friday, May 13, 1898. Don knew the location, had visited it several times in his youth, but had not been there for five years. Probably very few people are alive today who know the exact location.

So we started the ball rolling. We tried to locate Chuck Zehnder, a local newspaper reporter, who knew that we had been planning the trip for a long time and had purchased a metal detector in anticipation of finding some lead or brass at the site. No Zehnder, either at the newspaper office or at home. I remembered that Toy Atwood had a metal detector, so I borrowed his.

Don & Jeanette Wilcox inspect the plane.

We met Don at the home of Mark Predovich in East Carbon. Don had a big ten-wheeler truck full of cement and sand to take to the ranch. We left Mark's place at 8:10 p.m. and followed Don up the Bruin Point "freeway," being careful not to get too close so Don could back up to get around the curves. Reaching the top, we traveled about twenty dusty miles through seven gates, arriving at the ranch at 10:30 p.m., and we were in the sack by 11:30 p.m.

We were up early the next morning before dawn to photograph the beauty of the sunrise. (Tavaputs is a Ute word meaning sunrise.) We met our chartered 206 Cessna plane from Redtail Aviation out of Green River, Utah, at the Tavaputs landing strip. After chasing cattle off the 9,000-foot elevation runway, we took off at 8:15 a.m. In all her years at the ranch, Jeannette had always "chickened out" from flying off their dangerous high altitude strip because in the past, there had been fatalities there. But this day, she couldn't stand being left behind, so went along with Don, Maurine and me. The plane was crowded with pilot, four passengers, food boxes, camera bags, metal detector, plus supplies for Jim's (Don and Jeannette's son) family at their cow camp on the Ouray Ute Indian Reservation. The air was good, so we got off with no problem. We circled over the lower Range Creek area, spotting the Waldo Wilcox ranch and the confluence of Range Creek and the Green River.

In about twenty minutes, we landed at our destination on a straight strip of a narrow Jeep road atop a ridge at Moon Water Point on the Ute Indian Reservation on the east Tavaputs Plateau. Jim was waiting with one of his cowboys, a pickup truck and a Blazer. We left orders for the plane to return for us at 5 p.m. and drove to Jim's cow camp to greet his wife, Kelly; daughter, Emily, age three; little Jesse, age one and one half; and two more cowboys.

Jim and his cowboys took off on a cattle drive.

Don drove the Blazer with Jeannette, Kelly and her two children, Maurine and me. We went to McPherson Spring (named after Don's grandfather), where there were a couple of old fallen - in log cabins, one more ancient than the other. We then hiked several miles, with Don as guide, to Walker Draw and followed it down to Walker Rock, the outlaw camp site. Joe

Don & Jeanette Wilcox use metal detector at Walker Rock

Walker and three others had been camped in the shadow of Walker Rock that eventful morning in 1898. Walker and Herring were shot and killed in their bedrolls by a sheriff's posse from Price at dawn Friday, May 13th. Joe Walker is said to have got off a couple of shots from his six-shooter before he died.

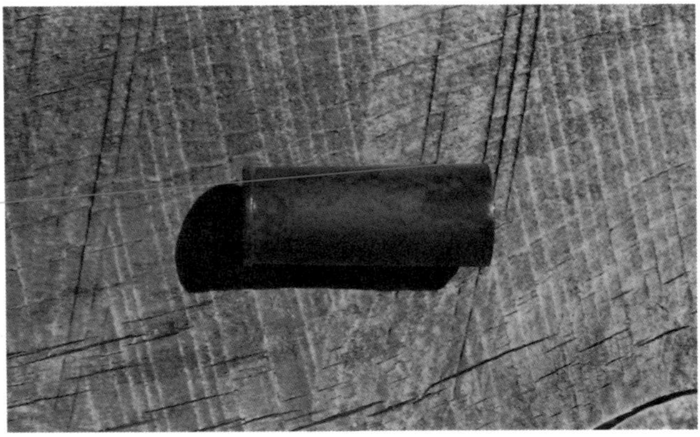

Joe Walker's last shot?

We turned on the metal detector and, almost at once, Don and Jeannette found a much-weathered Colt .45-caliber brass shell casing, located 3-4 inches beneath the surface. Joe Walker's last shot?

We waited while Don walked back to bring the car via an old road he had located in the upper end of Walker Draw, adjacent to an old abandoned log homesteader's cabin. While waiting for Don, we worked with the metal detector, getting lots of squawks, but no real finds.

The Ute Indian Tribe run their Ouray Reservation with a tight rein. It is located on the east Tavaputs Plateau and consists of a vast holding of many thousands of acres. Entrance to the reservation is by way of Vernal and Ouray, as the Utes have closed off the road that comes in from Thompson on the south. Jim Wilcox, Don's son, ran several hundred head of cattle on the reservation during the summer of 1987. Jim had obtained written permission for Don and our group to be on the reservation the weekend of September 11. However, in the hustle and bustle of getting away from Jim's cow camp that morning, we forgot to take the permit with us. Don had been a little nervous all day about that situation.

As we were coming out of Walker Draw to the "main road," there were two pickup trucks parked across the road. Six to eight Indians were out of their trucks drinking beer. They looked hostile, tough, and sullen. Most had long hair and some were wearing headbands. Don said, "Oh, oh, we are in trouble. Let me handle it." He got out of the Blazer, sauntered over to the group in his high-heeled boots, parlayed a few words in Ute and bragged about one of the Ute chiefs who used to work for the Wilcoxes. In a few minutes, they were all smiles and pulled their trucks out of our way.

Don Wilcox parleys with hostile Utes.

We heaved a sigh of relief and were soon at the spot to be picked up by the plane. We had to take off downwind and a little uphill on a warm afternoon. Being an ex-pilot, I could not help but notice that the stall warning device was screaming like hell as we barely cleared a rock outcrop on the ridge before we could drop down a little into the canyon to the west and pick up air speed. After my sphincters relaxed, I enjoyed the trip over Crandall Canyon, the Green River and the view of the Wilcox layout from the air. When a Cessna 206 lands on a 9,000-foot high rough airstrip at high speed, you think the landing gear and the whole damn plane are going to fall apart. Although it was Jeanette's first flight from their runway, nothing bothered her and she was as unconcerned as if she was on an old docile saddle horse.

We had a sumptuous steak and fixings dinner, relaxed in the luxury of a hot tub under the stars and went to bed to dream of Indians on the warpath, trigger happy lawmen and gun-fighting outlaws.

The end of a long to be remembered perfect day!

“Short Stacks” Bonus

Al Veltri

A Number of years ago, Al Veltri wrote a short article which was published in Carbon County: Eastern Utah's Industrialized Island. In it, he tells poignant stories of the feelings of an Italian kid and his visits to Helper. Al's folks came from Italy; his father worked in the mine and at the coke ovens in Sunnyside. Al is a pharmacist and operated the Veltri Drug in Helper for many years. He is now semi-retired and lives in Helper with his wife, Pena. He gave me permission to reprint his story verbatim.
Here it is:

On July 4, 1880, Teacum Pratt and his two wives, Sarah and Anna, settled at the mouth of Gordon Creek, then moved on to Helper in 1881. This is very exciting to me, and I hope to you people of this community, to know that Helper is 100 years old.

Phil Notarianni has said that Helper had sixteen to thirty-two nationalities and 136 businesses. Sitting home last night, I counted people I knew of sixteen different nationalities who live in Helper today. I feel sure, however, there are more than that.

Helper has a flavor and vintage that are very different from any other city in Utah. Phil called it the "hub" of Carbon County. If you will permit some personal reflection, I remember the "Entering Helper the Hub" sign when I used to come to Helper as a little boy with my mother to visit and shop. I loved to come to Helper. It was something special. It was very exciting. We lived in Sunnyside then. Once, I recall they had a Labor Day celebration when they blocked off Main Street from what was then Schram Johnson's Drug Store to the Strand Theatre for a street dance. I thought the whole town dancing in the street was absolutely fantastic!

Helper was the Broadway and Las Vegas of its time, a place with bright lights and businesses. Imagine that you are a coal miner from Castle Gate, Spring Canyon or Latuda. It's Saturday night, payday, and you come to town to find not only bright lights and cafes, but saloons, hotels, hot baths, clean beds, women, gambling, whiskey and dancing at the Rainbow Gardens.

Helper was also the Italian social center of Carbon County in those days. There were Italian lodges. My mother belonged to the Stella D'America and Women Moose Heart Lodge. She took great pride in wearing her lodge ribbons and emblems. The old-country Italians – our *commares* ("friends"), *paesanos* ("friends who lived in the same village or town in Italy") and cugini ("cousins") – all seemed to live in Helper. When we came to visit, my mother would bring a package of this or a bottle of that for so and so. When we returned home, we seemed to take a truckful of fresh fruits, vegetables, chickens, eggs, cheese, sausage, salami, bread and all sorts of goodies.

Spring Glen was like a paradise to me. There were orchards and farms, horses, cows, chickens, pigs, sheep, goats, pigeons and even a magpie. Here we played in the hayloft or wheat silo and smelled and ate hot bread from outdoor ovens.

We always had plum jam with hot bread. Every Italian family I know had plum trees in their yards. They couldn't throw the plums away so they made jam – lots and lots of jam. You won't catch me eating plum jam today. But if you drive around Helper, you still see fruit trees in the front yards, especially plum, but some apricot and peach.

Another thing I vividly remember was when they killed the pigs in the fall. Family groups and friends would gather; our fathers did the butchering, our mothers made the sausages, hams and bacon. There were pigs squealing, fires roaring, water boiling and kids running everywhere playing games. I think we used about everything in the pig except the squeal. They would give us the pig's bladder and we would blow it up and play ball games. We tasted many samples of fresh sausage.

The other big event in the fall was wine making. You always knew it was wine season because our teachers had grapes all over their desks. Walking home from school, we could smell the wine fermenting and see an aura of gnats or fruit flies surrounding the wooden box crates. After the grapes were used, the crates became cabins, rubber guns and go-carts.

I remember many neighborhood house parties, especially in Joe Bruno's basement. Dominic Albo would sing, dance and entertain us. We kids would eat, play games, sing and dance. They would throw quarters at our feet when we danced the tarantella (Italian folk dance).

The events that kept the Italians together were based mostly around the Catholic Church. Weddings, births, baptisms, first communions, confirmations and funerals – in fact, any reason to have a celebration. Once my dad told me about my niece, who was living in California and had just given birth to her first son. My father was upset because her husband didn't have cigars, candies, liquor and food to celebrate this important event. In Italy, he told me, they often say *"Vieni, vieni facema a Festa. Me filiata a chucha"* ("Come, come to my house everybody. Let's have a party. My donkey just gave birth to a baby foal"). We are losing our tradition of celebrating important events. In the early days, weddings and baptisms lasted three or four days.

If someone could capture the folklore in this area, it would be fantastic! Helper is full of colorful characters and personalities. This really happened to me: A lady called me up on the phone and said, "Eh, coumbah dis mizzi [name]. You pass my howz make deliver gimme $2.00 dizzi pill, $2.00 artrita, $3.00 pressure blood hi, $3.00 cold bladder, $3.00 sugar diarrhea. Eh maka lilly cheepa, huh!"

Phil pointed out that Helper is unique. I can't help but notice that we aren't doing much to preserve its uniqueness. We seem to have lost our pride in Helper. While I was attending the University of Utah, we lived in Price. The highway was then Helper's Main Street. Often I would stop at Vic Litizzette's L & A Drug to get an ice cream cone. The soda fountain was situated so that the soda clerk had her back to you when she stooped to get your ice cream. She had a very short uniform and when she bent over it became even shorter. I remember saying to myself that if I had a drug store I would never have a soda fountain like that. Well I am living in the town with the dreary main street, and I bought that very same fountain that I said I would never have!

So it may be true that parts of Helper are old and unattractive, but in many ways, the town is like a piece of old furniture that you were going to take to the dump. When you clean it up, polish it and shine it instead, it winds up not being a piece of junk, but a valuable piece of furniture.

How many places have a river running through the middle of town? There's a railroad on one side, a highway on the other, back streets with alleys, a swinging bridge, two tunnels with assorted graffiti, stone steps that go up 150 to 200 feet, hills, washes, parks and a dugway. It has character and personality, but it's going to be up to us to do something about it. Our river could look like a clear mountain fishing stream running through a small community where almost everyone could leisurely and conveniently walk to town to do his shopping. With some cleaning and policing and a little imagination, many positive things can be done. I don't expect Helper to become a very big business center, but it could be an attractive, pleasant residential area.

Dr. Albo gave a speech about Carbon County some time ago. He said something like, "When two people from Utah meet from cities or counties like Salt Lake, Weber, Dixie [i.e., Washington], Sanpete or Utah, there is a casual exchange of greetings or visiting; but when two people from Price, Helper or Carbon County meet it is different. There is an extra-special magic there." The people of Carbon County are our greatest resource. Reba Keele, in a speech at the College of Eastern Utah alumni banquet, said very much the same thing. Dr. Keele received a B.A. and an M.A. from Brigham Young University and a Ph.D. from Dartmouth and presently teaches at BYU. When asked, "Why did you go to CEU when you had an honors-at-entrance scholarship to practically any college you wanted to go to?" She said, "Well, I'm from Carbon County and I'm different because I am from Carbon County. Most people don't understand that."

So I think the Historical Society is trying to tell us something. We have a town full of history, personality and character. Hopefully we can do something to restore Helper's pride and dignity and make it an attractive community again.

Mr. Veltri is a retired pharmacist in Helper and a native of Sunnyside.

Dr. Andrew Dowd

During the second decade of the twentieth century, Dr. Andrew Dowd reigned supreme as a coal camp doctor at Sunnyside, Utah. He became well-known for his frequent caustic remarks.

At the close of his office hours one busy afternoon, he was confronted by a young male patient who had been waiting for him most of the afternoon so that he could talk to the doctor after the other patients had left. I can speak from experience that this was a dead giveaway to the doctor about the nature of the visit - it meant that the man had a real problem.

The man, who did not speak English too well, told Dr. Dowd that the visit was not for himself, but for a friend. His friend wanted a certain kind of medicine and would greatly appreciate it if the doctor would give him some medicine for his friend. The friend was quite ill and would indeed be thankful for the medicine which he would be happy to take to his friend.

Dr. Dowd looked at the man and said in a gruff, disgusted voice: "Oh hell, take your pants down and let's look at your friend!"

C.A. "Red" Knobbs

One Sunday morning about 11 a.m., in the late 1940s, I received a phone call from "Red" Knobbs who was then chief of police for the city of Helper. He stated that there was an emergency situation and wanted me to meet him at my office right away. As I waited for him, I pondered what the so-called emergency problem might be, expecting an injured prisoner from the Helper calaboose as had happened previously. I soon found out. Red was the patient and his face was a bloody mess. His nose was broken, both eyes were black and his lips were cut and swollen, besides abrasions on both cheeks and a bloody tongue. He was fit to be tied; he was well-known for his inflammable temper that matched his red hair and ruddy complexion. I tried to calm him down, without much luck. As I patched him up, I got the story. The previous Saturday night in Helper had been a wild one. About two o'clock in the morning, Red had been called to settle a drunken brawl in one of the bars. The main instigator of this commotion was a well-known Helper man named Pete and supposedly a friend of Red's. The chief tried to settle the squabble in an amiable manner, but to no avail. He became disgusted, eventually lost his temper, manhandled the man, put the cuffs on him and threw him in the clink. Then he went home to bed.

The next morning, he returned to the jail. The prisoner called to him and apologized for his actions the night before. He coaxed Red, in honeyed tones, to the bars of his cell, said that they were friends; he was ashamed of himself, etc. He repeated he was sorry, coaxed him closer and placed his arms astride Red's head, on his shoulders. Then he clinched his hands behind Reds neck and suddenly pulled the officer's face into the iron bars multiple times with great force.

No wonder Red was upset!

John B. "Jack" Kelley read the above story and called me on the phone to tell me another which I had heard, but forgotten.

It seems that on one very vigorous Helper Saturday night, Red was called to settle a tumultuous argument or fight in an upstairs bordello. Just as he started up the stairway, someone fired a pistol from the top. The bullet hit his lawman's shield and the notebook in his shirt pocket behind it and did no harm but to stagger him and dent his badge. Jack claims, as a kid, he was shown the dented emblem. So fate was kind to Red at times.

1950 - Steve J. Diamanti, Helper Ford dealer, gives keys to a new police car to Helper Chief of Police C.A."Red" Knobbs, officer Joe Myers looks on. Credit: Dr. Max Morgan

George Garavaglia

George Garavaglia was chief of police in Helper in the 1930s. He was noted for his uncanny ability to twist and mutilate the English language, both in interpretation and speech. Helper had a multitude of houses of ill repute. It was inevitable that some of the soiled doves would get in trouble and end up in the Helper City Jail. At times, as many as three or four might be incarcerated as guests in the jail at one time, perhaps after a disorderly Saturday night. There were no facilities to feed the inmates, so Chief Garavaglia would escort the group to the nearby McGonigal drugstore, which contained a small restaurant, for a frugal two meals a day repast. One day, he herded his frowsy group of females over to the drugstore for breakfast. They were seated at a table waiting for service, when one of the women asked Garavalagia if she could have some Kotex. He threw his hands in the air and shouted: "No, No, hella da No, - you eata da corna flakies likka everybodies else!"

This story is told about Chief Garavaglia during the turbulent times of the 1934 strike: The governor had sent the militia to Carbon County to quell the sometimes violent problems. Orders had been issued that there was to be no congregation of people on the streets of Helper or elsewhere. As Garavaglia patrolled the town one evening, he saw two men conversing on a street corner. He hurried toward them, threatening with his nightstick and yelling: "Braka up, braka up, one man to a bunch."

Visual Acuity

This episode happened in the late 1940s or the early 1950s. The man, a long-standing patient of mine, will be given the fictitious name of Blaine. He had one big problem: he had a congenital eye condition that caused his vision to be well below normal. In fact, he was considered industrially blind, with vision of a little less than 20/200 in each eye. He had been seen by several competent ophthalmologists, always with the diagnosis that nothing could be done to improve his vision.

He was about forty-five years of age, ambitious and a hard worker. He eked out a poor living for his family as a beekeeper. This was a seasonal situation and he always had financial difficulties. In an effort to better his position, he concocted what he thought was a brilliant idea. He had a friend by the name of Chidester who made a good living hauling gravel from a pit on Cedar Mountain for local consumption. This gravel was of a very high quality and in apparent demand. So Blaine decided he could maybe get rich if he went into the gravel hauling business.

He did not have a drivers license, having been rejected several times because of his poor vision. Undaunted, he went to the Price City Hall, where the driver's license tests were given in the upstairs hallway. He discovered that the man who gave the tests merely turned the eye chart to the wall when he was finished for the day. So Blaine returned several evenings in a row and thoroughly memorized the eye chart. He passed the test, thanks to his memory, for a chauffeur's license. He located a good used dump truck for $9000.00, which he purchased on a loan he inveigled from Bill Welsh, who operated an auto loan business.

On returning from his first trip to Cedar Mountain, he totaled his loaded rig on a bad curve, with no great damage to himself. Eventually, the entire story came out. Luckily, he had taken out insurance with Bill Welsh to cover payments in case anything went wrong. So Blaine got the experience, Bill Welsh got his money and I got the story.

Borzage

Joe Borzage was a stone mason. He had come to Carbon County from the Italian Alps and was much sought after because of his skill in rock work. There are still some remains of his artistry, for example the vandalized ruins of the "New Peerless" mine portal that faces the highway in Price Canyon above Castle Gate.

He married Jessie Behunin. Their conjugal life was somewhat tumultuous at times, mainly because of Joe's love of a well-known Carbon County concoction known as "Dago Red." Jessie did not approve, but Joe annually made his own wine, keeping several barrels in his basement so that he could imbibe daily of the cup that cheers of his own vintage. But on Saturday nights, he was wont to roam and would sneak out of the house to have company in his sought after pleasure, often to return in the wee small hours.

One Saturday night, he returned home to find himself locked out. He banged on the door and finally Jessie came to the entrance in her nightgown. She announced in a very disgusted voice, as she unlatched the screen: "Drunk again!" To which Joe replied: "Yeah, so am I!"

REFERENCES

1. Carr, Stephen L., The Historical Guide to Utah Ghost Towns - Salt Lake City; Western Epics, 1972.

2. Bender, Henry E., Jr., Uintah Railway, Berkeley, Calif., Howell-North, 1970.

3. Mingos, Howard., American Heros of the War in the Air, Lanciar Publishers, Inc., New York, 1943.

4 Notarianni, Phillip F. Editor, Carbon County, Eastern Utah's Industrialized Island, Utah State Historical Society, Salt Lake City, 1981.

5. Reynolds, Thursey; et al; Centennial Echos from Carbon County, Daughters of Utah Pioneers of Carbon County, 1948 (out of print).

6. Personal Interview: Bonto, Joe - Price, Utah, January 12, 1976. Population camps, number of employees, etc. Prolonged discussion.

7. Personal Interview: Corak, Milan and Antonia - Salt Lake City and Price, Utah. Frequent; up to and including 1995.

8. Personal Interviews; Milovich, John - Price, Utah. Many times over the years; even now, if I have a question I go ask John.

9. Personal Interview: Salzetti, Amando - Price, Utah, March 4, 1980. Tipple wages, bony pickers, etc., repeated discussions.

SUGGESTED READING ABOUT CARBON COUNTY & UTAH'S IMMIGRANTS

Balle, Wayne L., "I Owe My Soul," An Architectural and Social History of Kenilworth, Utah, Utah Historical Quarterly, 56 (Summer 1988).

Carr, Stephen L., The Historical Guide to Utah Ghost Towns, (Salt Lake City: Western Epics 1972).

Cederlof, A. Phillip, "The Peerless Coal Mines," Utah Historical Quarterly, 53 (Fall 1985).

Costa, Janeen Arnold, "A Struggle for Survival and Identity: Families in the Aftermath of the Castle Gate Mine Disaster," Utah Historical Quarterly, 56 (Summer 1988).

Dorman, J. Eldon, "Reminiscences of a Coal Camp Doctor," Carbon County, Eastern Utah's Industrialized Island, Utah State Historical Society, Phillip F. Notarianni, Editor, 1981.

Fraser, Marianne, "One Long Day that Went on Forever," Utah Historical Quarterly, 48 (Fall 1980).

Frazier, Russell G., "Bingham Canyon Through The Eyes of a Company Doctor," Utah Historical Quarterly, 33 (Fall 1965).

Hanson, Virginia, "I Remember Hiawatha," Utah Historical Quarterly, 40 (Summer 1972).

Noall, Claire, "Serbian-Austrian Christmas at Highland Boy," Utah Historical Quarterly, 33 (Fall 1965). (About Paul S. Richards, M.D.)

Papanikolas, Helen Zeese, "The Greeks of Carbon County," Utah Historical Quarterly, 22 (1954)

Papanikolas, Helen Zeese, "Life and Labor Among the Immigrants of Bingham Canyon," Utah Historical Quarterly, 33 (Fall 1965).
Papanikolas, Helen Zeese, "Toil and Rage in a New Land, The Greek Immigrants in Utah," Utah Historical Quarterly, 38 (Spring 1970).

Papanikolas, Helen Zeese, "Utah's Coal Lands, A vital example of how America became a Great Nation," Utah Historical Quarterly, 43 (1975).

Papanikolas, Helen Zeese, "Growing Up Greek in Helper, Utah," Utah Historical Quarterly, 48 (1980).

Papanikolas, Helen Zeese, "Women in the Mining Communities of Carbon County," in Philip Notarianni, ed. Carbon County, Eastern Utah's Industrialized Island, Salt Lake City, 1981.

Papanikolas, Helen Zeese, "Bootlegging in Zion: Making and Selling the Good Stuff," Utah Historical Quarterly, 53 (1985).

Papanikolas, Helen Zeese, Emily - George, (Salt Lake City, Utah, University of Utah Press, 1987).

Powell, Allan Kent, "Tragedy at Scofield," Utah Historical Quarterly, 41 (Spring 1973).

Powell, Allan Kent, The Next Time We Strike, (Logan, Utah, Utah State University Press, 1985).

Reynolds, Thursey J., et al., Centennial Echos from Carbon County, Daughters of Utah Pioneers of Carbon County, 1948 (out of print).

Most of these publications are available through the bookstore at the Utah State Historical Society, 300 Rio Grande, Salt Lake City, Utah 84101. Phone: (801) 533-3500.

REMARKS BY VARIOUS PEOPLE ABOUT "CONFESSIONS"

The greatest kind of folklore history by one of the state's best story tellers.
– "Chas" Peterson, St. George, Utah

I could not put it down. – Genevieve Rogers, Loveland, Colorado

I loved the book; it brought back memories of Carbon County and Joes Valley.
– David Salzette, Seattle Washington

What a wonderful trip back in time. – Betty Huff, Price, Utah

I can relate to beans three times a day. – Biff Lamma, Patagonia, Colorado

The funniest book I ever read. – Shannon Dimick, Price, Utah

The book reminds me of when as a kid, I had to go to bed in the winter on a screened-in sleeping porch. – John Vatsis, Dallas, Texas

A unique first-hand histroical account of living in another era.
– Nad and Martha Peterson, San Diego, California

This book has universal appeal to all people, but especially to coal miners everywhere. – Patrick Gallagher, Denver, Colorado

A book to pick up and read just for fun. – Many People

"Confessions" makes a great gift; they all like it and want more.
– Marge Sower, Price, Utah.

Some stories are enough to make you cry; others make you laugh.
– Leon and Erma Martin Yost, Jersey City, New Jersey

I enjoy other recent book, but love Confesssions of a Coal Camp Doctor.
– Kevin Jones, Salt Lake City, Utah

The book is great-one of a kind, just like the author.
– Nancy Taniguchi, Merced, California

Back cover photo by John R. Shupe.

All other uncaptioned photos are from the Dorman collection.